A HALF CENTURY AMONG THE SIAMESE AND THE LĀO

AN AUTOBIOGRAPHY

By

DANIEL McGILVARY, D.D.

WITH AN APPRECIATION BY

ARTHUR J. BROWN, D.D.

ILLUSTRATED

New York Chicago Toronto

Fleming H. Revell Company

London and Edinburgh

New York: 158 Fifth Avenue
Chicago: 125 N. Wabash Ave.
Toronto: 25 Richmond St., W.
London: 21 Paternoster Square
Edinburgh: 100 Princes Street

Daniel McGilvary

TO

MY WIFE

AN APPRECIATION

MISSIONARY biography is one of the most interesting and instructive of studies. It is, however, a department of missionary literature to which Americans have not made proportionate contribution. The foreign missionary Societies of the United States now represent more missionaries and a larger expenditure than the European Societies, but most of the great missionary biographies are of British and Continental missionaries, so that many Americans do not realize that there are men connected with their own Societies whose lives have been characterized by eminent devotion and large achievement.

Because I regarded Dr. McGilvary as one of the great missionaries of the Church Universal, I urged him several years ago to write his autobiography. He was then over seventy-five years of age, and I told him that he could not spend his remaining strength to any better advantage to the cause he loved than in preparing such a volume. His life was not only one of unusual length (he lived to the ripe age of eighty-three), but his missionary service of fifty-three years covered an interesting part of the history of missionary work in Siam, and the entire history, thus far, of the mission to the Lāo people of northern Siam. There is no more fascinating story in fiction or in that truth which is stranger than fiction, than the story of his discovery of a village of strange speech near his station at Pechaburī, Siam, his learning the language of the villagers, his long journey with his friend, Dr. Jonathan Wilson, into what was then the unknown region of northern Siam, pushing his little boat up the great river and pausing not until he had gone six hundred miles northward and arrived at the city of Chiengmai. The years that followed were years of toil and privation, of loneliness and sometimes of danger; but the missionaries persevered with splendid faith and courage until the foundations of a prosperous Mission were laid.

In all the marked development of the Lāo Mission, Dr. McGilvary was a leader—the leader. He laid the foundations of medical work, introducing quinine and vaccination among a people scourged by malaria and smallpox, a work which has now developed into five hospitals and a leper asylum. He began educational work, which is now represented by eight boarding schools and twenty-two elementary schools, and is fast expanding into a college, a medical college, and a theological seminary. He was the evangelist who won the first converts, founded the first church, and had a prominent part in founding twenty other churches, and in developing a Lāo Christian Church of four thousand two hundred and five adult communicants. His colleague, the Rev. Dr. W. C. Dodd, says that Dr. McGilvary selected the sites for all the present stations of the Mission long before committees formally sanctioned the wisdom of his choice. He led the way into regions beyond and was the pioneer explorer into the French Lāo States, eastern Burma, and even up to the borders of China. Go where you will in northern Siam, or in many sections of the extra-Siamese Lāo States, you will find men and women to whom Dr. McGilvary first brought the Good News. He well deserves the name so frequently given him even in his lifetime—"The Apostle to the Lāo."

It was my privilege to conduct our Board's correspondence with Dr. McGilvary for more than a decade, and, in 1902, to visit him in his home and to journey with him through an extensive region. I have abiding and tender memories of those memorable days. He was a Christian gentleman of the highest type, a man of cultivation and refinement, of ability and scholarship, of broad vision and constructive leadership. His evangelistic zeal knew no bounds. A toilsome journey on elephants through the jungles brought me to a Saturday night with the weary ejaculation: "Now we can have a day of rest!" The next morning I slept late; but Dr. McGilvary did not; he spent an hour before breakfast in a neighbouring village, distributing tracts and inviting the people to come to a service at our camp at ten o'clock. It was an impressive service,—under a spreading bo tree, with the mighty forest about us, monkeys curiously peering through the tangled vines, the huge elephants browsing the bamboo tips behind us, and the wondering people sitting on the ground, while one of the missionaries told the deathless story of redeeming love. But Dr. McGilvary was not present. Seventy-four years old though he was, he had walked three miles under a scorching sun to another village and was preaching there, while Dr. Dodd conducted the service at our camp. And I said: "If that is the way Dr. McGilvary rests, what does he do when he works?" Dr. McKean, his associate of many years, writes:

"No one who has done country evangelistic work with Dr. McGilvary can ever forget the oft-seen picture of the gray-haired patriarch seated on the bamboo floor of a thatch-covered Lāo house, teaching some one to read. Of course, the book faced the pupil, and it was often said that he had taught so many people in this way that he could read the Lāo character very readily with the book upside down. Little children instinctively loved him, and it is therefore needless to say that he loved them. In spite of his long snow-white beard, never seen in men of this land and a strange sight to any Lāo child, the children readily came to him. Parents have been led to God because Dr. McGilvary loved their children and laid his hands upon them. In no other capacity was the spirit of the man more manifest than in that of a shepherd. Always on the alert for every opportunity, counting neither time nor distance nor the hardship of inclement weather, swollen streams, pathless jungle, or impassable road, he followed the example of his Master in seeking to save the lost. His very last journey, which probably was the immediate cause of his last illness, was a long, wearisome ride on horseback, through muddy fields and deep irrigating ditches, to visit a man whom he had befriended many years ago and who seemed to be an inquirer."

Dr. McGilvary was pre-eminently a man who walked with God. His piety was not a mere profession, but a pervasive and abiding force. He knew no greater joy than to declare the Gospel of his blessed Lord to the people to whose up-lifting he had devoted his life. "If to be great is 'to take the common things of life and walk truly among them,' he was a great man—great in soul, great in simplicity, great in faith and great in love. Siam is the richer because Daniel McGilvary gave her fifty-three years of unselfish service." Mrs. Curtis, the gifted author of *The Laos of North Siam,* says of Dr. McGilvary: "Neither Carey nor Judson surpassed him in strength of faith and zeal of purpose; neither Paton nor Chalmers has outranked him in the wonders of their achievements, and not one of the other hundreds of missionaries ever has had more evidence of God's blessing upon their work."

Not only the missionaries but the Lão people loved him as a friend and venerated him as a father. Some of his intimate friends were the abbots and monks of the Buddhist monasteries and the high officials of the country. No one could know him without recognizing the nobility of soul of this saintly patriarch, in whom was no guile. December 6th, 1910, many Americans and Europeans celebrated the fiftieth anniversary of his marriage. The King of Siam through Prince Damrong, Minister of the Interior, sent a congratulatory message. Letters, telegrams, and gifts poured in from many different places. The Christian people of the city presented a large silver tray, on which was engraved: "The Christian people of Chiengmai to Dr. and Mrs. McGilvary, in memory of your having brought the Gospel of Jesus Christ to us forty-three years ago." The tray showed in relief the old rest-house where Dr. and Mrs. McGilvary spent their first two years in Chiengmai, the residence which was later their home of many years, the old dilapidated bridge, and the handsome new bridge which spans the river opposite the Christian Girls' School—thus symbolizing the old and the new eras.

The recent tours of exploration by the Rev. W. Clifton Dodd, D.D., and the Rev. John H. Freeman have disclosed the fact that the Lão peoples are far more numerous and more widely distributed than we had formerly supposed. Their numbers are now estimated at from twelve to sixteen millions, and their habitat includes not only the Lão States of northern Siam but extensive regions north and northeastward in the Shan States, Southern China, and French Indo-China. The evangelization of these peoples is, therefore, an even larger and more important undertaking than it was understood to be only a few years ago. All the more honour, therefore, must be assigned to Dr. McGilvary, who laid foundations upon which a great superstructure must now be built.

Dr. McGilvary died as he would have wished to die and as any Christian worker might wish to die. There was no long illness. He continued his great evangelistic and literary labours almost to the end. Only a short time before his death, he made another of his famous itinerating journeys, preaching the Gospel to the outlying villages, guiding perplexed people and comforting the sick and dying. He recked as little of personal hardship as he had all his life, thinking nothing of hard travelling, simple fare, and exposure to sun, mud, and rain. Not long after his return and after a few brief days of illness, he quietly "fell on sleep," his death the simple but majestic and dignified ending of a great earthly career.

The Lāo country had never seen such a funeral as that which marked the close of this memorable life. Princes, Governors, and High Commissioners of State sorrowed with multitudes of common people. The business of Chiengmai was suspended, offices were closed, and flags hung at half-mast as the silent form of the great missionary was borne to its last resting-place in the land to which he was the first bringer of enlightenment, and whose history can never be truly written without large recognition of his achievements.

Fortunately, Dr. McGilvary had completed this autobiography before his natural powers had abated, and had sent the manuscript to his brother-in-law, Professor Cornelius B. Bradley of the University of California. Dr. Bradley, himself a son of a great missionary to Siam, has done his editorial work with sympathetic insight. It has been a labour of love to him to put these pages through the press, and every friend of the Lāo people and of Dr. McGilvary is his debtor. The book itself is characterized by breadth of sympathy, richness of experience, clearness of statement, and high literary charm. No one can read these pages without realizing anew that Dr. McGilvary was a man of fine mind, close observation, and descriptive gifts. The book is full of human interest. It is the story of a man who tells about the things that he heard and saw and who tells his story well. I count it a privilege to have this opportunity of commending this volume as one of the books which no student of southern Asia and of the missionary enterprise can afford to overlook.

Arthur J. Brown.

156 Fifth Avenue, New York.

PREFACE

YEARS ago, in the absence of any adequate work upon the subject, the officers of our Missionary Board and other friends urged me to write a book on the Lāo Mission. Then there appeared Mrs. L. W. Curtis' interesting volume, *The Laos of North Siam,* much to be commended for its accuracy and its valuable information, especially in view of the author's short stay in the field. But no such work exhausts its subject.

I have always loved to trace the providential circumstances which led to the founding of the Lāo Mission and directed its early history. And it seems important that before it be too late, that early history should be put into permanent form. I have, therefore, endeavoured to give, with some fulness of detail, the story of the origin and inception of the Mission, and of its early struggles which culminated in the Edict of Religious Toleration. And in the later portions of the narrative I have naturally given prominence to those things which seemed to continue the characteristic features and the personal interest of that earlier period of outreach and adventure, and especially my long tours into the "regions beyond."

The appearance during the past year of Rev. J. H. Freeman's *An Oriental Land of the Free,* giving very full and accurate information regarding the present status of the Mission, has relieved me of the necessity of going over the same ground again. I have, therefore, been content to draw my narrative to a close with the account of my last long tour in 1898.

The work was undertaken with many misgivings, since my early training and the nature of my lifework have not been the best preparation for authorship. I cherished the secret hope that one of my own children would give the book its final revision for the press. But at last an appeal was made to my brother-in-law, Professor Cornelius B. Bradley of the University of California, whose birth and years of service in Siam, whose broad scholarship, fine literary taste, and hearty sympathy with our missionary efforts indicated him as the man above all others best qualified for this task. His generous acceptance of this work, and the infinite pains he has taken in the revision and editing of this book, place me under lasting obligations to him.

I wish to acknowledge my indebtedness to Dr. W. A. Briggs and to Rev. J. H. Freeman for the use of maps prepared by them, and to Dr. Briggs and others for the use of photographs.

DANIEL MCGILVARY.

April 6, 1911,
CHIENGMAI.

NOTE BY THE EDITOR

THE task which has fallen to me in connection with this book, was undertaken as a labour of love; and such it seems to me even more, now that it ends in sadness of farewell. It has not been an easy task. The vast spaces to be traversed, and the months of time required before a question could receive its answer, made consultation with the author almost impossible. And the ever-present fear that for him the night might come before the work could receive a last revision at his hands, or even while he was still in the midst of his story, led me continually to urge upon him the need of persevering in his writing—which was evidently becoming an irksome task—and on my part to hasten on a piecemeal revision as the chapters came to hand, though as yet I had no measure of the whole to guide me.

It is, therefore, a great comfort to know that my urgency and haste were not in vain; that all of the revision reached him in time to receive his criticism and correction—though his letter on the concluding chapter was, as I understand, the very last piece of writing that he ever did. How serene and bright it was, and with no trace of the shadow so soon to fall!

But the draft so made had far outgrown the possible limits of publication, and was, of course, without due measure and proportion of parts. In the delicate task of its reduction I am much indebted to the kind suggestions of the Rev. Arthur J. Brown, D.D., and the

Rev. A. W. Halsey, D.D., Secretaries of the Board of Foreign Missions of the Presbyterian Church, and of the Rev. W. C. Dodd, D.D., of the Lāo Mission, who, fortunately, was in this country, and who read the manuscript. For what appears in this book, however, I alone must assume the responsibility. "An autobiography is a personal book, expressive of personal opinion." And whether we agree with them or not, the opinions of a man like Dr. McGilvary, formed during a long lifetime of closest contact with the matters whereof he speaks, are an essential part not only of the history of those matters, but of the portrait of the man, and far more interesting than any mere details of events or scenes. On all grave questions, therefore, on which he has expressed his deliberate opinion, I have preferred to err on the side of inclusion rather than exclusion.

The plan adopted in this volume for spelling Siamese and Lāo words is intended to make possible, and even easy, a real approximation to the native pronunciation. Only the tonal inflections of native speech and the varieties of aspiration are ignored, as wholly foreign to our usage and, therefore, unmanageable.

The consonant-letters used and the digraphs *ch* and *ng* have their common English values.

The vowels are as follows:

Long ā as in *father*
ē as in *they*
ī as in *pique*
ō as in *rode*
ū as in *rude, rood*
aw as in *lawn*
ê as in *there* (without the *r*)

ô as in *world* (without the *r*)

û is the *high-mixed* vowel, not found in English. It may be pronounced as u.

Short a as in *about* (German *Mann*)—*not* as in *hat.*

e as in *set*

i as in *sit*

o as in *obey* (N. Eng. *coat*)—*not* as in *cot.*

u as in *pull, foot*—*not* as in *but.*

The last four long vowels have also their corresponding shorts, but since these rarely occur, it has not been thought worth while to burden the scheme with extra characters to represent them.

The diphthongs are combinations of one of these vowels, heavily stressed, and nearly always long in quantity—which makes it seem to us exaggerated or drawled—with a "vanish" of short *i, o,* (for *u*), or *a.* *ai* (=English long i, y) and *ao* (=English *ow*) are the only diphthongs with short initial element, and are to be distinguished from *âi* and *âo.* In deference to long established usage in maps and the like, *ie* is used in this volume where *ia* would be the consistent spelling, and *oi* for *awi.*

A word remains to be said concerning the name of the people among whom Dr. McGilvary spent his life. That name has suffered uncommonly hard usage, especially at the hands of Americans, as the following brief history will show. Its original form in European writing was *Lao,* a fairly accurate transcription by early French travellers of the name by which the Siamese call their cousins to the north and east. The word is a monosyllable ending in a diphthong similar to that heard in the proper names *Macão, Mindanão, Callão.* In French writing the name often appeared in the plural form, *les Laos;* the added *s,* however, being silent, made no difference with the pronunciation. This written plural, then, it would seem, English-speaking people took over without recognizing the fact that it was only plural, and made it their standard form for all uses, singular as well as plural. With characteristic ignorance or disregard of its proper pronunciation, on the mere basis of its spelling, they have imposed on it a barbarous pronunciation of their own—*Lay-oss.* It is to be regretted that the usage of American missionaries has been most effective in giving currency and countenance to this blunder—has even added to it the further blunder of using it as the name of the region or territory, as well as of the people. But the word is purely ethnical—a proper adjective like our words *French* or *English,* and, like these, capable of substantive use in naming either the people or their language, but not their land. Needless to say, these errors have no currency whatever among European peoples excepting the English, and they have very little currency in England. It seems high time for us of America to amend not only our false pronunciation, but our false usage, and the false spelling upon which these rest. In accordance with the scheme of spelling adopted in this work, the *a* of the name Lāo is marked with the macron to indicate its long quantity and stress.

CORNELIUS BEACH BRADLEY.

BERKELEY, CALIFORNIA,
December, 1911.

CONTENTS

ILLUSTRATIONS

I

CHILDHOOD AND YOUTH

HEREDITY and early environment exercise such a determining influence in forming a man's character and shaping his destiny that, without some knowledge of these as a clew, his after-life would often be unintelligible. And beyond these there is doubtless a current of events, directing the course of every man's life, which no one else can see so clearly as the man himself. In the following review of my early life, I have confined myself, therefore, to those events which seem to have led me to my life-work, or to have prepared me for it.

By race I am a Scotsman of Scotsmen. My father, Malcom McGilvary, was a Highland lad, born in the Isle of Skye, and inheriting the marked characteristics of his race. In 1789, when Malcom was eleven years old, my grandfather brought his family to the United States, and established himself in Moore County, North Carolina, on the headwaters of the Cape Fear River. The McGilvarys had but followed in the wake of an earlier immigration of Scottish Highlanders, whose descendants to this day form a large proportion of the population of Moore, Cumberland, Richmond, Robeson, and other counties of North Carolina. My father's brothers gradually scattered, one going to the south-western, and two to the northwestern frontier. My father, being the youngest of the family, remained with his parents on the homestead. The country was then sparsely settled; communication was slow and uncertain. The scattered members of the family gradually lost sight of one another and of the home. My mother belonged to the McIver clan—from the same region of the Scottish Highlands, and as numerous in North Carolina as the McGilvarys were scarce. She was born in this country not long after the arrival of her parents.

I was born May 16th, 1828, being the youngest of seven children. As soon after my birth as my mother could endure the removal, she was taken to Fayetteville, thirty-five miles distant, to undergo a dangerous surgical operation. The journey was a trying one. Anæsthetics were as yet unknown. My poor mother did not long survive the shock. She died on the 23d of November of that year.

Since feeding-bottles were not then in use, the motherless infant was passed around to the care of aunts and cousins, who had children of like age. Two aunts in particular, Catharine McIver and Margaret McNeill, and a cousin, Effie McIver, always claimed a share in me for their motherly ministrations till, at last, I could be turned over to my sister Mary. She, though but six years my senior, was old beyond her years; and the motherly care with which she watched over her little charge was long remembered and spoken of in the family.

When I was four years old, my father married his second wife, Miss Nancy McIntosh. The next nine years, till my father's death, June 8th, 1841, were spent in the uneventful routine of a godly family in a country home. My father's rigid ideas of family discipline were inherited from his Presbyterian ancestors in

Scotland, and his own piety was of a distinctly old-school type. He was a ruling elder in the church at Buffalo, Fayetteville Presbytery, in which office he was succeeded by my brother, Evander, and three others of his sons became elders in other churches. No pressure of business was ever allowed to interfere with family worship night and morning. A psalm or hymn from the old village hymnbook always formed part of the service. My father was an early riser, and, in the winter time, family worship was often over before the dawn. Almost every spare moment of his time he spent in reading Scott's Family Bible, the Philadelphia *Presbyterian*, or one of the few books of devotion which composed the family library. The special treasure of the book-case was the great quarto Illustrated Family Bible, with the Apocrypha and Brown's Concordance, published by M. Carey, Philadelphia, 1815. It was the only pictorial book in the library, and its pictures were awe-inspiring to us children—especially those in the Book of Revelation:—The Dragon Chained, The Beast with Seven Heads and Ten Horns, and the Vision of the Four Seals. These and the solemn themes of Russell's *Seven Sermons*—which on rainy days I used to steal away by myself to read—made a profound impression on me.

Scottish folk always carry the school with the kirk. Free schools were unknown; but after the crops were "laid by," we always had a subscription school, in which my father, with his large family, had a leading interest. The teacher "boarded around" with the pupils. Our regular night-task was three questions and answers in the Shorter Catechism—no small task for boys of ten or twelve years. My memory of the Catechism once stood me in good stead in after-life.

When examined for licensure by the Orange Presbytery, I was asked, "What is man's state by nature?" In reply I gave the answers to the nineteenth and twentieth questions in the Catechism. A perceptible smile passed over the faces of many of the presbyters, and Father Lynch said, "He is right on the Catechism. He will pass." In those days to be "right on the Catechism" would atone for many failures in Hodge or Turretin.

The church was at the village of Buffalo, four miles from our home, but no one of the family was expected to be absent from the family pew on "the Sabbath." Carriages were a later luxury in that region. Our two horses carried father and mother, with the youngest of the little folks mounted behind, till he should be able to walk with the rest.

The great event of the year was the camp-meeting at the Fall Communion. It served as an epoch from which the events of the year before and after it were dated. For weeks before it came, all work on the farm was arranged with reference to "Buffalo Sacrament"—pronounced with long *a* in the first syllable. It was accounted nothing for people to come fifteen, twenty, or even forty miles to the meetings. Every pewholder had a tent, and kept open house. No stranger went away hungry. Neighbouring ministers were invited to assist the pastor. Services began on Friday, and closed on Monday, unless some special interest suggested the wisdom of protracting them further. The regular order was: A sunrise prayer-meeting, breakfast, a prayer-meeting at nine, a sermon at ten, an intermission, and then another sermon. The sermons were not accounted of much worth if they were not an hour long. The pulpit was the tall old-fashioned box-pulpit with a sounding-board above. For want of room in the church, the two sermons on Sunday were preached from a stand in the open air. At the close of the second sermon the ruling elders, stationed in various parts of the congregation, distributed to the communicants the "tokens,"[1] which admitted them to the sacramental table. Then, in solemn procession, the company marched up the rising ground to the church, singing as they went:

> "Children of the Heavenly King,
> As ye journey sweetly sing."

It was a beautiful sight, and we boys used to climb the hill in advance to see it. When the audience was seated, there was a brief introductory exercise. Then a hymn was sung, while a group of communicants filled the places about the communion table. There was an address by one of the ministers, during the progress of which the bread and the wine were passed to the group at the table. Then there was singing again, while the first group retired, and a second group took its place. The same ceremony was repeated for them, and again for others, until all communicants present had participated. The communion service must have occupied nearly two hours. One thing I remember well—when the children's dinner-time came (which was after all the rest had dined), the sun was low in the heavens, and there was still a night service before us. Notwithstanding some inward rebellion, it seemed all right then. But the same thing nowadays would drive all the young people out of the church.

[1] The "token" was a thin square piece of lead stamped with the initial letter of the name of the church.

With some diffidence I venture to make one criticism on our home life. The "Sabbath" was too rigidly observed to commend itself to the judgment and conscience of children—too rigidly, perhaps, for the most healthy piety in adults. It is hard to convince boys that to whistle on Sunday, even though the tune be "Old Hundred," is a sin deserving of censure. An afternoon stroll in the farm or the orchard might even have clarified my father's vision for the enjoyment of his Scott's Bible at night. It would surely have been a means of grace to his boys. But such was the Scottish type of piety of those days, and it was strongly held. The family discipline was of the reserved and dignified type, rather than of the affectionate. Implicit obedience was the law for children. My father loved his children, but never descended to the level of familiarity with them when young, and could not sympathize with their sports.

But dark days were coming. Brother John Martin presently married and moved west. In August, 1840, an infant sister died of quinsy—the first death I ever witnessed. On June 8th, 1841, the father and "housebond" of the family was taken away. The inheritance he left his children was the example of an upright, spotless life—of more worth than a legacy of silver and gold. These we might have squandered, but that was inalienable.

At thirteen, I was small for my age—too small to do a man's work on the farm; and there was no money with which to secure for me an education. Just then occurred one of those casual incidents which often determine the whole course of one's life. Mr. Roderick McIntosh, one of my mother's cousins, being disabled for hard work on the farm, had learned the tailor's trade, and was then living in the village of Pittsboro, twenty-one miles away. His father was a neighbour of ours, and a man after my father's own heart. The two families had thus always been very intimate. While the question of my destiny was thus in the balance, this cousin, one day, while on a visit to his father, called at our house. He had mounted his horse to leave, when, turning to Evander, he asked, "What is Dan'l going to do?" My brother replied, "There he is; ask him." Turning to me, he said, "Well, Dan'l, how would you like to come and live with me? I will teach you a trade." I had never thought of such a thing, nor had it ever been mentioned in the family. But somehow it struck me favourably. Instinctively I replied, "I believe I should like it." A life-question could not have been settled more fortuitously. But it was the first step on the way to Siam and the Lāo Mission.

On the last day of August, 1841, I bade farewell to the old home, with all its pleasant associations. Every spot of it was dear, but never so dear as then. Accompanied by my brother Evander, each of us riding one of the old family horses, I started out for my new home. The departure was not utterly forlorn, since Evander was still with me. But the parting from him, as he started back next day, was probably the hardest thing I had ever experienced. I had to seek a quiet place and give vent to a flood of tears. For a time I was inexpressibly sad. I realized, as never before, that I was cut loose from the old moorings—was alone in the world. But the sorrows of youth are soon assuaged. No one could have received a warmer welcome in the new home than I did. There were two children in the family, and they helped to fill the void made by the separation.

Pittsboro was not a large village, but its outlook was broader than that of my home. The world seemed larger. I myself felt larger than I had done as a country boy. I heard discussion of politics and of the questions of the day. The county was strongly Whig, but Mr. McIntosh was an unyielding Democrat, and as fond of argument as a politician. According to southern custom, stores and shops were favourite resorts for passing away idle time, and for sharpening the wits of the villagers. The recent Presidential campaign of 1840 furnished unending themes for discussion in our little shop.

There was no Presbyterian church in Pittsboro at that time. The church-going population was divided between the Methodist and the Episcopalian churches, the former being the larger. With my cousin's family I attended the Methodist church. On my first Sunday I joined the Methodist Sunday School, and that school was the next important link in my chain of life. Its special feature was a system of prizes. A certain number of perfect answers secured a blue ticket; ten of these brought a yellow ticket; and yellow tickets, according to the number of them, entitled the possessor to various prizes—a hymnbook, a Bible, or the like. On the first Sunday I was put into a class of boys of my own age, at work on a little primer of one hundred and six questions, all answered in monosyllables. By the next Sunday I was able to recite the whole, together with the Lord's Prayer and the Apostles' Creed at the end. It was no great feat; but the teacher and the school thought it was. So, on the strength of my very first lesson, I got a yellow ticket, and was promoted to the next higher class. That stimulated my ambition, and I devoted my every spare hour to study. The next book was one of questions and answers on the four Gospels. They were very easy; I was able to commit to memory several hundred answers during the week. In a few Sundays I got my first prize; and it was not long before I had secured all the prizes offered in the school. What was of far more value than the prizes was the greater love for study and for the Scriptures which the effort had awakened in me, and a desire for an education. The shop was often idle; I had plenty of time for study, and made the most of it.

At one of the subsequent Quarterly Meetings, a Rev. Mr. Brainard, who had considerable reputation as a revivalist, preached one Sunday night a vivid and thrilling sermon on Noah's Ark and the Flood. So marked was the impression on the audience, that, at the close, according to the Methodist custom, "mourners" were invited to the altar. Many accepted the invitation. A young friend sitting beside me was greatly affected. With streaming eyes he said, "Dan'l, let us go, too," rising up and starting as he spoke. After a few moments I followed. By this time the space about the altar was well filled. There was great excitement and no little confusion—exhortation, singing, and prayer going on all at once. A number of persons made profession of religion, and soon my young friend joined them. He was full of joy, and was surprised to find that I was not so, too. The meetings were continued night after night, and each night I went to the altar. As I look back upon it from this distance, it seems to me that, with much exhortation to repent and believe, there was not enough of clear and definite instruction regarding the plan of salvation, or the offices and work of Christ. One night, in a quiet hour at home, the grounds and method of a sinner's acceptance of Christ became clear to me, and He became my Lord.

Soon after, when invitation was given to the new converts to join the church as probationers, I was urged by some good friends to join with the rest; and was myself not a little inclined to do so. It was no doubt the influence of my cousin that enabled me to withstand the excitement of the revival and the gentle pressure of my Methodist friends, and to join, instead, my father's old church at Buffalo. But I owe more than I shall ever know to that Sunday School, and since then I have always loved the Methodist Church. Meanwhile the prospects for an education grew no brighter, though Mr. Brantley, then a young graduate in charge of the Pittsboro Academy, but afterward a distinguished Baptist minister of Philadelphia, gave me a place in his school at idle times; and a Dr. Hall used to lend me books to read.

When the opportunity for acquiring an education finally came, it was as unexpected as a clap of thunder out of a blue sky. The celebrated Bingham School, now in Asheville, North Carolina, was then, as now, the most noted in the South. It was started by Rev. William Bingham in Pittsboro, North Carolina, in the closing years of the eighteenth century. It was moved to Hillsboro by his son, the late William J. Bingham, father of the present Principal. The school was patronized by the leading families of the South. The number of pupils was strictly limited. To secure a place, application had to be made a year or more in advance.

My surprise, therefore, can well be imagined, when one day Baccus King, a young boy of the town, walked into the shop with a letter addressed to Master Daniel McGilvary from no less a personage than William J. Bingham, the great teacher and Principal. At first I thought I was the victim of some boyish trick. But there was the signature, and the explanation that followed removed all doubt. Nathan Stedman, an influential citizen of Pittsboro, was an early acquaintance and friend of Mr. Bingham. He had visited the school in person to secure a place for his nephew, young King, and had brought back with him the letter for me. What Mr. Bingham knew of me I never discovered. No doubt Mr. Stedman could have told, though up to that time I had never more than spoken with him. Be that as it may, there was the letter with its most generous offer that I take a course in Bingham School at the Principal's expense. He was to board me and furnish all necessary expenses, which, after graduation, I was to refund by teaching. If I became a minister of the Gospel, the tuition was to be free; otherwise I was to refund that also. To young King's enquiry what I would do, I replied, "Of course, I shall go." My cousin, Mr. McIntosh, was scarcely less delighted than I was at the unexpected opening.

The invitation to attend Bingham School came in the fall of 1845, when I was in my eighteenth year. There were then only two weeks till the school should open. I had little preparation to make. A pine box painted red was soon got ready to serve as a trunk, for my wardrobe was by no means elaborate. Mr. Stedman kindly offered me a seat with Baccus and a friend of his who was returning to the school. On the way Baccus' friend entertained us with stories of the rigid discipline, for this was in the days when the rod was not spared. I had no fears of the rod, but I trembled lest I should not sustain myself as well as such great kindness demanded. It might be a very different thing from winning a reputation in a Methodist Sunday School.

It was dusk when we reached The Oaks. The family was at supper. Mr. Bingham came out to receive us. He told Baccus' friend to take him to his own old quarters, and, turning to me, said, "I have made arrangements for you to board with Mr. C., and to room with Mr. K., the assistant teacher, till my house is finished, when you are to live with us. But we are at supper now. You must be hungry after your long ride. Come in and eat with us." After supper, Mr. Bingham went with me to my boarding-house, and introduced me to my hosts and to my chum, David Kerr. He welcomed me, and said he thought we should get along finely together. We not only did that, but he became a warm friend to whom I owed much. So I was in the great Bingham School, overwhelmed with a succession of unexpected kindnesses from so many quarters! What did it all mean?

My highest anticipations of the school were realized. If there ever was a born teacher, William J. Bingham was one. Latin and Greek were taught then by a method very different from the modern one. Before a sentence was read or translated, the invariable direction was—master your grammar. In grammar-drill Mr. Bingham could have no superior. Bullion's Grammars and Readers were the text-books. The principal definitions were learned practically verbatim. The coarse print was required of all in the class. The older pupils were advised to learn notes, exceptions, and all. I never became so familiar with any other books as with that series of grammars. We were ex-

WILLIAM J. BINGHAM

pected to decline every noun and adjective, alone or combined, from nominative singular to ablative plural, backwards or forwards, and to give, at a nod, voice, mood, tense, number, and person of any verb in the lesson. These exercises became at last so easy that they were great fun. Even now, sixty years later, I often put myself to sleep by repeating the old paradigms.

It may seem that my estimate of Mr. Bingham is prejudiced by my sense of personal obligation to him for his kindness. Yet I doubt not that the universal verdict of every one who went there to study would be that he should be rated as one of the world's greatest teachers. The South owes much to him for the dignity he gave to the profession of teaching. No man ever left a deeper impress on me. Thousands of times I have thanked the Lord for the opportunity to attend his school.

I was graduated from the school in May, 1849, a few days before I was twenty-one years old. On leaving my kind friends at The Oaks, I was again at sea. It will be remembered that, by my original agreement, I was booked for teaching—but I had no idea where. Once more the unexpected happened. In the midst of negotiations for a school in the southern part of the state, I was greatly surprised at receiving an offer from one of the prominent business men of my own town, Pittsboro, to assist me in organizing a new school of my own there. With much doubt and hesitation on my part—for there were already two preparatory schools in the place—the venture was made, and I began with ten pupils taught in a little business office. The number was considerably increased during the year. But when the second year opened, I was put in charge of the Academy, whose Principal had resigned. Here, in work both pleasant and fairly profitable, I remained until the four years for which I had agreed to stay were up.

I had by no means reached my ideal. But, as my friends had predicted, it had been a success. Some of my warmest supporters were sure that I was giving up a certainty for an uncertainty, in not making teaching my life-work. It had evidently been the hope of my friends from the first that I would make Pittsboro my home, and build up a large and permanent school there. But my purpose of studying for the ministry had never wavered, and that made it easier for me to break off.

During these four years my relations with the newly organized Presbyterian church had been most pleasant and profitable. There was no resisting the appeal that I should become ruling elder. The superintendency of the Sunday School also fell naturally to me, and opened up another field of usefulness. The friendship formed with the pastor, the Rev. J. H. McNeill, is one of the pleasant memories of my life.

One feature of the church connection must not be passed over. Neither of the other elders was so circumstanced as to be able to attend the meetings of the Orange Presbytery. Three of the leading professors in the University were members of the Presbytery, and all the leading schools within its bounds were taught by Presbyterian ministers or elders. To accommodate this large group of teachers, the meetings were held in midsummer and midwinter. Thus it fell to my lot to represent the Pittsboro church at the Presbytery during nearly the whole of the four years of my stay in Pittsboro. As it was then constituted, its meetings were almost equal to a course in church government. The Rev. J. Doll, one of the best of parliamentarians, was stated clerk. A group of members such as the two Drs. Phillips, father and son, Dr. Elisha Mitchell, of the University, and many others that could be named, would have made any assembly noted. Professor Charles Phillips, as chairman of the committee on candidates for the ministry, came into closer touch with me than most of the others. He afterwards followed my course in the Seminary with an interest ripening into a friendship which continued throughout his life.

The meetings of the Presbytery were not then merely formal business meetings. They began on Wednesday and closed on Monday. They were looked forward to by the church in which they were to be held as spiritual and intellectual feasts. To the members themselves they were seasons of reunion, where friendships were cemented, and where wits were sharpened by intellectual conflicts, often before crowded congregations.

Union Seminary, now of Richmond, Virginia, has always been under the direction of the Synods of North Carolina and Virginia; and there were strong reasons why students from those Synods should study there. They were always reminded of that obligation. But the high reputation of Drs. Hodge and Alexander was a strong attraction toward Princeton. My pastor and Professor Phillips, chairman of the committee in charge of me, had both studied there. So I was allowed to have my preference. No doubt this proved another stepping-stone to Siam. Union Seminary was not then enthusiastic in regard to foreign missions, as it has since become. At the last meeting of Presbytery that I was to attend, Dr. Alexander Wilson moved that, inasmuch as Orange Presbytery owned a scholarship in Princeton Seminary, I be assigned to it. To my objection that I had made money to pay my own way, he replied, "You will have plenty of need of your money. You can buy books with it." I followed the suggestion and laid in a good library.

II

MINISTERIAL TRAINING

I ENTERED Princeton Seminary in the fall of 1853. I did not lodge in the Seminary building, but, through the kindness of Rev. Daniel Derouelle—whom, as agent of the American Bible Society, I had come to know during his visits to Pittsboro—I found a charming home in his family. There were, of course, some disadvantages in living a mile and a half away from the Seminary. I could not have the same intimate relations with my fellow students which I might have had if lodged in the Seminary. But I had the delightful home-life which most of them missed altogether. And the compulsory exercise of two, or sometimes three, trips a day, helped to keep me in health throughout my course. I became, indeed, a first-rate walker—an accomplishment which has since stood me in good stead in all my life abroad.

Being from the South, and not a college graduate, as were most of the students, I felt lonesome enough when, on the first morning of the session, I entered the Oratory and looked about me without discovering a single face that I knew. But at the close of the lecture some one who had been told by a friend to look out for me, touched me on the shoulder, made himself known, and then took me off to introduce me to J. Aspinwall Hodge, who was to be a classmate of mine. No man ever had a purer or a better friend than this young man, afterward Dr. J. Aspinwall Hodge; and I never met a friend more opportunely.

Of our revered teachers and of the studies of the Seminary course there is no need to speak here. Our class was a strong one. Among its members were such men as Gayley, Mills, Jonathan Wilson, Nixon, Lefevre, and Chaney. Of these Gayley and Mills were already candidates for missionary work abroad. In other classes were Robert McMullen and Isidore Loewenthal, destined to become martyrs in Cawnpore and Peshawur. Many were the stirring appeals we heard from these men. Dr. Charles Hodge, too, had given a son to India; and he never spoke more impressively than when he was pleading the cause of foreign missions. Princeton, moreover, because of its proximity to New York and to the headquarters of the various missionary societies established there, was a favourite field for the visits of the Secretaries of these organizations, and of returned missionaries. A notable visit during my first year was that of Dr. Alexander Duff, then in his prime. No one who heard him could forget his scathing criticism of the church for "playing at missions," or his impassioned appeals for labourers.

So the question was kept constantly before me. But during the first two years, the difficulty of the acquisition of a foreign language by a person not gifted in his own, seemed an obstacle well-nigh insuperable. Conscience suggested a compromise. Within the field of Home Missions was there not equal need of men to bring the bread of life to those who were perishing without it? With the object of finding some such opportunity, I spent my last vacation, in the summer of 1855, in Texas as agent of the American Sunday School Union.

Texas afforded, indeed, great opportunities for Christian work; but in the one object of my quest—a field where Christ was not preached—I was disappointed. In every small village there was already a church—often more than one. Even in country schoolhouses Methodists, Baptists, and Cumberland Presbyterians had regular Sunday appointments, each having acquired claim to a particular Sunday of the month. Conditions were such that the growth of one sect usually meant a corresponding weakening of the others. It was possible, of course, to find local exceptions. But it is easier even now to find villages by the hundred, with three, four, and even five Protestant churches, aided by various missionary societies; where all the inhabitants, working together, could do no more than support one church well. This may be necessary; but it is surely a great waste.

From this trip I had just returned with these thoughts in my mind, and was entering upon my senior year, when it was announced that Dr. S. R. House, a missionary from Siam, would address the students. Expectation was on tiptoe to hear from this new kingdom of Siam. The address was a revelation to us all. The opening of the kingdom to American missionaries by the reigning monarch, Mahā Mongkut—now an old story—was new then, and sounded like a veritable romance. My hesitation was ended. Here was not merely a village or a parish, but a whole kingdom, just waking from its long, dark, hopeless sleep. Every sermon I preached there might be to those who had never heard that there is a God in heaven who made them, or a Saviour from sin.

The appeal was for volunteers to go at once. None, however, of the men who had announced themselves as candidates for service abroad were available for Siam. They were all pledged to other fields. The call found Jonathan Wilson and myself in much the same state of expectancy, waiting for a clear revelation of duty. After anxious consultation and prayer together, and with Dr. House, we promised him that we would give the matter our most serious thought. If the Lord should lead us thither, we would go.

Meanwhile the Rev. Andrew B. Morse had been appointed a missionary to Siam, and the immediate urgency of the case was thus lightened. Shortly before the close of my Seminary course, in 1856, there came to me a call to the pastorate of two contiguous churches, those of Carthage and of Union, in my native county in North Carolina. The call seemed a providential one, and I accepted it for one year only. My classmate, Wilson, soon after accepted a call to work among the Indians in Spencer Academy.

My parish was an admirable one for the training of a young man. The church at Union was one of the oldest in the state. The church at Carthage, five miles away, was a colony from Union. No distinct geographical line separated the two. Many of the people regularly attended both. That, of course, made the work harder for a young pastor. The extreme limits of the two parishes were fifteen miles apart. But these were church-going folk, mostly of Scottish descent—not "dry-weather Christians." The pastorate had been vacant a whole year.

At the first morning service the church was crowded to its utmost capacity. Some came, no doubt, from curiosity to hear the new preacher; but most of them were hungry for the Gospel. They had all known my father; and some had known me—or known of me

—from boyhood. I could not have had a more sympathetic audience, as I learned from the words of appreciation and encouragement spoken to me after church—especially those spoken by my brother, who was present.

The year passed rapidly. The work had prospered and was delightful. In it I formed the taste for evangelistic touring, which was afterwards to be my work among the Lāo. There had been a number of accessions in both churches. It was easy to become engrossed in one's first charge among a people so sympathetic, and to overlook far-away Siam. Indeed, I had become so far influenced by present surroundings as to allow my name to be laid before a meeting of the congregation with a view to becoming their permanent pastor. Their choice of me was unanimous. Moreover, I had been dismissed from my old Presbytery to the one within whose bounds my parish was. The regular meeting of the latter was not far off, when arrangements were to be made for my ordination and installation.

As the time drew near, do what I might, my joy in accepting the call seemed marred by the thought of Siam. I learned that the Siamese Mission, instead of growing stronger, was becoming weaker. Mr. Morse's health had completely broken down during his first year in the field. He was then returning to the United States. Mrs. Mattoon had already come back an invalid. Her husband, after ten years in Siam, was greatly in need of a change; but was holding on in desperation, hoping against hope that he might be relieved.

The question of my going to Siam, which had been left an open one, must now soon be settled by my accepting or declining. I needed counsel, but knew not on what earthly source to call. When the question of Siam first came up in Princeton, I had written to leading members of the Orange Presbytery for advice, stating the claims of Siam so strongly that I was sure these men would at least give me some encouragement toward going. But the reply I had from one of them was typical of all the rest: "We do not know about Siam; but we do know of such and such a church and of such and such a field vacant here in Orange Presbytery. Still, of course, it *may* be your duty to go to Siam." In that quarter, surely, there was no light for me. So I devoted Saturday, August 1st, to fasting and prayer for guidance. In the woods back of the Carthage church and the Academy, the decision was finally reached. I would go.

Next morning I stopped my chief elder on his way to church, and informed him of my decision. After listening to my statement of the case, he replied, "Of course, if it is settled, there's nothing more to be said." It chanced that Mr. Russell, my former assistant in the Pittsboro Academy, had just finished his theological course; and, wholly without reference to the question pending in my mind, had arranged to preach for me that day. The session was called together before service, was notified of my decision, and was reminded that the preacher of the day would be available as a successor to me. He preached a good sermon, had a conference with the session afterwards, and was virtually engaged that day. The following week brought notice of my appointment as missionary to Siam.

The last communion season of that year was one of more than usual interest. The meetings began on

Friday. Since the minds of the congregation were already on the subject of foreign missions, and since Dr. McKay, from my home church, had been appointed by the Synod to preach on that subject at its coming session in Charlotte, I prevailed upon him to preach to us the sermon that he had prepared. The text was from Romans x:14, "How shall they hear without a preacher?" No subject could have been more appropriate to the occasion. It produced a profound impression. Some were affected to tears.

The sermon was a good preparation for the communion service that followed. At the night service there was deep seriousness throughout the congregation, and a general desire to have the meetings continued. On Monday there was an unexpectedly large congregation. At the busiest season of the year farmers had left their crops to come. The meetings soon grew to be one protracted prayer-meeting, with occasional short applications of Scripture to the questions which were already pressing upon our minds.

Finally, after the meetings had been continued from Friday until Wednesday week, they were reluctantly brought to a close; both because it seemed unwise to interrupt longer the regular life of the community, and also because the leaders no longer had the voice to carry them on. As a result of the meetings, there were about eighty accessions to the two Presbyterian churches, as well as a number to other churches. Many asked if I did not see in the revival reason to change my mind and remain. But the effect on me was just the opposite. It was surely the best preparation I could have had for the long test of faith while waiting for results in Siam.

Inasmuch as my certificate of dismissal had never

been formally presented to the Fayetteville Presbytery, I preferred to return it to my old Orange Presbytery, and to receive my ordination at its hands. On December 11th, the Presbytery met at my old home in Pittsboro. The installation of a foreign missionary was new to the Presbytery, as well as to the church and the community. When the ordaining prayer was ended, there seemed to be but few dry eyes in the congregation. It was a day I had little dreamed of sixteen years before, when I first came to Pittsboro an orphan boy and an apprentice. I felt very small for the great work so solemnly committed to me. Missionary fields were further off in those days than they are now, and the undertaking seemed greater. The future was unknown; but in God was my trust—and He has led me.

III

BANGKOK

ON reaching New York I went directly to the Mission House, then at 23 Centre Street. As I mounted the steps, the first man I met on the landing was Jonathan Wilson. We had exchanged a few letters, and each knew that the other had not forgotten Siam; but neither expected to meet the other there. "Where are you going?" said one. "I am on my way to Siam," said the other. "So am I," was the reply. In the meantime he had married and, with his young wife, was in New York awaiting passage. We took the first opportunity that offered, the clipper ship *David Brown,* bound for Singapore, and sailing on March 11th, 1858.

Sailors have a tradition that it is unlucky to have missionaries on board; but the weather was propitious throughout, and the voyage a prosperous one. We three were the only passengers, and we proved to be good sailors. Our fare was reasonably good. We had plenty of good reading, and soon settled down to steady work. The ship was somewhat undermanned; and this fact was given as an excuse for not having service on Sundays. But we had a daily prayer-meeting throughout the voyage, with just a sufficient number present to plead the promise: "Where two or three are gathered together in my name." We also had free access to the men in the forecastle when off duty.

We had the excitement of an ocean race with a twin

ship of the same line, which was to sail a week after us. As we reached Anjer Straits on the seventy-eighth day out, a sail loomed up which proved to be our competitor. She had beaten us by a week! Ten days later we reached Singapore, where, indeed, we met no brethren, but were met by welcome letters from Siam. Like Paul at the Three Taverns, "we thanked God and took courage." One of the letters ran thus:

> "Those were good words that came to our half-discouraged band—the tidings that we are to have helpers in our work. . . . In our loneliness we have sometimes been tempted to feel that our brethren at home had forgotten us. But we rejoice to know that there are hearts in the church which sympathize with us, and that you are willing to come and participate with us in our labours and trials, our joys and sorrows, for we have both."

We were fortunate to secure very early passage for Bangkok. On Friday, June 18th, we reached the bar at the mouth of the Mênam River. The next day we engaged a small schooner to take us up to Bangkok. With a strong tide against us, we were not able that evening to get further than Mosquito Point—the most appropriately-named place in all that land—only to learn that we could not reach Bangkok until Monday afternoon. There was no place to sleep on board; and no sleeping would have been possible, had there been a place. By two o'clock in the morning we could endure it no longer;—the mosquito contest was too unequal. At last we found a man and his wife who would take us to the city in their two-oared skiff.

Fifty years' residence in Siam has not surpassed the romance of that night's ride. Leaving our goods behind, we seated ourselves in the tiny craft. With gunwales but two inches above the water's edge, we skimmed along through a narrow winding canal overhung with strange tropical trees. The moon was full, but there was a haze in the air, adding weirdness to things but dimly seen. The sight of our first Buddhist monastery, with its white columns and grotesque figures, made us feel as if we were passing through some fairyland.

Just at dawn on Sunday morning, June 20th, 1858, we landed at the mission compound. Our quick passage of only one hundred days took our friends by surprise. Dr. House, roused by our voices on the veranda, came *en déshabillé* to the door to see what was the matter. Finding who we were, the eager man thrust his hand through a vacant square of the sash, and shook hands with us so, before he would wait to open the door. We were in Bangkok! It was as if we had waked up in a new world—in the Bangkok to which we had looked forward as the goal of our hopes; which was to be, as we supposed, the home of our lives.

The Rev. Mr. Mattoon was still at his post, awaiting our coming. Mrs. Mattoon and her daughters had been compelled to leave for home some time before our arrival. And not long thereafter Mr. Mattoon followed them on his furlough, long overdue. Besides the two men of our own mission, we found in Bangkok the Rev. Dan B. Bradley, M.D., who was conducting a self-supporting mission; Rev. S. J. Smith, and Rev. R. Telford of the Baptist mission.

Since neither Bangkok nor Lower Siam proved to be my permanent home, I shall content myself with a very summary account of the events of the next three years.

The first work of a new missionary is to acquire the language of the country. His constant wish is, Oh for a gift of tongues to speak to the people! As soon as a teacher could be found, I settled to work at my *kaw, kă, ki, kī*.[1] No ambitious freshman has such an incentive for study as has the new missionary. It is well if he does not confine himself to grammar and dictionary, as he did in the case of his Latin, Greek, and Hebrew. Pallegoix's *Dictionarium Linguae Thai*, and his short *Grammar* in Latin, were all the foreign helps we had. The syntax of the language is easy; but the "tones," the "aspirates," and "inaspirates," are perplexing beyond belief. You try to say "fowl." No, that is "egg." You mean to say "rice," but you actually say "mountain."

A thousand times a day the new missionary longs to open his mouth, but his lips are sealed. It is a matter of continual regret that he cannot pour out his soul in the ardour of his first love, unchilled by the deadening influences to which it is sure to be subjected later. But the delay is not an unmitigated evil. He is in a new world, in which he is constantly reminded of the danger of giving offence by a breach of custom as unalterable as the laws of the Medes and Persians. A bright little boy runs up and salutes you. You stroke his long black hair, only to be reminded by one of your seniors—"Oh! you must *never* do that! It is a mortal offence to lay your hand on a person's head." So, while you are learning the language, you are learning other things as well, and of no less importance.

In the mission school there was a class of bright boys named Nê, Dit, Chûn, Kwāi, Henry, and one girl, Tūan. To my great delight, Dr. House kindly turned them over to me. It made me think I was

[1] The first exercise of the Siamese Spelling-book.

doing something, and I really was. I soon became deeply interested in these children. Nê grew to be an important business man and an elder in the church; Tũan's family became one of the most influential in the church. Her two sons, the late Bun It and Elder Bun Yĩ of the First Church in Chiengmai, have been among the very best fruits of the mission; though my personal share in their training was, of course, very slight. In the September after our arrival there was organized the Presbytery of Siam, with the four men of the mission as its constituent members. During the first two years, moreover, I made a number of tours about the country—sometimes alone, oftener with Dr. House, and once with Mr. Wilson.

I had the pleasure of meeting His Majesty the King of Siam, not only at his birthday celebrations, to which foreigners were invited, but once, also, at a public audience on the occasion of the presentation of a letter from President James Buchanan of the United States. This was through the courtesy of Mr. J. H. Chandler, the acting United States Consul. Two royal state barges were sent down to the Consulate to receive the President's letter and the consular party. Siamese etiquette requires that the letter be accorded the same honour as would be given the President in person. In the first barge was the letter, placed in a large golden urn, with a pyramidal cover of gold, and escorted by the four officers who attend upon His Majesty when he appears in public. In the second barge was the consular party.

After a magnificent ride of four miles up the river, we were met at the palace by gilded palanquins for the members of the party, while the letter, in a special palanquin and under the golden umbrella, led the way to the Palace, some quarter of a mile distant. At the Palace gate a prince of rank met us, and ushered us into the royal presence, where His Majesty sat on his throne of gold, richly overhung with gilded tapestry. Advancing toward the throne, and bowing low, we took our stand erect, while every high prince and nobleman about us was on bended knees, not daring to raise his eyes above the floor.

The Consul then read a short introductory speech, stepped forward, and placed the letter in the extended hands of the King. Having glanced over it, the King handed it to his secretary, who read it aloud, His Majesty translating the substance of it to the princes and nobles present. The King then arose, put his scarf about his waist, girded on his golden sword, came down, and shook hands with each of the party. Then, with a wave of his hand, he said, "We have given President Buchanan the first public reception in our new palace," adding, "I honour President Buchanan very much." He escorted the party around the room, showing us the portraits of George Washington, President Pierce, Queen Victoria, and Prince Albert. Then, turning to the proper officer, he directed him to conduct us to an adjoining room to partake of a luncheon prepared for us; and, with a bow, withdrew.

After "tiffin," we were escorted to the landing as we had come, and returned in like state in the royal barge to the Consulate. Altogether it was a notable occasion.

Of the tours undertaken in Lower Siam, the one which led to the most lasting results was one in 1859 to Pechaburī, which has since become well known as one of our mission stations. For companion on this trip I had Cornelius Bradley, son of the Rev. Dr. Brad-

MAHĀ MONKUT,
KING OF SIAM, 1851-1872

ley of Bangkok. Shortly before this a rising young nobleman, and a liberal-minded friend of foreigners, had been assigned to the place ostensibly of lieutenant-governor (Pra Palat) of Pechaburī, but practically of governor. He was a brother of the future Regent; had been on the first embassy to England; and at a later period became Minister for Foreign Affairs. At our call, His Excellency received us very kindly, and before we left invited us to dine with him on the following evening.

The dinner was one that would have done credit to any hostess in America. I was still more surprised when, at the table, addressing me by a title then given to all missionaries, he said, "Maw" (Doctor), "I want you to come and live in Pechaburī. You have no family. I will furnish you a house, and give you every assistance you need. You can teach as much Christianity as you please, if only you will teach my son English. If you want a school, I will see that you have pupils." I thanked him for the offer, but could only tell him that I would think the matter over. It might be, after all, only a Siamese cheap compliment. It seemed too good to be true. It was, however, directly in the line of my own thoughts. I had come to Siam with the idea of leaving the great commercial centres, and making the experiment among a rural population like that of my North Carolina charge.

The next day the Pra Palat called on us at our *sălă*,[1] and again broached the subject. He was very anxious to have his son study English. In my mission

[1] A public rest-house or shelter, such as Buddhist piety provides everywhere for travellers, but especially in connection with the monasteries.

work I should be untrammelled. Before leaving us, he mentioned the matter again. It was this time no courteous evasion when I told him I would come if I could.—What did it all mean?

I returned to Bangkok full of enthusiasm for Pechaburī. The more I pondered it, the greater the offer seemed to be. Beyond my predilection for a smaller city or for rural work, I actually did not like Bangkok. Pechaburī, however, was beyond the limits of treaty rights. Permission to establish a station there could be had only by sufferance from a government not hitherto noted for liberality. Here was an invitation equivalent to a royal permit, and with no further red tape about it. I could see only one obstacle in the way. The senior member of the mission —the one who was naturally its head—I feared would not approve. And he did, indeed, look askance at the proposition. He doubted whether we could trust the promises made. And then to go so far away alone! But I thought I knew human nature well enough to trust that man. As to being alone, I was willing to risk that. Possibly it might not be best to ride a free horse too freely. I would go with my own equipment, and be at least semi-independent; though the Palat had said that he did not mind the expense, if only he could get his son taught English.

There could at least be no objection to making an experimental visit, and then continuing it as long as might seem wise. Pechaburī is within thirty hours of Bangkok. If taken sick, I could run over in a day or two. With that understanding, and with the tacit rather than the expressed sanction of the mission, I began to make preparations.

At last my preparations were complete, even to

baking bread for the trip. I had fitted up a touring-boat of my own, and had engaged captain and boatmen; when, on the day before I was to start, cholera, which for some time had been sporadic in Bangkok, suddenly became epidemic. Till then Dr. James Campbell, physician to the British Consulate, and our medical authority, thought that with caution and prudence I might safely go. A general panic now arose all over the land. Dr. Bradley came to tell me that deaths were occurring hourly on the canal by which I was to travel. To go then would be to tempt providence. I had earnestly sought direction, and it came in a way little expected.

The first man I met next morning was Dr. House, coming home from Mr. Wilson's. He had been called in the night to attend Mrs. Wilson, who had been suddenly attacked with "the disease," as the natives euphemistically call it, being superstitiously afraid of uttering the name. Dr. House had failed to check it, and sent me to call Dr. Campbell. But he was not at home, and did not get the message till near noon. By that time the patient had reached the stage when collapse was about to ensue. The disease was finally arrested, but Mrs. Wilson was left in a very precarious condition.

Meanwhile her little daughter Harriet was also taken ill, and for a time the life of both mother and daughter was in suspense. The child lingered on till May 13th, when she was taken to a better clime. On July 14th the mother, too, ceased from her suffering, and entered on her everlasting rest.

During these months, of course, all thoughts of Pechaburi had been abandoned; nor would it then have been deemed wise to travel during the wet season. Before the next dry season came, Bangkok began to have more attractions, and I had become less ambitious to start a new station alone. On the 11th of September I became engaged to Miss Sophia Royce Bradley, daughter of the Rev. D. B. Bradley, M.D. On December 6th, 1860, we were married. In my wife I found a helpmeet of great executive ability, and admirably qualified for the diversified work before us. It was something, too, to have inherited the best traditions of one of the grand missionaries of his age.[1]

Samrē, our mission station in Bangkok, was four miles distant from the heart of the city. We greatly needed a more central station for our work. Dr. Bradley offered us the use of a house on his own premises—one of the most desirable situations in Bangkok—if we would come and live there. The mission accepted his generous offer. With reluctance I resigned whatever claim I might have to be the pioneer of the new station at Pechaburī. We were settled, as it would seem, for life, in Bangkok.

[1] Dr. Bradley's life would be the best history we could have of Siam during its transition period. He left a voluminous diary, and it was from his pen that most of the exact information concerning Siam was long derived.

IV

PECHABURĪ—THE CALL OF THE NORTH

BY this time the mission generally had become interested in the establishment of a new station at Pechaburī. Dr. and Mrs. House were designated for the post. The Doctor actually went to Pechaburī; procured there, through the help of our friend the Palat, a lot with a house on it; and thus committed the mission to the project. But the day before he was to start homeward to prepare for removal thither, he was so seriously hurt by a fall from his horse that he was confined to his bed for several months. It was even feared that he was permanently disabled for active life. A new adjustment of our personnel was thus necessitated. Dr. Mattoon had just returned from the United States with the Rev. S. G. McFarland, the Rev. N. A. McDonald, and their wives. Dr. Mattoon could not be spared from Bangkok, nor was he enthusiastic over the new station. Mr. McDonald had no desire for such experiments. Both Mr. and Mrs. McFarland were anxious to move, but were too new to the field to be sent out alone. They were urgent that we should go with them. My opportunity had come. So, early in June, 1861, we broke up the first home of our married life, and, in company with the McFarlands, moved on to our new home and our new work.

Our friend, the Pra Palat, seemed pleased that we

had come, after all. His slight knowledge of English had been learned as a private pupil from Mrs. McGilvary's own mother. He was glad, whenever he had leisure, to continue his studies with Mrs. McGilvary. Mr. McFarland preferred school work. He took the son that I was to have taught, and left me untrammelled to enter upon evangelistic work. The half-hour after each evening meal we spent in united prayer for guidance and success. Two servants of each family were selected as special subjects of prayer; and these, in due time, we had the pleasure of welcoming into the church.

Of the incidents of our Pechaburī life I have room for but a single one. As we were rising from the dinner-table one Sunday shortly after our arrival, we were surprised to see a man coming up the steps and crossing the veranda in haste, as if on a special errand. He led by the hand a little boy of ten or twelve years, and said, "I want to commit this son of mine into your care. I want you to teach him." Struck by his earnest manner, we drew from him these facts: He was a farmer named Nāi Kawn, living some five miles out in the country. He had just heard of our arrival, had come immediately, and was very glad to find us.

We asked whether he had ever met a missionary before. No, he said, but his father—since dead—had once met Dr. Bradley, and had received a book from him. He had begged other books from neighbours who had received them but did not value them. Neither did he at first, till the great cholera scourge of 1849, when people were dying all around him. He was greatly alarmed, and learned from one of the books that Pra Yēsū heard prayer in trouble, and could save from sin. For a long time he prayed for light, until, about three years ago, he believed in Jesus, and was now happy in heart. He had heard once of Dr. Bradley's coming to Pechaburī, but not until he was gone again. He preached to his neighbours, who called him "Kon Pra Yēsū" (Lord Jesus' man). He had prayed for Dr. Bradley and the missionaries; he had read the story of Moses, the Epistle to the Romans, the Gospel of John, a tract on Prayer, and "The Golden Balance"; and he believed them. He could repeat portions of Romans and John verbatim; and he had his son repeat the Lord's Prayer.

My subject at the afternoon service was Nicodemus and the New Birth. Nāi Kawn sat spellbound, frequently nodding assent. At the close we asked him to speak a few words; which he did with great clearness. On being questioned as to the Trinity, he replied that he was not sure whether he understood it. He gathered, however, that Jehovah was the Father and Ruler; that the Son came to save us by dying for us; and that the Holy Spirit is the Comforter. The difference between Jesus and Buddha is that the latter entered into Nirvana, and that was the last of him; while Jesus lives to save. He even insisted that he had seen a vision of Jesus in heaven. His other experiences were characterized by such marks of soberness that we wondered whether his faith might not have been strengthened by a dream or a vision.

This incident, coming so soon after our arrival, greatly cheered us in our work. His subsequent story is too long to follow out in detail here. His piety and his sincerity were undoubted. He lived and died a Christian; yet he never fully identified himself with the church. He insisted that he had been baptized by the Holy Ghost, and that there was no need of further baptism. Not long after this Dr. Bradley and Mr. Mattoon visited Pechaburi, examined the man, and were equally surprised at his history.

What changed our life-work from the Siamese to the Lāo? There were two principal causes. The various Lāo states which are now a part of Siam, were then ruled by feudal princes, each virtually sovereign within his own dominions, but all required to pay a triennial visit to the Siamese capital, bringing the customary gifts to their suzerain, the King of Siam, and renewing their oath of allegiance to him. Their realms served, moreover, as a "buffer" between Siam and Burma. There were six of these feudal principalities. Five of them occupied the basins of five chief tributaries of the Mênam River; namely—in order from west to east—Chiengmai, Lampūn, Lakawn, Prê, and Nān. The sixth was Lūang Prabāng on the Mê Kōng River. The rapids on all these streams had served as an effectual barrier in keeping the northern and the southern states quite separate. There was no very frequent communication in trade. There was no mail communication. Official despatches were passed along from one governor to the next. Very little was known in Bangkok about the Lāo provinces of the north. A trip from Bangkok to Chiengmai seemed then like going out of the world. Only one Englishman, Sir Robert Schomburgk of the British Consulate in Bangkok, had ever made it.

Of these Lāo states, Chiengmai was the most important. After it came Nān, then Lūang Prabāng (since ceded to the French), Lakawn, Prê, and Lampūn. The Lāo people were regarded in Siam as a very warlike race; one chieftain in particular being famed

PAGODA OF WAT CHÊNG, BANGKOK

as a great warrior. They were withal said to be suspicious and unreliable.

Almost the only visible result of my six months' stay within the city of Bangkok, after my marriage, was the formation of a slight acquaintance with the Prince of Chiengmai and his family. Just before my marriage he had arrived in Bangkok with a great flotilla of boats and a great retinue of attendants. The grounds of Wat Chêng monastery, near to Dr. Bradley's compound, had always been their stopping-place. The consequence was that, of all the missionaries, Dr. Bradley had become best acquainted with them and most deeply interested in them. He earnestly cultivated their friendship, invited them to his printing-office and to his house, and continually preached unto them the Gospel. They were much interested in vaccination, which he had introduced, and were delighted to find that it protected them from smallpox.

The day after our marriage, in response to a present of some wedding cake, the Prince himself, with his two daughters and a large train of attendants, called on us in our new home. This was my first introduction to Chao Kăwilōrot and his family, who were to play so important a rôle in my future life. All that I saw of him and of his people interested me greatly. During the short time we remained in their neighbourhood, I made frequent visits to the Lāo camp. The subject of a mission in Chiengmai was talked of, with apparent approval on the part of the Prince. My interest in Pechaburī was increased by the knowledge that there was a large colony of Lāo [1] there. These were cap-

[1] The application of this name is by no means uniform throughout the peninsula. From Lūang Prabăng southward along the eastern frontier, the tribes of that stock call themselves Lāo, and are so

tives of war from the region of Khōrāt, bearing no very close resemblance to our later parishioners in the north. At the time of our stay in Pechaburī, the Lāo in that province were held as government slaves, engaged all day on various public works—a circumstance which greatly impeded our access to them, and at the same time made it more difficult for them to embrace Christianity. Neither they nor we dared apply to the government for the requisite sanction, lest thereby their case be made worse. Our best opportunity for work among them was at night. My most pleasant memories of Pechaburī cluster about scenes in Lāo villages, when the whole population would assemble, either around a camp-fire or under the bright light of the moon, to listen till late in the night to the word of God. The conversion of Nāi Ang, the first one from that colony, anticipated that of Nān Inta, and the larger ingathering in the North.

But there was more than a casual connection between the two. My labours among them increased the desire, already awakened in me, to reach the home of the race. Here was another link in the chain of providences by which I was led to my life-work. The time, however, was not yet ripe. The available force of the mission was not yet large enough to justify further expansion. Moreover, our knowledge of the

called by their neighbours. But the central and western groups do not acknowledge the name as theirs at all, but call themselves simply Tai; or if a distinction must be made, they call themselves Kon Nūa (Northerners), and the Siamese, Kon Tai (Southerners). The Siamese, on the other hand, also call themselves Tai, which is really the race-name, common to all branches of the stock; and they apply the name Lāo alike to all their northern cousins except the Ngio, or Western Shans. Nothing is known of the origin of the name, but the same root no doubt appears in such tribal and geographical names as Lawā, Lawa, Lawō—the last being the name of the famous abandoned capital now known as Lophburi.—Ed.

Lāo country was not such as to make possible any comprehensive and intelligent plans for a mission there. The first thing to do was evidently to make a tour of exploration. The way to such a tour was opened in the fall of 1863. The Presbytery of Siam met in Bangkok early in November. I had so arranged my affairs that, if the way should open, I could go north directly, without returning to Pechaburī. I knew that Mr. Wilson was free, and I thought he would favour the trip. This he readily did, and the mission gave its sanction. So I committed my wife and our two-year-old daughter to the care of loving grandparents, and, after a very hasty preparation, we started on the 20th of November in search of far-away Chiengmai.

The six-oared touring-boat which I had fitted up in my bachelor days was well adapted for our purpose as far as the first fork of the Mênam. The Siamese are experts with the oar, but are unused to the setting-pole, which is well-nigh the only resource all through the upper reaches of the river. It was sunset on a Friday evening before we finally got off. But it was a start; and it proved to be one of the straws on which the success of the trip depended. The current against us was very strong; so we slept within the city limits that night. We spent all day Saturday traversing a canal parallel with the river, where the current was weaker. It was sunset before we entered again the main stream, and stopped to spend Sunday at a monastery. To our great surprise we found that the Prince of Chiengmai—of whose coming we had had no intimation—had camped there the night before, and had passed on down to Bangkok that very morning. We had missed him by taking the canal!

We were in doubt whether we ought not to return and get a letter from him. A favourable letter would be invaluable; but he might refuse, or even forbid our going. If we may judge from what we afterwards knew of his suspicious nature, such probably would have been the outcome. At any rate, it would delay us; and we had already a passport from the Siamese government which would ensure our trip. And, doubtless, we did accomplish our design with more freedom because of the Prince's absence from his realm. It was apparently a fortuitous thing that our men knew of the more sluggish channel, and so missed the Lāo flotilla. But it is quite possible that upon that choice depended the establishment of the Lāo mission.

All went well until we reached the first fork at Pāknam Pō. There the water came rushing down like a torrent, so swift that oars were of no avail. We tried first one side of the stream and then the other, but all in vain. Our boatmen exchanged their oars for poles. But they were awkward and unaccustomed to their use. The boat would inevitably drift down stream. The poor boatmen laughed despairingly at their own failure. At last a rope was suggested. The men climbed the bank, and dragged the boat around the point to where the current was less swift. But when, as often happened, it became necessary to cross to the other side of the river, the first push off the bank would send us into water so deep that a fifteen-foot pole could not reach bottom. Away would go the boat some hundreds of yards down stream before we could bring up on the opposite bank. We reached Rahêng, however, in nineteen travelling days—which was not by any means bad time.

In our various journeyings hitherto we had controlled our own means of transportation. Henceforth we were at the mercy of native officials, to whose temperament such things as punctuality and speed are altogether alien. From Rahêng the trip by elephant to Chiengmai should be only twelve days. By boat, the trip would be much longer, though the return trip would be correspondingly shorter. We had a letter from Bangkok to the officials along the route, directing them to procure for us boats, elephants, or men, as we might need. We were in a hurry, and, besides, were young and impulsive. The officials at Rahêng assured us that we should have prompt despatch. No one, however, seemed to make any effort to send us on. The governor was a great Buddhist, and fond of company and argument. He could match our Trinity by a Buddhist one: Putthō, Thammō, Sangkhō—Buddha, the Scriptures, the Brotherhood. Men's own good deeds were their only atonement. The one religion was as good as the other. On these subjects he would talk by the hour; but when urged to get our elephants, he always had an excuse. At last, in despair, we decided to take our boatmen and walk. When this news reached the governor, whether from pity of us, or from fear that some trouble might grow out of it, he sent word that if we would wait till the next day, we should have the elephants without fail.

We got the elephants; but, as it was, from preference I walked most of the way. Once I paid dear for my walk by getting separated from my elephant in the morning, losing my noonday lunch, and not regaining my party till, tired and hungry, I reached camp at night. Our guide had taken a circuitous route to avoid a band of robbers on the main route which I had followed! This was my first experience of elephant-riding. We crossed rivers where the banks were steep, and there was no regular landing. But whether ascending or descending steep slopes, whether skirting streams and waterfalls, one may trust the elephant's sagacity and surefootedness. The view we had from one of the mountain ridges seemed incomparably fine. The Mê Ping wound its way along the base beneath us, while beyond, to right and to left, rose range beyond range, with an occasional peak towering high above the rest. But that was tame in comparison with many mountain views encountered in subsequent years.

We were eight days in reaching Lakawn,[1] which we marked as one of our future mission stations. On being asked whether he would welcome a mission there, the governor replied, "If the King of Siam and the Prince of Chiengmai approve." At Lakawn we had no delay, stopping there only from Friday till Monday morning. Thence to Lampūn we found sālās, or rest-houses, at regular intervals. The watershed between these towns was the highest we had crossed. The road follows the valley of a stream to near the summit, and then follows another stream down on the other side. The gorge was in places so narrow that the elephant-saddle scraped the mountain wall on one side, while on the other a misstep would have precipitated us far down to the brook-bed below.

[1] A corruption of Nakawn (for Sanskrit *nagara*, capital city), which is the first part of the official name of the place, Nakawn Lampāng. The Post Office calls it Lampāng, to distinguish it from another Nakawn (likewise Lakawn in common speech), in the Malay Peninsula—the place known to Europeans as Ligor. The general currency of this short name, and its regular use in all the missionary literature, seem to justify its retention in this narrative.—Ed.

At Lampūn my companion was not well, so that I alone called on the authorities. The governor had called the princes together to learn our errand. They seemed bewildered when told that we had no government business, nor were we traders—were only teachers of religion. When the proper officer was directed to send us on quickly, he began to make excuses that it would take two or three days. Turning sharply upon him, the governor asked, "Prayā Sanām, how many elephants have you?" "Four," was the response. "See that they get off to-morrow," was the short reply. He meekly withdrew. There was evidently no trifling with that governor. One day more brought us to Chiengmai—to the end of what seemed then a very long journey. As we neared the city, Mr. Wilson's elephant took fright at the creaking noise of a water-wheel, and ran away, crashing through bamboo fences and trampling down gardens. Fortunately no one was hurt.

We reached the city on January 7th, 1864, on the forty-ninth day of our journey. The nephew of the Prince had been left in charge during the Prince's absence. He evidently was in doubt how to receive us. He could not ignore our passport and letter from Bangkok. On the other hand, why did we not have a letter from the Prince? Our story of missing him through choosing the canal instead of the main river might or might not be true. If the deputy were too hospitable, his Prince might blame him. So he cut the knot, and went off to his fields. We saw no more of him till he came in to see us safely off.

The elder daughter of the Prince had accompanied her father to Bangkok, but the younger daughter was at home. She was a person of great influence, and was by nature hospitable. Things could not have been better planned for our purpose. The princess remembered me and my wife from her call on us after our wedding. She now called on us in person with her retinue; after that everybody else was free to call. It is not unlikely that that previous acquaintance redeemed our trip from being a failure. Our sālā was usually crowded with visitors. We had an ideal opportunity of seeing the heart of the people. They lacked a certain external refinement seen among the Siamese; but they seemed sincere and more religious. Buddhism had not become so much a matter of form. Many of the older people then spent a day and a night, or even two days, each month fasting in the monasteries. There was hope that if such people saw a better way, they would accept it. One officer, who lived just behind our sālā, a great meritmaker, was a constant visitor. Years afterward we had the pleasure of welcoming him to the communion of the church.

From every point of view the tour was eminently successful. Many thousands heard the Gospel for the first time. In our main quest we were more than successful. We were delighted with the country, the cities, the people. Every place we came to we mentally took possession of for our Lord and Master. In Chiengmai we remained only ten days; but one day would have sufficed to convince us. I, at least, left it with the joyful hope of its becoming the field of my life-work.

From the first we had planned to return by the river through the rapids. But the prince in charge was very averse to our going by that route. We knew that the route positively made no difference to him personally. He had only to give the word, and either elephants or boats would be forthcoming. Was he afraid of our spying out the road into the country? At last we were obliged to insist on the wording of our letter, which specially mentioned boats. Then he offered us one so small that he probably thought we would refuse it. But we took it; and our captain afterwards exchanged it for a larger one. We made a swift passage through the famous rapids, and reached Bangkok on January 30th, 1864.

The first news that we heard on our arrival was that Mrs. Mattoon was obliged to leave at once for the United States, and that Mr. Wilson was to take his furlough at the same time. This, of course, ended all plans for any immediate removal to Chiengmai. We hastened to Pechaburī, where the McFarlands had been alone during our absence. Three years were to pass before our faces were again turned northward.

V

THE CHARTER OF THE LĀO MISSION

IN the meantime, with two children added unto us, we were become a family much more difficult to move. We liked our home and our work. At the age of thirty-nine, to strike out into a new work, in a language at least partly new, was a matter not to be lightly undertaken. Might it not be better that Mr. Wilson should work up in the United States an interest in the new mission, should himself select his associates in it, and that I should give up my claim to that place? It was certain that three families could not be spared for Chiengmai. More than one day was spent, under the shade of a great tree behind Wat Noi, in thought on the subject, and in prayer for direction.

Finally—though it was a hard thing to do—I wrote to Mr. Wilson, then in the United States, suggesting the plan just stated. Feeling sure that it would commend itself to him, I considered the door to Chiengmai as probably closed to me. In the meantime Mr. Wilson had married again; and on the eve of his return wrote to me that he had failed to get another family to come out with him, and was discouraged about the Chiengmai mission. Probably the time had not yet come, etc., etc. I was delighted to get that letter. It decided me to go to Chiengmai, the Lord willing, the following dry season, with only my own family, if need be. Dr. Mattoon and Dr. House were absent on furlough. Mr. Wilson and I would be the senior members of the mission. The Board had already given its sanction. The mission in Bangkok meanwhile had been reinforced by the arrival of the Georges and the Cardens. On the return of those then absent on furlough, one of these families could join the McFarlands in Pechaburī, and yet there would be four families in Bangkok. Such a combination of favourable circumstances might not occur again.

When Mr. Wilson arrived in Bangkok in the fall of 1866, a letter was waiting for him, asking him to visit us in Pechaburī to talk over the question. On his arrival we spent one Sunday in anxious consultation. He was still eager to go to Chiengmai, but could not go that year. His preference would be that we should wait another year.—But that might be to lose the opportunity. So next morning, leaving Mr. and Mrs. Wilson to visit with my family, I hurried over to Bangkok. There was no time to be lost. The Prince of Chiengmai had been called down on special business, and was soon to return. The whole plan might depend on him—as, in fact, it did.

It was after dark on Tuesday night when I reached Dr. Bradley's, taking them all by surprise. I made known my errand. Another long and anxious consultation followed. I knew that Dr. Bradley's great missionary soul would not be staggered by any personal considerations. It would be but the answer to his own prayers to see a mission planted in Chiengmai. In his heart he was glad that it was to be planted by one of his own family. Earnest prayer was offered that night at the family altar for guidance in the negotiations of the following day, and for a blessing on the mission that was to be.

On Wednesday, after an early breakfast, Dr. Bradley accompanied me to our mission. My colleagues, McDonald, George, and Carden, were easily induced to consent. Mr. McDonald said that he would not go himself; but if I were willing to risk my family, he would not oppose the scheme, and would vote to have Mr. Wilson follow me the next year. Thus another obstacle was removed.

Taking Mr. McDonald and Mr. George with us, we proceeded next to the United States Consulate, where Mr. Hood readily agreed to give his official and personal aid. The two greatest obstacles remained yet: the Siamese government and—as it turned out in the end—the Lāo Prince[1] also. The Consul wrote immediately to the King, through our former Pechaburī friend, who had recently been made Foreign Minister, a formal request for permission to open a station in Chiengmai. It was Friday evening when the reply

[1] The Lāo ruler was a feudal vassal of the King of Siam, governing an important frontier province, and granted, within that province, some of the powers which are usually thought of as belonging to sovereignty—notably the power of life and death in the case of his immediate subjects. His title, Pra Chao, like its English parallel, Lord, he shared with the deity as well as with kings; though the Kings of Siam claim the added designation, "*Yū Hūa*," "at the head," or "Sovereign." By the early missionaries, however, he was regularly styled "King," a term which to us misrepresents his real status, and which leads to much confusion both of personality and of function. Meantime both title and function have vanished with the feudal order of which they were a part, leaving us free to seek for our narrative a less misleading term. Such a term seems to be the word Prince, thus defined in Murray's Dictionary (*s. v.* II. 5):—"The ruler of a principality or small state, actually, nominally, or originally, a feudatory of a king or emperor." The capital initial should suffice generally to distinguish the Prince who is ruler from princes who are such merely by accident of birth.—Ed.

came that the decision did not rest with the King. He could not force a mission upon the Lāo people. But the Lāo Prince was then in Bangkok. If he gave his consent, the Siamese government would give theirs. He suggested that we have an audience with the Prince, at which His Majesty would have an officer in attendance to report directly to him.

So on Saturday morning at ten o'clock we all appeared at the landing where the Lāo boats were moored, asking for an audience with the Prince. We were invited to await him in the sālā at the river landing. In a few moments His Highness came up in his customary informal attire—a *phānung* about his loins, no jacket, a scarf thrown loosely over his shoulders, and a little cane in his hand. Having shaken hands with us, he seated himself in his favourite attitude, dangling his right leg over his left knee. He asked our errand. At Mr. Hood's request Dr. Bradley explained our desire to establish a mission station in Chiengmai, and our hope to secure his approval. The Prince seemed relieved to find that our errand involved nothing more serious than that. The mission station was no new question suddenly sprung upon him. We had more than once spoken with him about it, and always apparently with his approbation. To all our requests he now gave ready assent. Yes, we might establish ourselves in Chiengmai. Land was cheap; we need not even buy it. Timber was cheap. There would be, of course, the cost of cutting and hauling it; but not much more. We could build our houses of brick or of wood, as we pleased. It was explained, as he already knew, that our object was to teach religion, to establish schools, and to care for the sick. The King's secretary took down the replies of the Prince to our questions. The Consul expressed his gratitude, and committed my family to his gracious care. We were to follow the Prince to Chiengmai as soon as possible.

Such was the outward scene and circumstance of the official birth of the Lāo mission. In itself it was ludicrous enough: the audience chamber, a sālā-landing under the shadow of a Buddhist monastery; the Consul in his official uniform; the Prince *en déshabillé;* our little group awaiting the answer on which depended the royal signature of Somdet Phra Paramendr Mahā Mongkut authorizing the establishment of a Christian mission. The answer was, Yes. I was myself amazed at the success of the week's work. On the part both of the Siamese government and of the Lāo Prince, it was an act of grace hardly to be expected, though quite in keeping with the liberality of the truly great king who opened his country to civilization and to Christianity. And the Lāo Prince, with all his faults, had some noble and generous traits of character.

Later in the day I called alone to tell the Prince that as soon as I could after the close of the rainy season, I would come with my family. After the intense excitement of the week, I spent a quiet Sabbath in Dr. Bradley's family, and on Monday morning could say, as did Abraham's servant, "Hinder me not, seeing the Lord hath prospered me." Taking the afternoon tide, I hastened home to report the success of my trip, to close my work in Pechaburī, and to make preparation for a new station, which was soon to be a new mission.

The work in hand was easily turned over to Mr. McFarland, an earnest and successful worker, who had

REV. DAN BEACH BRADLEY, M.D.
1872

KĀWILŌROT, PRINCE OF CHIENGMAI
(ABOUT 1869)

become specially gifted in the Siamese language. The Presbytery was to meet in Bangkok in November. The last busy weeks passed rapidly away. At their end we bade good-bye to our home and friends in Pechaburī.

Friends in Bangkok gave us their hearty assistance. The Ladies' Sewing Society made a liberal contribution to the new mission. Dr. James Campbell supplied us with medicines and a book of instructions how to use them. The German Consul gave us a Prussian rifle for our personal protection. All our missionary friends added their good wishes and their prayers.

We had great difficulty in securing suitable boats and crews for the journey. On January 3d, 1867, we embarked, leaving Mr. and Mrs. Wilson to follow us the next year. Mr. George accompanied us as far as Rahêng. The trip is always a slow one, but we enjoyed it. My rifle was useful in securing pelicans and other large birds for food. Once I fired into a large flock of pelicans on the river and killed three with a single shot. Fish everywhere abounded. My shotgun furnished pigeons and other small game. The trip afforded fine opportunity for evangelistic work. Nothing of the sort had ever been done there save the little which Mr. Wilson and I had attempted on our earlier trip.

Rahêng was reached in four weeks. There we dismissed the boats that had brought us from Bangkok, and procured, instead, two large ones of the sort used in up-country travel. We should have done better with three of smaller size. We spent nearly a month in toiling up the thirty-two rapids. At one of them we were delayed from Friday noon till Tuesday afternoon. At another, to avoid the furious current of the main river, we attempted a small channel at one side. As we slowly worked our way along, the water in our channel became shallower and shallower, till we had to resort to a system of extemporized locks. A temporary dam was built behind the boat. The resulting slight rise of water would enable us to drag the boat a little further, till again it was stranded—when the process would have to be repeated. After two days of hard work at this, our boatmen gave up in despair. A Chiengmai prince on his way to Bangkok found us in this extremity, and gave us an order to secure help at the nearest village. To send the letter up and to bring the boatmen down would require nearly a week. But there was nothing else to do.

My rifle helped me somewhat to while away the time of this idle waiting. We could hear tigers about us every night. I used to skirt about among the mountain ridges and brooks, half hoping to shoot one of them. Since my rifle was not a repeater, it was no doubt best that my ambition was not gratified. Once, taking a Siamese lad with me, I strayed further and returned later than usual. It was nearly dark when we got back to the boats, and supper was waiting. Before we had finished our meal, the boatmen caught sight of the glowing eyes of a tiger that had followed our trail to the further bank of the river, whence we had crossed to our boat.

One of the boat captains professed to be able to call up either deer or tiger, if one were within hearing. By doubling a leaf together, and with thumb and finger on either side holding the two edges tense between his lips while he blew, he would produce a sound so nearly resembling the cry of a young goat or deer, that a doe within reach of the call, he claimed, would run to the rescue of her young, or a tiger, hearing it, would run to secure the prey. The two captains and I one day went up on a ridge, and, selecting an open triangular space, posted ourselves back to back, facing in three directions, with our guns in readiness. The captain had sounded his call only two or three times, when suddenly a large deer rushed furiously up from the direction toward which one of the captains was facing. A fallen log was lying about twenty paces off on the edge of our open space. The excited animal stopped behind it, his lower parts concealed, but with back, shoulder, neck, and head fully exposed. Our captain fired away, but was so excited that he would have missed an elephant. His bullet entered the log some six inches below the top. In an instant the deer was gone. We found not far off the spot where evidently a young deer had been devoured by a tiger. We tried the experiment a number of times later, but with no success.

After we had waited two days and nights for help from the village above, on the third night the spirits came to our rescue. Either with their ears or in their imaginations, our crew heard strange noises in the rocks and trees about them, which they interpreted as a warning from the spirits to be gone. Next morning, after consultation together, they made another desperate effort, and got the boats off. It was still several days before we met the men that came down in response to the prince's order. But some of the worst rapids were yet before us. We could hardly have got through without their aid.

The efforts of a single crew, it must be remembered, are utterly inadequate to bring a boat up through any of these rapids. Only by combining two or three crews can the boats be brought up one by one. Some of the men are on the bank, tugging at the tow-rope while they clamber over rocks and struggle through bushes. Some are on board, bending to their poles. Others are up to their waists in the rushing water, by main force fending off the boat from being dashed against the rocks. On one occasion I myself had made the passage in the first boat, which then was left moored in quieter waters. The crew went back to bring up the second boat, in which were my wife and children. With anxious eyes I was watching the struggle; when, suddenly, in the fiercest rush of the current, the men lost control of her. Boat and passengers were drifting with full force straight against a wall of solid rock on the opposite bank. It seemed as if nothing could save them. But one of the fleetest boatmen, with rope in hand, swam to a rock in midstream, and took a turn of the rope about it, just in time to prevent what would have been a tragedy.

At night, about camp-fires on the river bank, we were regaled by the boatmen with legends of the country through which we were passing. One of these legends concerned the lofty mountain which rises above the rapid called Kĕng Soi, where we were camped. The story was that on its summit there had been in ancient times a city of *sētis* (millionaires), who paid a gold *fûang* (two dollars) a bucket for all the water brought up for their use. It was said that remains of their city, and particularly an aged cocoanut tree, were still to be seen on the summit.

. Since it would take our boatmen at least two days to surmount that rapid, I resolved to attempt the ascent, and either verify or explode the story. Starting at early dawn with my young Siamese, zigzagging back and forth on the slope all that long forenoon, I struggled upward—often despairing of success, but ashamed to turn back. At last we stood on the top, but it was noon or later. We spent two or three hours in search of the cocoanut tree or other evidence of human settlement, but all in vain. I was satisfied that we were the first of human kind that had ever set foot on that lofty summit. We had brought lunch—but no water! Most willingly would we have given a silver *fûang* for a draught.

The legend of the rapids themselves was one of the most interesting. At the edge of the plain above the rapids there is pointed out a wall of rock dropping fully a hundred feet sheer to the water's edge. The story goes that in ancient times a youth made love to the Prince's daughter. The course of true love did not run smooth; the father forbade the suit. The lovers resolved to make their escape. The young man mounted his steed with his bride behind him, and together they fled. But soon the enraged father was in hot pursuit. They reached the river-brink at the top of the precipice, with the father in plain sight behind them. But there the lover's heart failed him. He could not take that leap. The maiden then begged to exchange places with her lover. She mounted in front; tied her scarf over her eyes; put spurs to the horse; and took the fatal leap. To this day the various rapids are mostly named from various portions of the equipage which are supposed to have drifted down the stream and lodged upon the rocks.

Lāo witchcraft was another favourite theme of our Rahêng boatmen. They were very much afraid of the magical powers of wizards; and evidently believed that the wizards could readily despatch any who offended them. They could insert a mass of rawhide into one's stomach, which would produce death, and which could not be consumed by fire when the body was cremated. They could make themselves invisible and invulnerable. No sword could penetrate their flesh, and a bullet fired at them would drop harmless from the mouth of the gun.

But we have lingered too long among the rapids. Some distance above the last one the mountains on either side recede from the river, and enclose the great plain of Chiengmai and Lampūn. Both passengers and boatmen draw a long breath of relief when it opens out. The glorious sun again shines all day. The feathery plumes of the graceful bamboo clumps are a delight to the eye, and give variety to the otherwise tame scenery. But the distant mountains are always in sight.

The season was advancing. The further we went, the shallower grew the stream. Long before we reached Chiengmai, we had to use canoes to lighten our boats; but presently a seasonable rise in the river came to our aid. On Saturday evening, April 1st, 1867, we moored our boats beside a mighty banyan tree, whose spreading arms shaded a space more than a hundred feet wide. It stands opposite the large island which forty years later the government turned over to Dr. McKean of our mission for a leper asylum. Stepping out a few paces from under its shade, one could see across the fields the pagoda-spires of Chiengmai. There, prayerfully and anxiously, we spent the thirteenth and last Sunday of our long journey, not knowing what the future might have in store for us.

A REST BETWEEN RAPIDS IN THE GORGE OF THE MÊ PING RIVER

POLING UP THE MÊ PING RIVER

VI

CHIENGMAI

ON Monday morning, April 3d, 1867, we reached the city. We had looked forward to the arrival as a welcome rest after the long confinement of our journey in the boat. But it was only the beginning of troubles. We were not coming to an established station with houses and comforts prepared by predecessors. The Prince was off on a military expedition, not to be back for over a month. Till he came, nothing could be done. We could not secure a house to shelter us, for there was none to be had. Just outside the eastern gate of the city, however, a sālā for public use had recently been built by an officer from Rahêng, to "make merit," according to Buddhist custom. He had still a quasi claim upon it, and, with the consent of the Prince's representative, he offered it to us. It was well built, with tile roof and teak floor, was enclosed on three sides, and opened in front on a six-foot veranda. In that one room, some twelve feet by twenty, all our belongings were stored. It served for bedroom, parlour, dining-room, and study. In it tables, chairs, bedstead, organ, boxes, and trunks were all piled one upon another. A bamboo kitchen and a bathroom were presently extemporized in the yard. That was our home for more than a year.

The news of the arrival of white foreigners soon spread far and wide. It was not known how long they would remain; and the eagerness of all classes to get sight of them before they should be gone was absolutely ludicrous, even when most annoying. "There is a white woman and children! We *must* go and see them." Our visitors claimed all the immunities of backwoodsmen who know no better. In etiquette and manners they well deserved that name. Within a few feet of the sălă was a rickety plank-walk leading over marshy ground to the city. Everybody had to pass that way, and everybody must stop. When the veranda was filled, they would crowd up on the ground in front as long as they could get sight of anybody or anything. If to-day the crowd prevented a good view, they would call to-morrow. The favourite time of all was, of course, our meal-time, to see how and what the foreigners ate. Almost never in the daytime could we sit down to a quiet meal without lookers-on. It was not uncommon for our visitors to pick up a knife or a fork or even the bread, and ask what that was. "They don't sit on the floor to eat, nor use their fingers, as we do!"

This, however, is only one side of the picture. In one sense we were partly to blame for our discomfort. We could soon have dispersed the crowd by giving them to understand that their presence was not wanted. But we ourselves were on trial. If we had got the name of being ill-natured or ungracious, they would have left us, probably never to return. No. This was what we were there for. It gave us constant opportunities from daylight till dark to proclaim the Gospel message. The first and commonest question, who we were and what was our errand, brought us at once to the point. We were come with messages of mercy and with offer of eternal life from the great God and Saviour. We were come with a revelation of our Heavenly Father to His wandering and lost children. While the mass of our visitors came from curiosity, some came to learn; and many who came from curiosity went away pondering whether these things were so. Friendships also were formed which stood us in good stead afterwards when we sorely needed friends. During our time of persecution these persons would come in by stealth to speak a word of comfort, when they dared not do so openly.

As the annoyance of those days fell most heavily on the nerves of my wife, it was a comfort to learn afterwards that possibly the very first convert heard the Gospel message first from her lips, while she was addressing a crowd of visitors very soon after our arrival. Reference will be made to him later, but it may be said here that from the day when he first heard the news, he never again worshipped an idol.

Whatever was their object in coming to see us, we soon gave every crowd, and nearly every visitor, to understand what we had come for. We had come as teachers—primarily as teachers of a way of salvation for sinners. And we never addressed a crowd of thoughtful men or women who did not readily confess that they were sinners, and needed a saviour from sin. But we were not merely teachers of religion, though primarily such. We could often, if not usually, better teach religion—or, at least, could better lead up to it—by teaching geography or astronomy. A little globe that I had brought along was often my text.

I presume that most Christian people in America have a very crude idea of the method of preaching the Gospel often, or, perhaps, generally, used by missionaries, particularly in new fields. If they think that the bell is rung, that the people assemble in orderly fashion, and take their seats, that a hymn is sung, prayer offered, the Scripture read, a sermon delivered, and the congregation dismissed with the doxology and benediction,—they are very much mistaken. All that comes in time. We have lived to see it come in this land—thanks to God's blessing upon work much more desultory than that. Long after the time we are now speaking of, one could talk of religion to the people by the hour, or even by the day; one might sing hymns, might solemnly utter prayer, in response to inquiry as to how we worshipped—and they would listen respectfully and with interest. But if public worship had been announced, and these same people had been invited to remain, every soul would have fled away for fear of being caught in some trap and made Christians without their consent, or for fear of being made to suffer the consequences of being reputed Christians before they were ready to take that step. Forty years later than the time we are now speaking of, I have seen people who were standing about the church door and looking in, driven quite away by the mere invitation to come in and be seated.

In one sense our work during the first year was very desultory. I had always to shape my instruction to the individuals before me. It would often be in answer to questions as to where was our country; in what direction; how one would travel to get there; could one go there on foot; and so on. Or the question might be as to the manners and customs of our nation; or it might be directly on religion itself. But as all roads lead to Rome, so all subjects may be turned to Christ, His cross, and His salvation.

Of the friends found in those early days I must

mention two. One was Princess Bũa Kam, the mother of the late and last Lão Prince, Chao Intanon. At our first acquaintance, she formed for us a warm friendship that lasted till her death. Nor could I ever discover any other ground for her friendship than the fact that we were religious teachers. She was herself a devout Buddhist, and continued to the last her offerings in the monasteries. I believe that the Gospel plan of salvation struck a chord in her heart which her own religion never did. From Buddha she got no assurance of pardon. The assurance that pardon is possible in itself seemed to give her hope, though by what process a logical mind could hardly see, so long as she held on to a system which, as she confessed, did not and could not give pardon. She was always pleased to hear the story of the incarnation, the birth, life, and miracles of Christ. She was deeply touched by the recital of His sufferings, persecutions, and death. Illustrations of the substitutionary efficacy of His sufferings she readily understood. She acknowledged her god to be a man who, by the well-nigh endless road to nirvãna, had ceased to suffer by ceasing to exist. The only claim he had to warrant his pointing out the way to others was the fact that he had passed over it himself. There was one ground, however, on which she felt that she might claim the comfort both of the doctrines which she still held and of ours, too. A favourite theory of hers—and of many others—was that, after all, we worship the same God under different names. She called hers Buddha, and we call ours Jehovah-Jesus.

She had by nature a woman's tender heart. Benevolence had doubtless been developed in her by her religion, till it had become a second nature. The gifts she loved to make were also a means of laying up a store of merit for the future. She was most liberal in sending us tokens of remembrance. These were not of much value. A quart of white rice, a few oranges, cucumbers, or cocoanuts on a silver tray, were so customary a sight that, if ever any length of time elapsed without them, we wondered if the Princess were ill. And, on the other hand, if for any cause my calls were far apart, she would be sure to send to enquire if I were ill. The "cup of cold water" which she thus so often pressed to our lips, I am sure, was given for the Master's sake.

Another remarkable friendship formed during that first year was that of a Buddhist monk, abbot of the Ūmōng monastery. As in the other case, there was no favour to ask, no axe to grind. He never made a request for anything, unless it were for a book. But the little novice who attended him almost always brought a cocoanut or some other small present for us. Very early in our acquaintance he came to see that the universe could not be self-existent, as Buddhism teaches. On his deeply religious nature the sense of sin weighed heavily. He was well versed in the Buddhist scriptures, and knew that there was no place for pardon in all that system. He understood the plan of salvation offered to men through the infinite merit of Jesus Christ. At times he would argue that it was impossible. But the thought that, after all, it might be possible, afforded him a gleam of hope that he saw nowhere else; and he was not willing to renounce it altogether.

During the dark months that followed the martyrdom of our native Christians, when many who were true friends deemed it unwise to let their sympathy

TEMPLE OF THE OLD TĀI STYLE OF ARCHITECTURE, CHIENGMAI

be known, the good abbot visited us regularly, as, indeed, he continued to do as long as he lived. At times I had strong hopes that he would leave the priesthood. But he never could quite see his way to do that, though he maintained that he never ceased to worship Jesus. The only likeness, alas! that I have of his dear old face is a photograph taken after death, as his body lay ready for cremation. Unto whom, if not unto such true friends of His as these, was it said, "I was a hungered, and ye gave Me meat; I was thirsty, and ye gave Me drink; I was in prison, and ye visited Me.—Inasmuch as ye have done it unto one of the least of these My brethren, ye have done it unto Me"?

VII

PIONEER WORK

THE military expedition in which the Prince was engaged detained him in the field until some time in May. It was one of many unsuccessful attempts to capture a notorious Ngīo chieftain who, turning outlaw and robber, had gathered about him a band of desperadoes, with whom he sallied forth from his mountain fastness, raiding innocent villages and carrying off the plunder to his stronghold, before any force could be gathered to withstand or to pursue him. In this way he kept the whole country in constant alarm during the earlier years of our stay in Chiengmai. What made matters worse was the fact—as the Lāo firmly believed—that he had a charmed life, that he could render himself invisible, and that no weapon could penetrate his flesh. Had not the stockade within which he had taken shelter been completely surrounded one night by a cordon of armed men, and at dawn, when he was to have been captured, he was nowhere to be found? Such was the man of whom we shall hear more further on.

At the Lāo New Year it is customary for all persons of princely rank, all officers and people of influence, to present their compliments to the Prince in person, and to take part in the ceremony of "Dam Hūa," by way of wishing him a Happy New Year. Because of the Prince's absence in the field, this ceremony could not be observed at the regular time; but it was none the less brilliantly carried out a few days after his return. The name, Dam Hūa, means "bathing the head" or "head-bath," and it is really a ceremonial bathing or baptism of the Prince's head with water poured upon it, first by princes and officials in the order of their rank, and so on down to his humblest subjects.

The first and more exclusive part of the ceremony took place in the palace, where I also was privileged to offer my New Year's greetings with the rest. The great reception-hall was crowded with the Prince's family and with officials of all degrees. The air was heavy with the fragrance of flowers which loaded every table and stand. All were in readiness with their silver vessels filled with water, awaiting His Highness' appearance. At length an officer with a long silver-handled spear announced his coming. The whole company received him with lowest prostration after the old-time fashion. Seeing me standing, he sent for a chair, saying that the ceremony was long, and I would be tired. The Court Orator, or Scribe, then read a long address of welcome to the Prince on his return from his brilliant expedition, with high-sounding compliments on its success. Then there was a long invocation of all the powers above or beneath, real or imaginary, not to molest, but instead to protect, guide, and bless His Highness' person, kingdom, and people, with corresponding curses invoked on all his enemies and theirs. Then came the ceremonial bath, administered first by his own family, his relatives, and high officials—he standing while vase after vase of water was poured on his head, drenching him completely and flooding all the floor. It is a ceremony not at all unpleasant in a hot climate, however unendurable it might be in colder regions.

This was the beginning. According to immemorial custom, a booth was prepared on a sand-bar in the river. To this, after the ceremony in the palace, the Prince went in full state, riding on an elephant richly caparisoned with trappings of solid gold, to receive a like bath at the hands of his loyal subjects—beginning, as before, with some high nobles, and then passing on to the common people, who might all take part in this closing scene of the strange ceremony.

I was not in the concourse at the river, but watched the procession from our sālā, the Prince having said to me that he would call on his return. This he did, making us a nice little visit, taking a cup of tea, and listening to the playing of some selections on the organ. He asked if I had selected a place for a permanent station, and suggested one or two himself. But I was in no hurry, preferring to wait for the judgment of Mr. Wilson on his arrival. Meanwhile I was assured that I might remain in the sālā, and might put up a temporary house to receive the new family. When I requested his consent to the employment of a teacher, he asked whom I thought of employing. I mentioned the name of one, and he said, "He is not good. I will send you a better one,"—and he sent me his own teacher.

It was a very auspicious beginning. I knew that neither the Siamese nor the Lāo trusted the Prince very thoroughly; yet every time that I saw him it seemed to me that I might trust him. At any rate, I did not then look forward to the scenes that we were to pass through before three years were gone.

After the first curiosity wore off, many of those who came to our sālā were patients seeking medical treatment. The title "Maw" (doctor) followed me from Bangkok, where all missionaries, I believe, are still so called. This name itself often excited hopes which, of course, were doomed to disappointment. To the ignorant all diseases seem equally curable, if only there be the requisite skill or power. How often during those first five years I regretted that I was not a trained physician and surgeon! My only consolation was that it was not my fault. When my thoughts were first turned towards missions, I consulted the officers of our Board on the wisdom of taking at least a partial course in preparation for my work. But medical missions had not then assumed the importance they since have won. In fact, just then they were at a discount. The Board naturally thought that medical study would be, for me at least, a waste of time, and argued besides that in most mission fields there were English physicians. But it so happened that eleven years of my missionary life have been spent in stations from one hundred to five hundred miles distant from a physician. So, if any physician who reads this narrative is inclined to criticise me as a quack, I beg such to remember that I was driven to it—I had to do whatever I could in the case of illness in my own family; and for pity I could not turn away those who often had nothing but superstitious charms to rely on. It was a comfort, moreover, to know that in spite of inevitable disappointments, our practice of medicine made friends, and possibly enabled us to maintain the field, at a time when simply as Christian teachers we could not have done so. Even Prince Kāwilōrot himself conceded so much when, after forbidding us to remain as missionaries, he said we might, if we wished, remain to treat the sick.

In such a malarial country, there is no estimating the boon conferred by the introduction of quinine alone. Malarial fevers often ran on season after season, creating an anæmic condition such that the least exertion would bring on the fever and chills again. The astonishment of the people, therefore, is not surprising when two or three small powders of the "white medicine," as they called it, taken with much misgiving, would cut short the fever, while their own medicines, taken by the potful for many months, had failed. The few bottles of quinine which it had been thought sufficient to bring with me, were soon exhausted. The next order was for forty four-ounce bottles; and not till our physicians at length began to order by the thousand ounces could a regular supply be kept on hand. I have often been in villages where every child, and nearly every person, young or old, had chills and fever, till the spleen was enlarged, and the whole condition such that restoration was possible only after months of treatment.

There was another malady very common then—the goitre—which had never been cured by any remedy known to the Lāo doctors. I soon learned, however, that an ointment of potassium iodide was almost a specific in the earlier stages of the disease. That soon gave my medicine and my treatment a reputation that no regular physician could have sustained; for the people were sure that one who could cure the goitre must be able to cure any disease. If I protested that I was not a doctor, it seemed a triumphant answer to say, "Why, you cured such a one of the goitre." Often when I declined to undertake the treatment of some disease above my skill, the patient would go away saying, "I believe you could, if you would."

One other part of my medical work I must mention here, since reference will be made to it later. The ravages of smallpox had been fearful, amounting at times to the destruction of a whole generation of children. The year before our arrival had witnessed such a scourge. Hardly a household escaped, and many had no children left. I was specially interested to prevent or to check these destructive epidemics, because the Prince had seen the efficacy of vaccination as practised by Dr. Bradley in Bangkok, and because I felt sure that what he had seen had influenced him to give his consent to our coming. One of the surest ways then known of sending the virus a long distance was in the form of the dry scab from a vaccine pustule. When once the virus had "taken," vaccination went on from arm to arm. Dr. Bradley sent me the first vaccine scab. It reached me during the first season; and vaccination from it ran a notable course.

The Karens and other hill tribes are so fearful of smallpox that when it comes near their villages, they all flee to the mountains. Smallpox had broken out in a Lâo village near a Karen settlement. The settlement was at once deserted. Meanwhile the news of the efficacy of vaccination had reached the Lâo village, and they sent a messenger with an elephant to beg me to come and vaccinate the entire community. Two young monks came also from an adjoining village, where the disease was already raging. These two I vaccinated at once, and sent home, arranging to follow them later when their pustules should be ripe. From them I vaccinated about twenty of the villagers. During the following week the Karens all returned, and in one day I vaccinated one hundred and sixty-three persons. It was a strange sight to see four generations all vaccinated at one time—great-grandfathers holding out their withered arms along with babes a month old.

Success such as this was naturally very flattering to one's pride; and "pride goeth before a fall." I had kept the Prince informed of the success of my attempt, and naturally was anxious to introduce vaccination into the palace. The patronage of the palace would ensure its introduction into the whole kingdom. Having a fine vaccine pustule on the arm of a healthy white infant boy, I took him to the palace to show the case to the Prince's daughter, and to her husband, who was the heir-apparent. They had a little son of about the same age. The parents were pleased, and sent me with the child to the Prince. As soon as he saw the pustule, he pronounced it genuine, and was delighted. His younger daughter had lost a child in the epidemic of the year before, and the family was naturally very anxious on the subject. He sent me immediately to vaccinate his little grandson.

I returned to the palace of the son-in-law, and very carefully vaccinated the young prince on whom so many hopes were centred. I watched the case daily, and my best hopes seemed realized. The pustules developed finely. All the characteristic symptoms appeared and disappeared at the proper times. But when the scab was about to fall off, the little prince was taken with diarrhœa. I felt sure that a little paregoric or some other simple remedy would speedily set the child right, and I offered to treat the case. But half a dozen doctors—most of them "spirit-doctors" —were already in attendance. The poor child, I verily believe, was dosed to death. So evident was it that the unfortunate outcome could not have been the result of vaccination, that both the parents again and again assured me that they entertained no such thought. But all diseases—as was then universally believed among the Lāo—are the result of incurring the displeasure of the "spirits" of the family or of the clan. The "spirits" might have taken umbrage at the invasion of their prerogative by vaccination.

No doubt some such thought was whispered to the Prince, and it is not unnatural that he should at least have half believed it. In his grief at the loss of his grandson, it is easy to see how that thought may have fanned his jealousy at the growing influence of the missionaries.

No year ever passed more rapidly or more pleasantly than that first year of the mission. We were too busy to be either lonesome or homesick, although, to complete our isolation, we had no mails of any sort for many months. Our two children, the one of three and the other of six years, were a great comfort to us. When we left Bangkok it was understood that a Mr. C. of the Borneo Company was to follow us in a month on business of their teak trade. He had promised to bring up our mail. So we felt sure of getting our first letters in good time. Since he would travel much faster than we, it was not impossible that he might overtake us on the way. But April, May, and June passed, and still no word of Mr. C. or of the mails he was bringing. In July we received a note from him, with a few fragments of our long looked-for mail. He had been attacked by robbers below Rahêng, himself had received a serious wound, and his boat had been looted of every portable object, including our mail-bag. Fortunately the robbers, finding nothing of value to them in the mail, had dropped as they fled some mutilated letters and papers, which the officers in pursuit picked up, and which Mr. C. forwarded to us. Otherwise we should have had nothing. We could at least be devoutly thankful that we had traversed the same river in safety.

It was long before we were sure that Mr. Wilson and his family were coming at all that year. It was at least possible that any one of a thousand causes might delay them, or even prevent their coming altogether. Their arrival on February 15th, 1868, was, of course, a great event.

Not long after this we were eagerly awaiting a promised visit from our old associate and friend, Dr. S. R. House. Both Mrs. Wilson and Mrs. McGilvary were expecting shortly to be confined, and the good doctor was making the tedious journey that he might be on hand to help them with his professional skill in the hour of their need. Our dismay can be imagined, when, one day, there appeared, not the doctor, but his native assistant, with a few pencilled lines from the doctor, telling us that he was lying in the forest some four or five days distant, dangerously, if not fatally, gored by an elephant. We were not to come to him, but were to stand by and attend to the needs of our families. He begged us to pray for him, and to send him some comforts and medicines.

The accident happened on this wise: The doctor had been walking awhile for exercise behind his riding elephant, and then attempted to pass up beside the creature to the front. The elephant, startled at his unexpected appearance, struck him to the ground with a blow of his trunk, gored him savagely in the abdomen, and was about to trample him under foot, when the driver, not a moment too soon, got the creature again under control. With rare nerve the doctor cleansed the frightful wound, and sewed it up by the help of its reflection in a mirror, as he lay on his back on the ground. He despatched the messenger to us; gave careful instructions to his attendants as to what they should do for him when the inevitable fever and delirium should come on; and resigned himself calmly to await whatever the outcome might be.

The situation was, indeed, desperate. We could not possibly hope to reach him before the question of life or death for him would be settled; nor could he be brought to us. The best we could do was to get an order from the Prince for a boat, boatmen, and carriers, and despatch these down the river, committing with earnest prayer the poor sufferer to the all-loving Father's care. The doctor was carried on a bamboo litter through the jungle to the Mê Ping River, and in due time reached Chiengmai convalescent, to find that the two expected young missionaries had arrived in safety before him. After a month's rest he was able to return to Bangkok; but not until he had assisted us in organizing the First Presbyterian Church of Chiengmai.

In the *Presbyterian Record* for November, 1868, will be found an interesting report from the doctor's pen. Naturally he was struck with the predominance of demon-worship over Buddhism among the Lāo. We quote the following:

"Not only offerings, but actually prayers are made to demons. I shall never forget the first prayer of the kind I ever heard. . . . We had just entered a dark defile in the mountains, beyond Mûang Tôn, and had come to a rude, imageless shrine erected to the guardian demon of the pass. The owner of my riding-elephant was seated on the neck of the big beast before me. Putting the palms of his hands together and raising them in the attitude of worship, he prayed: 'Let no evil happen to us. We are six men and three elephants. Let us not be injured. Let nothing come to frighten us,' and so on. On my way down the river, at the rapids and gloomy passes in the mountains the boatmen would land, tapers would be lighted, and libations would be poured, and offerings of flowers, food, and betel would be made to the powers of darkness."

The doctor speaks also of "the favour with which the missionaries were received, the confidence they had won from all classes, the influence of their medicines, and the grand field open for a physician." He frankly says, "I must confess that though at one time I did have some misgivings whether, all things considered, the movement was not a little premature, I now, being better able to judge, greatly honour the Christian courage and enterprise which undertook the work; or rather bless God who inspired Mr. McGilvary's heart, and made his old Princeton friend, Mr. Wilson, consent to join him in thus striking out boldly into an untried field. It will prove, I trust, a field ready to the harvest."

VIII

FIRST-FRUITS

DURING the first three months after Mr. Wilson's arrival we were so occupied with mission work and with family cares that we had not made choice of the lot which the Prince had promised to give us. On the very day that Dr. House left us, however, the Prince came in person, selected, and made over to us our present beautiful mission compound on the east bank of the Mê Ping. He would not allow us to offer any compensation; but, learning afterwards that the native owners had received no remuneration, we secretly paid them. Mr. Wilson began at once to erect temporary bamboo buildings, and soon moved to the new compound. Since it was difficult for me to spare time for further work of building for myself, and since the old location was an ideal one for meeting the people, I moved with my family from the sālā into the bamboo house the Wilsons had occupied, and we made it our home for the next two years.

Mr. Wilson was greatly interrupted in his work by sickness in his family. Little Frank had fallen ill on the journey from Bangkok, and continued to suffer during all these months. His death on November 17th, 1868, was a heavy stroke to us all. In vain we combined our slight medical skill, and searched our books of domestic medicine for his relief. It was pitiful enough to see the natives die, with the sad feeling in our hearts that a physician might have saved their lives. But the death of one of our own number, so soon after the trying experiences early in the year, emphasized, as nothing else could have done, our appeals for a physician. Yet it was not until 1872 that we welcomed the first physician appointed to our mission.

During this time raids were continually being made into the Lāo country by the renegade Ngĭo chieftain already spoken of. Five hundred men from Prê, and one thousand from Lakawn were drafted for the defence of the city, and were stationed near our compound. Thus hundreds of soldiers and workmen furnished us an ever-changing audience. All we had to do, day or night, was to touch the organ, and people would crowd in to hear. The dry season of 1868-69 was, therefore, an exceptionally good one for our work. We had constant visitors from other provinces, who would converse with us by the hour, and, on returning to their homes, would carry the news of our presence and of our work.

In the fall of 1868 occurred two events which, widely different as they might seem to be, were in reality closely connected, and of much importance in their bearing on the mission. One was a total eclipse of the sun on August 17th, and the other was the conversion of Nān Inta, our first baptized convert. I well remember his tall figure and thoughtful face when he first appeared at our sālā, shortly after our arrival in Chiengmai. He had a cough, and had come for medicine. He had heard, too, that we taught a new religion, and wished to enquire about that. Some soothing expectorant sufficiently relieved his cough to encourage him to make another call. On each visit religion was the all-absorbing topic. He had studied Buddhism, and he diligently practised its precepts. As an abbot he had led others to make offerings for the monastery worship, and he had two sons of his own in the monastic order. But Buddhism had never satisfied his deep spiritual nature. What of the thousands of failures and transgressions from the results of which there was no escape? The doctrine of a free and full pardon through the merits of another, was both new and attractive to him, but it controverted the fundamental principle of his religion.

We had some arguments, also, on the science of geography, on the shape of the earth, on the nature of eclipses, and the like. What he heard was as foreign to all his preconceived ideas as was the doctrine of salvation from sin by the death of Christ. Just before the great eclipse was to occur I told him of it, naming the day and the hour when it was to occur. I pointed out that the eclipse could not be caused by a monster which attacked the sun, as he had been taught. If that were the cause, no one could foretell the day when the monster would be moved to make the attack. He at once caught that idea. If the eclipse came off as I said, he would have to admit that his teaching was wrong on a point perfectly capable of being tested by the senses. There would then be a strong presumption that we were right in religion as well as in eclipses. He waited with intense interest for the day to come. The sky was clear, and everything was favourable. He watched, with a smoked glass that we had furnished, the reflection of the sun in a bucket of water. He followed the coming of the eclipse, its progress, and its passing off, as anxiously as the wise men of old followed the star of

Bethlehem—and, like them, he, too, was led to the Saviour.

Early the next morning he came in to see me. His first words were, "Mên tê" (It's really true). "The teacher's books teach truth. Ours are wrong." This confident assurance had evidently been reached after a sleepless night. A complete revolution had taken place in his mind; but it was one that cost him a severe struggle. His only hope had rested on the teachings of Buddha, and it was no light thing to see the foundation of his hope undermined. The eclipse had started an ever-widening rift. He began, as never before, to examine the credentials of Christianity. He soon learned to read Siamese in order to gain access to our Scriptures. We read the Gospel of John together. He studied the Shorter Catechism. He had a logical mind, and it was never idle. Whenever we met, if only for a few moments, he always had some question to ask me, or some new doubt to solve. When tempted to doubt, he fell back on the eclipse, saying, "I know my books were wrong there. If the Gospel system seems too good to be true in that it offers to pardon and cleanse and adopt guilty sinners, and give them a title to a heavenly inheritance, it is simply because it is divine, and not human." While the truth dawned gradually on his mind, the full vision seemed to be sudden. His own account was that afterwards, when walking in the fields and pondering the subject, it all became very plain to him. His doubts all vanished. Henceforth for him to live was Christ; and he counted all things but loss for the excellency of the knowledge of Him.

The conversion of Nān Inta was an epoch in the history of the mission. The ordinary concourse of visitors might be for medicine, or it might be from mere curiosity. But when one of the most zealous Buddhists, well known by members of the royal family, openly embraced Christianity, the matter began to assume a different aspect. What was more remarkable still was that he urged his two sons to abandon the monastic order. The Prince's younger daughter, herself a strong Buddhist, told me that this was to her convincing evidence of his sincerity. Whether Christianity were true or false, he certainly believed it true. It was the height of ambition for every Lāo father to have a son in the order. If he had none of his own, he often would adopt one and make him a monk. But here was one of the most devout of them urging his own sons to come out and be Christians! We regarded it as a favourable circumstance that the patron and protector of this our first convert was high in princely rank. Nān Inta's defection from Buddhism produced a profound impression among all classes. Emboldened by his example, secret believers became more open. Not the number alone, but the character of the enquirers attracted attention.

The second convert was Noi Sunya, a native doctor from a village eight miles to the east. He has the enviable distinction of never having postponed the Gospel offer. He was the chief herdsman in charge of the Prince's cattle. Coming to the city on an errand, he called at our sālā to see what was the attraction there. As in the case of so many others, it was the good news of pardon for a sinsick soul that arrested his attention. On his return in the afternoon he called again to make fuller enquiry concerning "the old, old story of Jesus and His love." He promised to return on Sunday. Promises of that sort so often fail, that we were surprised and delighted to see him early on Sunday morning. We had an earnest talk together before the time came for public worship. He remained through the afternoon, and spent the night with us. In answer to a final exhortation before he left us in the morning, he said, "You need not fear my going back. I feel sure I am right." He was willing to sell all—even life itself, as it proved—for the pearl of great price. He went home, called his family together, and began family worship that very night. Only four brief months after this his labours were ended by the executioner's stroke, and he wore the martyr's crown.

The third, Sên Yā Wichai, has already been mentioned as receiving his first instruction in Christianity from the "mother teacher," as Mrs. McGilvary was called, during the very first month of the mission. He then received the great truth of the existence of God and of man's accountability to Him. He was an officer living six days' journey to the north, and was under the jurisdiction of the Prince of Lampūn. On his visit a year later, he received further instruction, was baptized, and returned to tell his neighbours what he had found. They only laughed at him for his oddity in refusing to join in the Buddhist worship, and in offerings to the spirits.

The fourth was Nān Chai, a neighbour and friend of Noi Sunya, and destined to suffer martyrdom along with him. He, too, was an ex-abbot, and, therefore, exempt from government work. He was a good scholar, and was employed by Mr. Wilson as a teacher. When he became a Christian, he was strongly tempted to hold on still to his position in the monastery, explaining that he would not himself engage in the worship, but would only sweep the buildings and keep the grounds in order for others. But when his duty was pointed out to him, he readily gave up his position, and was enrolled for regular government service. Here were four noble and notable men at once deserting the Buddhist faith! No wonder it became an anxious question whereunto this was to grow.

IX

MARTYRDOM

IN the course of these events our second year of work in Chiengmai had come to its end. We were now beyond the middle of the year 1869. As some indefinable sense of oppression in the air gives warning of the approaching storm, so there were ominous hints, and even some dark forebodings. Our Christian people—who understood far better than we did both the character of their rulers and the significance of furtive looks and innuendoes—were anxious. But they stood firm, and their faith strengthened ours.

In the light of subsequent events we now know that the most dangerous element in the gathering storm was the angry surprise of the Prince himself at the discovery that the old order seemed actually passing away under his very eyes; that his will was no longer supreme in men's minds, nor always consulted in their actions—this and the deep treachery and ruthless cruelty of his nature which it brought into play. But there were other sinister influences at work also, and among them we must not overlook that of a certain Portuguese adventurer, Fonseca by name. He was a thoroughly unprincipled man, who, having played his game in Bangkok and lost, had worked himself into the favour of the Prince during his recent visit to the capital, and had accompanied him on his return to Chiengmai. The Prince was persuaded that this man could be of great service to him in the two matters which were then causing him most disquietude; namely, the defence of certain lawsuits involving large sums of money, brought against him in the British Consular Court by Burmese timber merchants; and the getting rid of the missionaries. These last were more in Fonseca's way than they were in the Prince's. He could accomplish his ends more readily if they were not there.

The most plausible excuse that could be offered for desiring to be rid of the missionaries was the failure of the rice crop that year. In the early part of the season there was no rain at all. When at last the fields had been planted, one of the worst floods ever known in that region destroyed all the lowland rice. Then, finally, the rains ceased prematurely, and the upland crop was cut off by drought. The presence of the missionaries in the country had offended the spirits, and they had withheld the rain. Such was the pretext urged in a petition sent to Bangkok to have the missionaries removed. The specific address of the petition to the Minister for Foreign Affairs and the United States Consul leads one to suspect that the matter was directed by some one who understood the order of official business much better than did the Lāo Prince.

The Minister forwarded the document to Mr. McDonald, the acting Vice-Consul at the time. Mr. McDonald replied to the Minister that there must be some mistake about it. It appeared that the scarcity of rice complained of had begun the year before the arrival of the missionaries; it was not confined to Chiengmai, but extended over all the northern provinces. He added roguishly, however, that he would strictly enjoin the American missionaries to be very careful in future not to cause any famine. Of all this secret plotting we were entirely ignorant at the time, and learned of it only long afterwards. While these plots were developing, I was frequently visiting the Prince, and all our relations with him were apparently satisfactory. But we knew that he was under the influence of a wily and unprincipled adversary.

The other matter in which Fonseca was supposed to be able to help his patron out of difficulties even more pressing, was the Burmese lawsuits pending before the British Consul. But the British government was the last party to permit officious meddling with its public business from such a quarter. It is presumed that there was evidence of his interference with official correspondence. This much is certain—a peremptory demand was made on the Siamese government for his recall. The official order sent up was too emphatic to be neglected. The man was sent out of the country in quite different style from that in which he entered it. This man is known to have been present at the consultation relative to the mission. If the jealousy and suspicion on the part of the Prince did not originate with him, there is no doubt that he at least worked on the Prince's suspicious nature, increasing his jealousy of the growing popularity of the mission, and leading him to think that it would be wise to stop it in its incipiency.

Yet even when the blow was about to fall, we could not believe that the Prince was so treacherous as to plan to drive us out of the country, at the same time that he continued to treat us so kindly, and would even come to dine with us. We could not believe that the younger Princess, who had a predominating influence over her father, could encourage one of the Christians to put himself under her protection, only that he might the more surely be sent to his death a day or two later. We could not believe that an excursion down the river had been planned by the Prince, only that he might be out of reach when the executions should take place. We were still incredulous, even after we received reliable information from the agent of the Borneo Company that he had heard the Prince and a certain high officer consulting together to stop our work. The plan which he reported was to expel the converts from the country, giving their wives and children the option to follow them or to remain. After all, that would not have been so great a disaster. These men had no great possessions to lose. Their banishment would only plant the Gospel in other provinces or other lands.

When, in September, 1869, just before the fatal stroke, the Prince started on what purported to be a three weeks' fishing trip, we thought that his absence would give us a respite from our present fears, and would afford him leisure for better thoughts. As his boats pushed off, we waved him a parting good-bye from the shore. His first business was at Lampūn, to secure the co-operation of the governor of that province in ridding the country of the new religion. Inasmuch as Sên Yā Wichai, the third convert mentioned above, was a Lampūn officer, it was thought prudent in his case to secure the action of his own immediate superior. He was at once sent for, and was condemned to death, but was saved by his young master, the governor's son, on the plea that he was a backwoodsman, and knew no better.

Of the deep designs against us and our work we were thus either ignorant or incredulous till, on the evening of September 13th, just before dark, our night watchman came to us with the common excuse for leaving us, that some relative was dead or dying, and insisting that he must go immediately. In vain we urged that he must not leave us thus in the lurch. As a final argument, we threatened to dock him of a month's wages. But wages were nothing to him then. "All that a man hath will he give for his life." While we talked to him, he had reached the gate and was gone. So, also, fled the cook and the coolie, leaving only one blind Ngīo who had taken refuge with us.

Mr. Wilson then lived across the river on the new premises, and it was not until the next day that we learned that all his people, too, had fled in like manner and at the same hour. We went to Prayā Tēpasing, the Prince's executive officer, to enquire the cause. He feigned surprise, and professed entire ignorance of any designs against the Christians. He said, however, that the Prince had given an order that the inhabitants of certain villages should bring in each a hewn slab of timber to repair the stockade. Possibly the scare might have somehow arisen from that. We were aware of the order, and had told the Christians that if pressed for time to procure the timber, they might each take a slab of ours. We now told the Prayā that we would ourselves be responsible for the timbers required of them. To assure us with regard to our servants, the Prayā sent for our cook, gave him a letter assuring his safety, and threatened, besides, to have him flogged if he deserted us. The cook remained with us all through these troubles, until we could find another to take his place. For some reason

Mr. Wilson did not avail himself of this offer. He and Mrs. Wilson got on as they could without servants for several months.

We now know that the order for the execution of the Christians had been given long before by that same Prayā Tēpasing—in such fear of the Prince was the highest officer in the realm! Not only had our servants vanished—there was a sudden cessation of our visitors as well. Few even dared to come for medicine for fear of being suspected of becoming Christians. There were, however, a few notable exceptions, the abbot of the Ūmōng monastery being the most conspicuous.

During the following week Mr. Wilson waded out across the flooded country to the home of Nān Chai, his teacher. But his family did not dare to give any information concerning him. To tell what they knew would cost their lives also—so they had been told. He then went on another mile to Noi Sunya's home, with the same result. The wives of both these men pretended to believe that their husbands had gone to the city to visit us. Mr. Wilson noticed that one of the women had tears in her eyes as she spoke. Puzzled rather than satisfied by the result of the visit, Mr. Wilson returned with the hope that, after all, the men were still alive, and that we yet should see them in the land of the living.

It was two weeks before our suspense was broken by the certainty of their death. On Sunday morning, September 26th, a Ngīo friend and neighbour of the martyrs called at my house. After looking all about him, he asked where the Christians were. I told him there seemed to be a mystery about them that we could not unravel, but we hoped they were secreting themselves in safety somewhere. Seeing that I was really ignorant of their fate, he came close up to me, and looking around again to assure himself that no one was near, he asked, "If I tell you, will you promise never to betray me?" Having demanded and received an emphatic promise equivalent to an oath, he drew his hand significantly across his neck, and whispered, "That is the way." His gesture was too well understood in that reign to leave any doubt as to what was meant. The man had really come on a sad and dangerous errand of kindness. As soon as it was accomplished, he hurried away, evidently fearing that the birds of the air might hear it, or that some breeze might waft it to the palace.

On Monday morning Mr. Wilson and I went again to the Prayā. He could now no longer lie for his master as to the fact of the execution of the men, but he offered the flimsy excuse that it was because they had not brought in their slabs on time. We were then obliged to charge him with patent falsehood. He knew that they were executed for no crime whatever, but only for being Christians. Poor man! He seemed somewhat ashamed; but what could he do? He was not at heart a bad man, as his letter of protection for the cook showed. The lives of two peasants were no great matter in those days. He had been so trained to execute every behest of his master, that it scarcely occurred to him that he ought to hesitate at this.

But it was some relief to know the worst, and to know that it was known that we knew it. Before this we had been obliged to feign hopes that we hardly believed ourselves. Now we could speak openly. The Prince had not yet returned from his fishing trip; so we went to his elder daughter and her husband, afterward Prince Intanon. In their position they could not say much; but they did say that what the Prince had done was not right, and that they did not approve of the act.

One outcome of the situation was a flood of the wildest rumours—some of them, no doubt, started on purpose to frighten us away. One of these touched us in a most tender point. One of our most faithful servants, who had been with us from the very first, was desirous of visiting Bangkok. So we arranged to have him go down in charge of a boat that was to bring up our supplies for the year. By him we sent a large package of letters written before we had reason to suspect so serious an outcome of the troubles that were brewing. While we could not conceal some gloomy forebodings, our reports were, on the whole, full of hope for the speedy progress of the Gospel. The boat left for Bangkok a few days after the Prince started on his fishing trip. Presently it was reported that the boat had been intercepted, and that this man, with his wife, his son, and his son's family, even down to a little grandchild of two years old, had been killed, and the boat broken to pieces and burned.

Although such atrocity seemed beyond belief, yet a number of circumstances combined to give the report credibility. Why, for instance, was the long, unusual trip down the river taken just before our boat was to start? What did it mean that, after the murder of the Christians was known, no sum of money could induce a Lāo man to take a letter to Bangkok? If the story of the fate of our messenger were true, the act was the act of a madman—and there is no telling what a madman may not do. He was in a position to keep us from escaping; and if he had really gone so far as that, he evidently did not intend that we should be heard from alive.

For a time we virtually resigned ourselves to what seemed inevitable fate. When we could get no letters sent, we actually began writing the history of those days on the margins of books in our library, so that, if we were never heard from again, some of the precedent circumstances of our end might thus, perhaps, come to light. It was a great relief, therefore, when an influential Burmese, knowing our situation, offered to carry a letter through to our friends in Bangkok.

On September 29th, when the letters carried by the Burmese were written, we were still under the impression that our boatman had been murdered, and that neither he nor the letters and reports carried by him had been heard from. It was the knowledge that these rumours were false, and that he had passed Rahêng in safety, that first relieved our minds. So, too, his arrival in Bangkok gave our friends there the first assurance of our safety. With this explanation the letters themselves will give the best idea of our situation in those dark days. The following is from a letter of Dr. S. R. House to our Mission Board in New York, printed in the *Presbyterian Record* of February, 1870. It is dated November 11th, 1869.

"Since our last mail was despatched, tidings have been received from the mission families in North Laos which have greatly distressed and alarmed us, causing no little anxiety for their personal safety. This outburst of persecution from which they are now suffering must have been quite unlooked for, for their letters down to September 10th were full of encouragement. Never had the king and the princes [1]

[1] That is the Prince of Chiengmai and the nobility. These terms are so used generally throughout this correspondence.—Ed.

seemed more friendly; never had their prospects seemed brighter. Seven interesting converts had been baptized since the year began, and they had just been enjoying a wonderfully favourable opportunity to make the gospel message known to the people from every part of the kingdom. . . . What has caused this sudden change in the demeanour of the king of Chiengmai toward our missionaries there, does not appear. . . .

"Thus far they seem to have had no apprehension for themselves personally; but the next letter, of two days' later date, indicates that something had occurred or had come to their knowledge which led them to believe that their own lives were in jeopardy. On September 29th Mr. McGilvary writes hurriedly to his father-in-law, Rev. D. B. Bradley, M.D., of the A. M. A. mission as follows:—

"'Dear Father and Mother:—We write to tell you that we may be in great danger. If you never hear from us more, know that we are in heaven. Send some one up here to look after our Christians, and do not, we beg you, grieve over the loss of our lives. Two of our church members died at the martyr's stake on the 14th of September. Warrants are out for the others. What is before us we do not know. We are all peaceful, and very happy. We have written letters giving the full facts, but dare not send them for fear of their interception.

"'Lung Puk left here on the 12th direct for Bangkok. Should he never reach you, you may fear the worst for us. . . . He had a large mail with our reports, etc. Should worst come to worst, we have counted the cost beforehand, and our death will not be in vain. Love to all the dear ones. Good-bye, dear father, mother, brothers, sisters, and friends—perhaps till we meet in heaven!'"

Dr. House then continues:

"That these letters—the last one especially—awakened our deepest solicitude, I need not assure you. The brethren from the Pechaburī station reached Bangkok, to attend the annual session of Presbytery, the very day the startling tidings came; and anxious were our deliberations, and earnest our prayers in behalf of those brethren beloved and their helpless families. A month had then elapsed since the date of the letters. Were they still in the land of the living?

"It was deemed advisable that some of our number should proceed as far up the river as possible—to Rahêng at least—to learn the existing state of things and extend all possible assistance. After consultation this service devolved on Bros. McDonald and George.

"Owing to the peculiar allegiance which holds the Lāo tribes tributary to the Siamese, it was thought best not to press any doubtful treaty rights and claims through the United States Consul—that is, the protection they would be entitled to claim anywhere on the soil of Siam proper—but to throw ourselves on the friendliness and good-will of the Siamese Government as old residents here, most of us, who are greatly troubled lest harm should befall our friends who are living in one of their tributary states. What could they do to help us?

"The deputation, consisting of Dr. Bradley, Mr. McDonald, Mr. George, and myself, were most kindly received by the new Regent of the kingdom, the late Prime Minister—were received in every respect as friends, and the best endeavours of the Siamese Government were promised. A government official would be despatched at once bearing a letter to the king of Chiengmai, enjoining on him to give protection to the missionaries. But the Regent added, 'It is difficult to deal with a man so moody and arbitrary as this Chief of Chiengmai. He is like King Theodore of Abyssinia.'—This too significant comparison had already suggested itself in anything but an agreeable way to ourselves.

"The Siamese move slowly at the best, and the brethren who have consented to go on this errand so full of perplexity and possible peril started several days before the royal messenger's preparations were completed. We are waiting with the greatest solicitude further tidings. I must say from what I know of the character of the man in whose hands and at whose mercy they are, that I have great fears. Others here, however, are confident that no harm can come to them personally."

The following, from a note of mine to the Board, will throw further light on our letter to our friends and on our situation. It was dated October 31st, while we were anxiously waiting for the reply to our letters.

. . . "But the particular fact that filled us with deepest anxiety when we sent that note to Bangkok, was a rumour that the king had, in person, stopped a boat in charge of our old servant whom we had sent down to Bangkok after money and supplies, and had put him, his wife, and all the boatmen to death. That rumour was currently believed here, and we had so many questions asked us about them by persons in high and in low station, that we were constrained almost to believe it. And if that had been done, we knew not what would come next. Of course we had serious apprehensions regarding our own safety; yet our duty was clear. However dangerous our position, we felt that flight would be more dangerous. . . . Our strength was to sit still. . . .

"After waiting a month in suspense about our servants, we have just learned, on pretty good authority, that they were not murdered. They have been reported as having passed Rahêng. In a few days we shall know the truth. If they are safe, our greatest fears were groundless. We wait to see the Lord's purpose in reference to this people. We yet believe they are purposes of mercy. The excitement has somewhat died down, and we have daily many visitors. But there is great fear of the authorities. No one feels safe; no one knows what will come next."

I quote from a letter of Mr. Wilson to the Board the following account of the suffering and death of the martyrs, written January 3d, 1870, after all the various rumours had been sifted, and the facts were clearly known. Meantime the Commission referred to in the letter of Dr. House had come, and this letter was brought to Bangkok by it on its return. This letter and the one cited just above were printed in the *Foreign Missionary* for March and for May, 1870.

"Till within a very short time before their execution, we had no apprehension that any serious obstacle would be thrown in the way of the Lāo becoming Christians. All the baptisms had taken place publicly. The number, and some of the names, of the Christians had been given in answer to questions asked by the younger daughter of the king, and by others of royal blood. We had become convinced that the king must know that some of his people had become disciples of Jesus. His two daughters had assured Mr. McGilvary that no one should be molested for becoming Christians. With such an assurance from the highest princesses in the land, we flattered ourselves that the king would tolerate Christianity. The fearlessness, also, with which all but Nān Chai professed Christ, made us feel that there was no danger to the life of any one who had received baptism.

"Nān Chai, however, seemed anxious. Some two months before his baptism he requested us to write to Bangkok and get the King of Siam to make proclamation of religious toleration. Not a month before his baptism he asked me, 'If the king should call me and ask, "Are you a disciple of Jesus?" would it be wrong to say "No"?' We knew that for some time he had loved the Saviour, but he was following Him tremblingly. His position as overseer (ex-abbot) of the monastery made his renunciation of Buddhism a more noticeable event, and rendered him more liable to persecution than some of the others. I may here state that those who, after leaving the monastery, are appointed overseers of the temple, are, by virtue of their position, exempt from the call of their masters to do government work. Nān Chai belonged to this class. His resignation of this post when he became a Christian, both proved his sincerity, and made him a mark for Buddhist hate and reproach.

"Noi Sunya's work was to tend the king's cattle, and in this way he performed his share of public service. He also worked a farm, and was a physician. He was of a genial disposition and cheerful temper, always looking on the bright side of life, happy himself, and trying to make others happy. He was thus a general favourite. His reception of the truth was hearty and childlike. How his face beamed with joy that communion Sabbath! Next day, Monday, September 6th, about noon, he started for his walk of nine miles across the plain to Mê Pō Kā. In bidding him goodbye we little thought we should see his face no more.

"Our teacher, Nān Chai, came in the following Thursday, somewhat sad because the head man of his village was urging him for some government work and supplies that were then being raised for the army. After resigning the oversight of the temple, being virtually without a master, he had come in to the city to put himself under the king's younger daughter. On Saturday morning, the 11th, she gave him his protection papers, for which he paid the usual three rupees. Some ten days before, when Mr. McGilvary had called with him in reference to this matter, he had, at the princess' request, made a statement of his Christian faith, even to the repeating of a prayer.

"On that same Saturday afternoon a message came from the head man of the village for Nān Chai's immediate return home. The message was so urgent that he concluded not to wait for the accustomed Sabbath morning worship. Knowing that there was a disposition on the part of some of the public officers to find fault with the Christians, I thought it best for him to go home, and not return to us till quiet should be restored. He seemed very sad, and said that his master was disposed to oppress him. All that I could say did not rouse him from his depression. He took leave of us about ten o'clock at night. When we awoke on Sabbath morning, he was gone. We know now that shortly after the princess had given him her letters of protection on Saturday morning, she despatched a messenger to the head man of the village ordering Nān Chai's arrest. Imagine that Sabbath morning's walk of nearly nine miles, much of the way through water nearly knee-deep! Dear gentle heart, full of care and fear!

"He reached home about noon. After dinner he called upon the head man of the village; but no one knew the nature of the conference. He was permitted to sleep at home that night. Next morning came the order from the chief man of the district for the overseers of the temples and those doing the king's own work to appear at his house.

This order included, of course, both our brethren, Noi Sunya and Nān Chai. But to make their attendance doubly sure, armed men were sent with clubs and pikes to conduct them to the appointed rendezvous. Noi Sunya took leave of his wife and six children in tears. He knew what that call and those clubs and spears meant. When they reached the house of the district chief, they found a large armed force ready to receive them. When arrested at their homes they had been charged with refusing to do the king's work. But now Nān Chai was asked, 'Are you an overseer of a temple?' He answered, 'I was, but am not now.' 'Have you entered the religion of the foreigners?' 'Yes.' Noi Sunya was asked the same question, to which he also answered 'Yes.'

"They were then seized, and after further examination were told that they had been condemned to death. While Nān Chai was giving the reason of the faith that was in him, one of the examiners kicked him in the eye, leaving it bloodshot and causing it to swell till the eye was closed. The arms of the prisoners were tied behind their backs. Their necks were compressed between two pieces of timber (the death-yoke) tied before and behind so tightly as painfully to impede both respiration and the circulation of the blood. They were thus placed in a sitting posture near a wall, and cords were passed through the holes in their ears and tied to a beam above. In this constrained and painful position—not able to turn their heads or bow them in slumber—they remained from Monday afternoon till Tuesday morning about ten o'clock, when they were led out into the jungle and executed.

"When Nān Chai was arrested, his wife started on a run to inform us, supposing that he would be brought to the city to undergo a regular trial. In that case she hoped the missionaries could ensure his release. She had arrived in sight of our house, when a messenger from the head man of the village overtook her, and informed her that if she called on us, it would be at the risk of her life. She returned immediately, to join him at the district chief's house; but was informed that if she made the least demonstration of grief, she too would be put to death. She sat down by her husband for a time. They conversed together as opportunity offered, being narrowly watched by the merciless guard. The prisoners both said, 'Oh, if the missionaries were here, we should not have to die!' Nân Chai's last words to his wife were, 'Tell the missionaries that we die for no other cause than that we are Christians.' One of the guards angrily asked what he had said. She saw that it was best for her to retire, and they parted.

"When Nān Chai knew that he and his comrade were doomed, he said to one of the officers, 'You will kill us; we are prepared. But I beg you not to kill those who are in the employ of the missionaries. They are not Christians, and are not prepared to die.' What a triumph of faith in this once fearful disciple! What a noble forgetfulness of self in that earnest request for the lives of others!

"And now, after a long and weary night of painful watching, the morning of Tuesday, the 14th, dawns upon them. The hour is come. They are led out into the lonely jungle. They kneel down. Nān Chai is asked to pray. He does so, his last petition being, 'Lord Jesus, receive my spirit.' The tenderness of the scene melts his enemies to tears. The heads of the prisoners—prisoners for Jesus' sake—are drawn back by slightly raising the cruel yoke they have worn for more than twenty hours. The executioner approaches with his club. Nān Chai receives the stroke on the front of the neck. His body sinks to the ground a corpse. . . . Noi Sunya receives upon the front of his neck five or six strokes; but life is still not extinct. A spear is thrust into his heart. His body is bathed in blood, and his spirit joins that of his martyred brother. Their bodies were hastily buried. Their graves we may not yet visit. . . .

"Only a few days before his death Nān Chai wrote, at Mrs. Wilson's request, a little slip which she forwarded to her friends as a specimen of the Lao language. The last line—the last, no doubt, that he ever wrote—contained the following words 'Nān Chai dai rap pen sit lêo. Hak Yēsū nak' (Nān Chai has become a disciple. He loves Jesus much)."

X

THE ROYAL COMMISSION

AFTER the despatch of our hurried notes by the Burmese on September 29th, 1869, we felt reasonably sure that our friends would learn the news of our situation, and we were in a measure relieved. But at that time we still believed the reports about the murder of Lung Puk. In fact, it was these reports, which we had just heard before writing the letters sent by the Burmese, that caused the great anxiety expressed in them. But though we poured out our hearts and unburdened our fears to our friends, no one in Chiengmai outside of our two families ever knew the fears that agitated our breasts. For two months or more we still feared that we might be treacherously murdered under colour as though it were done by robbers or dacoits. We knew not on lying down at night what might happen before dawn.

One of the hardest things of the situation was that, in the presence of our own dear children, we felt obliged to speak to each other of these matters by signs alone, since it seemed wise to conceal our fears from them. When we had native callers, or in our visits to the natives, we preached to them just as if nothing had happened. Some that we know were sent as spies to see what we were doing and what we were planning to do, had nothing to report except the Gospel message which they had heard.

Then was the time when a few tried friends endeared themselves forever to us. Among these was the Princess Būa Kam, and the abbot of the Ūmōng monastery, both of whom have been mentioned before. The silver plate with a little rice or fruit from the Princess never ceased to come; and the abbot often made an excuse of errands elsewhere in our neighbourhood that he might have occasion to call and express his sympathy.

One incident which occurred before the various rumours had been cleared up, though well-nigh tragic at the time, seemed afterward amusing enough. After the appalling treachery of the younger daughter of the Prince in regard to Nān Chai, while professing constantly such personal friendship for us, we naturally regarded her with profound distrust. What, then, was our surprise, when, one night in the darkest time of our troubles, a summons came for me to go at once to her palace with the officer who brought the message. I was by no means to wait till morning, and I could get no clue to the object of the summons. But it was almost a royal command. Whatever it might mean, nothing would be gained by refusal; so I promised at once to go. But a difficulty arose. My wife positively refused to let me go alone. If the worst were to come, she would be there to see it.

So the children were left in bed, and off we walked three-fourths of a mile in the dark to the palace. We found it brilliantly lighted up. Was it for the final act? But our fears were soon allayed. The Princess received us as she always had done—probably a little surprised to see Mrs. McGilvary with me. A foreign rug was spread for us, and soon was produced a formidable package of documents in English, which the Princess wanted us to translate! They were from the court in Maulmein, and had reference to the law-suits. They had just arrived, and she could not wait till morning. We glanced over them, gave her the substance of them, and promised that if she would send her scribe down next day, we would translate them. She was relieved to find that there was nothing more formidable in them—and so were we. The whole interview did not last more than fifteen minutes; and when ready to return, we were escorted home by servants with lanterns.

For a time we had very few visitors even for medicine. But the monasteries were always open, and we were welcomed in nearly all the homes of the princes. I regularly called on the Prince. When he was in a pleasant mood, I had pleasant conversations with him. If I found him moody or busy, I paid my respects and retired. His elder daughter and her husband were always pleasant, and she was always interested to talk on the subject of religion.

Another friendship formed the year before was then a great comfort to us, though no one could really help us. A wealthy Chinese, who had charge of collecting nearly all the revenue of the government, had been shot in the city of Lampūn, eighteen miles away. A messenger with an elephant was sent, begging me to come at once. It seemed at first impossible for me to go, but finally I did so. The ball had entered below the knee while the man was lying down, had followed the bone, and had lodged in the soft part of the thigh. It was extracted, and I remained there till the patient was out of danger. The wife, a Siamo-Chinese, was a merchant, and acted as our banker for ten years. At this writing, the family has not yet forgotten the service rendered.

But our hourly thoughts were directed to Bangkok. What would be the outcome of our letters? We were continually asked what we were going to do. Our reply was that, of course, we intended to remain. There was no telegraph then, nor even a monthly mail. It was not till November 26th that the first news of what was doing in our behalf reached us. It was brought by messengers sent on in advance to notify the government that a Royal Commissioner had arrived in Lampūn, with two foreigners and a train of eighteen elephants and fifty-three attendants. They were to be in Chiengmai the next day. No intimation, however, was given as to what the object of the Commission was. But plainly it must be a matter of no slight importance.

Early on the morning of the 27th every one was on the alert. A body of men under the direction of an officer were scrubbing the old sālā next door to us, for the letter had asked that preparations be made for the party. A prince whispered in our ears to enquire whether we knew what the "Kā Lūang" was coming for. But we knew as little as he did. We were so hopeful, however, that we began to prepare for our guests, too. The whole place seemed in an attitude of expectancy. The sudden arrival of a Kā Lūang was not an everyday occurrence. And then the two foreigners—two "white kolās"!

In the afternoon the curiosity of every one was gratified by the arrival of the long train with the Commissioner at its head. The two "white kolās" were none other than our associates in the Siamese mission, the Rev. N. A. McDonald, and the Rev. S. C. George. Were ever guests more welcome! The story was soon told of the receipt of our letters in Bangkok, and of the negotiations which had resulted in their coming with a Royal Commissioner and with a "Golden Seal," as the royal letter is called. We now knew definitely that the Commissioner had come on the business of the mission and the treatment of the Christians. But our brethren did not know the contents of the royal letter. No human sagacity could yet predict what turn affairs would take. Was the mission to be securely established, or were we to be escorted safely out of the country? The Commissioner immediately notified the Prince of his arrival with the "Golden Seal," and awaited His Highness' pleasure. The Prince's curiosity and anxiety were guarantee that there would be no delay. Nine o'clock next morning was named as the hour for the audience. The Commissioner notified us to be ready. An officer was sent with a palanquin to escort the "Golden Seal" under the golden umbrella to the palace.

Mr. Wilson and I, of course, joined the procession. On reaching the grand reception hall at the palace, we encountered such an array of princely state as we had never before seen among the Lāo. Every prince, princess, and officer who could come was already there. I quote from Mr. McDonald's official report to the Board, dated February 2d, 1870, an account of the audience. (*Presbyterian Record,* June, 1870.)

"The next morning after our arrival the Regent's letter was conducted in state to the palace under the royal umbrella, and the golden tray containing it was placed on a stand near the middle of the hall. Very soon the king entered the hall apparently calm, but pale with suppressed rage. We arose and bowed to him, and then resumed our seats. The Siamese officers, however, remained prostrate before him, as did every other one in the hall. The king immediately broke the seal and handed the letter to the Siamese secretary to read. After the reading of the letter he looked up, evidently quite relieved, and remarked, 'This letter does not amount to so much. It gives the missionaries privilege to remain if they wish, or to go if they prefer.'"

Mr. McDonald, then, as a member of the Commission, addressed the King, referring to the kindness with which the missionaries had been received by him on their arrival—which was in keeping with the favour shown them in Bangkok, and with the beneficent nature of their work—but regretting that late difficulties had made their stay unpleasant. Among other things he referred to the desertion of their servants. But neither he nor the royal letter made the slightest reference to the murder of the Christians. Mr. McDonald then proceeds:

"What I said did not seem to rouse him. He continued to suppress his rage, and replied, 'As to servants, he had never placed any hindrance. He had put to death a couple of fellows—a thing which he had a right to do, since they had failed to do their allotted government work. But that was his own business.'"

The Prince evidently thought that the affair was ended, and was preparing to close the audience, greatly relieved that the one dreaded point had not been referred to either in the letter or in the conference. But to stop there would have been an inexcusable blunder on our part. Not only had the good name of the Christians been tarnished, but our own also, if we had made all this great fuss about nothing. It was a difficult thing to face the Prince before his whole court, and charge him with falsehood; but he had driven us to it. If he had not lied, we had. For once we were called upon to stand before kings for His name's sake; and I believe that words were given to me to speak.

I said that I was sorry to be compelled to say that the Prince knew that he had not spoken the truth. There was not a man or woman in that audience, nor in the whole country, who did not know that those two men had been put to death for no other pretended reason than that they were Christians. It was done and was proclaimed to be done as a warning to others. They had not refused to do government work. The charge that they had failed to get the slabs for the stockade was a subterfuge. There was not a word of truth in it, as the officer through whom it was done, then present, well knew. When these men received the order to get the slabs, they started immediately, but were at once arrested, and were not allowed to get them. In no sense were they dealt with as criminals. On that very day (over three months after the order), not one-fifth of the men in the province had as yet brought in their timbers, and nothing was said about it. In this country it was an unheard-of thing, even for the gravest offences, to decoy men out from their homes into the jungle, and to kill them there with no pretence of a trial. There was a Sanām (Court), there were regular officers of law, even down to the executioner. In the case of these men, not a single form of law had been observed. By the Prince's own order they had been treacherously arrested, led out into the jungle, and cruelly clubbed to death in the presence of a lawless mob by a ruffian hired to do it.

The old man looked on me in mingled astonishment and rage. Possibly till then he thought we had not been able to learn the facts and particulars in the case. More likely he thought that no one would dare thus openly and publicly to expose them. But what was said had the desired effect. Up to this point the Prince's position had been impregnable. To assault it successfully would have required the production of evidence; and no man in the country, high or low, would have dared to testify against him. But this unexpected challenge was more than he could endure. He flung all caution to the winds. In an instant his sole defence was abandoned. Mr. McDonald says:

"'Yes,' he said, 'he had killed them because they had embraced the Christian religion. And he would continue to kill every one who did the same. Leaving the religion of the country was rebellion against him, and he would so treat it. If the missionaries would remain to treat the sick, they might do so. But they must not make Christians; they must not teach the Christian religion. If they did, he would expel them from the country' . . . At one time I feared that he might become uncontrollable, and break over all restraints, and do us some personal injury. The Siamese officer also was alarmed for our safety."

Matters now had been brought to a crisis. The Christians had been proved to be not malefactors, but martyrs. We now understood each other, and all parties understood the situation. The Prince's bravado before the Commissioner in one sense was politic. He had read between the lines of the King's letter that the Siamese were afraid of him; and he was quite willing to have it so. On the other hand, his attitude might have the effect of convincing them that he was a dangerous man, to be dealt with accordingly —and I believe it did.

But, as Mr. McDonald goes on to say, "It was useless to attempt any further argument. The missionaries merely told him that it was their intention to remain. The conversation then turned to other subjects, and the Prince became more calm. After returning to the house of Mr. McGilvary, and after anxious consultation and prayer, it was considered best to abandon the mission for a time."

The Commissioner strongly advised us to withdraw. Mr. McDonald was naturally timid, and hardly felt safe till he was fairly out of the country. He and Mr. George were sure that it would not be safe for us to remain a single day after the Commissioner departed; and Mr. Wilson agreed with them. Such, then, was the report made to the Board, and the number of the *Record* from which we have quoted above announced the dissolution of the mission.

The news of the scene in the palace spread like wildfire over the city. We had scarcely reached home when our neighbours and friends began to send us secret messages that it would be foolish to remain. The Prince was like a lion bearded in his den. When the Commissioner left there was no telling what he might do. The Commissioner naturally felt some responsibility for our safety, and desired to have us return with him. I so far consented as to allow the Commissioner to send word to the Prince that we would retire as soon as we conveniently could. Yet, from what I knew of the feeling of the people toward us, I could not see that it was the will of Providence that the mission should be abandoned. Nor did I believe that it would be hazardous to remain. The Prince evidently had no thought of actually renouncing his allegiance to Siam. He had been directed to see to our safety, if we wished to remain. I think, too, that I understood him better than did either our own friends or the Commissioner. His bluster at the audience was for effect. It was more than probable that, after sober thought, he himself would realize that he had gone too far. Before the coming of the Commissioner he had been summoned to Bangkok; he was at that time busy preparing boats for the journey, and was soon to start. He was too shrewd a man to wish us to appear there before him as witnesses against him. It was, I thought, more than probable that he would meet more than half-way any advance made toward him, though we could not expect him to make the advance himself.

Next morning before breakfast Mr. Wilson came over to have a long walk and talk with me. He did not wish to express his fears before our children. He argued with all his logic that it was better to go while we safely could. His idea was to retire to Rahêng, where we would be under the direct protection of the Siamese government; for, after yesterday's scene, he was sure we never could be safe in Chiengmai. So far as he was concerned, I thought it a good idea. He might go, and I would remain—at least as long as I could. He felt, however, that he would be to blame if any disaster happened to us. From all responsibility on that score I freely exonerated him. As I viewed the case, our personal risk was at an end so soon as the situation should be known in Bangkok. The Prince would no longer dare either to do anything or to cause anything to be done *secretly,* as once we feared he would. Therefore, notwithstanding the bluster of the day before, fear for our personal safety had little weight with me. But quite apart from the question of danger, there was much to be said in favour of Mr. Wilson's going to Rahêng. The place was an important one for missionary work. The result might possibly be a station in both places, instead of in

Chiengmai alone. His departure might seem some concession to the wishes of the Prince—would show less determination to thwart his known will. If there were any danger in remaining, it would be less for one family than for two. All I wanted was time to see the Lord's will. At any rate, I was not willing to depart without having an audience with the Prince alone. Against this it was urged that the Prince had a special grudge against me, because of the vaccination of his little grandson, and that this would be increased by my having angered him the day before. But of this I was not afraid. The parents of the dear child had begged me never to think that they blamed me for it. As to what had happened the day before, I believed the Prince's respect for me was higher than it would have been had I allowed him to bluff us with his barefaced lie. The result of our walk was that Mr. Wilson agreed to have me call on the Prince the next day, though Mr. McDonald maintained that for himself he would not risk it.

So, next morning, I called at the palace at an hour when I knew I should find the Prince alone with his head-wife. And, just as I expected, he received me with unwonted cordiality. I referred to the friendship between him and my father-in-law, Dr. Bradley; to his cordial consent given to our coming to his country to teach the Christian religion and to benefit his people in other ways; to his kind reception of us when we came; to his granting us a place for a home; and to his many other acts of kindness. We had come to him as friends, and I could not bear we should part as enemies. As I had anticipated, his whole manner showed that he was pleased at my advance. That, too, he said, was his desire. We might remain at least till after his return from Bangkok, and take all the time needed for a comfortable departure. I thanked him for his consideration, and told him that Mr. Wilson would probably go at once. We shook hands and parted as if the scene in the palace had never occurred. I had won my point. What I wanted was time, and I had gained it. The Prince could not possibly return in less than six months' time—it might be much longer.

In a few days our friends left us. Having no faith in the success of my new negotiations, or possibly thinking that I might be caught in a trap, they reported to the Board, as we have seen, that the mission was broken up—as technically it was. This last turn of affairs was merely a private arrangement between the Prince and myself.

Had the matter not passed beyond our power, I doubtless should have been credulous enough, or weak enough, to prefer that no further action should be taken by our friends in Bangkok. I did write to Dr. Bradley and to our mission to pursue a pacific policy, and to show the Prince all kindness, as, indeed, I knew they would. But I learned afterwards that their advances were hardly received with courtesy. Mr. George, who asked permission to send by some one of the numerous fleet of boats some parcels to us, was given to understand that the things would not be needed, as the Prince expected both families to leave Chiengmai upon his return.

XI

DEATH OF KĀWILŌROT

THE Commissioner's report of the attitude assumed by the Prince showed the Siamese government that the man in control of the northern provinces was of a spirit and temper that might be difficult to curb—that might at any time throw everything into confusion. Hitherto it had been their policy to strengthen his hands to any degree not inconsistent with his loyalty. Siam and Burma had long been rivals and enemies. A strong buffer-state in the north had been a necessity to Siam. But conditions were changed. Burma was now under English control, and had ceased to be a disturbing factor in the problem. A change in Siamese policy as regards the North was inevitable.

When the news of the murder of the Christians became known in Bangkok, our friends there deferred to the wishes of the Siamese government as expressed by the Regent—whose goodwill to the mission and to ourselves no one doubted. No steps, therefore, were taken to have the United States officially represented on the Commission. In this we believe our friends were providentially led. But Dr. House's letter does not state, what was also the fact, that the United States Consul, in whose presence the Lāo Prince had given his official sanction to the establishment of the mission, was anxious that the United States should be so represented. And when that Commission so signally failed to accomplish anything satisfactory, it was the Consul's turn to say to our friends, "I told you so."

Because, as they themselves expressed it, of the lawless nature of the Lāo Prince, and the consequent difficulty of protecting foreigners so far away, our Siamese friends would then have preferred to have us recalled. In fact, that was their first thought. The first draft of the letter prepared to be sent by the Commission actually contained the stipulation that we be safely conveyed back to Siam proper. It was only the indomitable perseverance of Dr. Bradley—who frankly declared that he would rather have no such letter sent at all—that secured the omission of that clause, and left the way open for the possible continuance of the mission. So, when the Commission returned to Bangkok, and it was known that the Lāo Prince was soon to follow them, General Partridge, the United States Consul, immediately took up the case, and insisted that the Siamese government give guarantee for the fulfilment of promises publicly made by its vassal in the presence of officials of both governments. "Before this you could say, 'He is like a tiger in the jungle; we cannot control him.' But when he reaches Bangkok, he is in your power. You can then make your own terms regarding his return."

How this negotiation was conducted, I am not aware. But from the *Presbyterian Record* of September, 1870, we learn that the Consul carried his point:

"Dr. House sends us word that the Siamese government has extended its protection over the missionaries in Chiengmai; they are not to be molested in their work. As the king of Chiengmai is tributary to Siam, this decision will no doubt be respected. This king is not likely to live long, and he will be succeeded by his son-in-law, a prince who has shown a friendly interest in the missionaries. The intervention of the Siamese government was obtained by the U. S. Consul, Gen. Partridge, not at the instance of the missionaries, but he took the ground of treaty stipulations between Siam and our country, which accorded the right of protection to American citizens."

From the *Foreign Missionary* of September, 1870, we quote the following extract from the *Bangkok Summary*, doubtless from the pen of Dr. Bradley:

"I am very happy to learn from the most reliable authority that His Grace the Regent has been pleased to commit the American citizens in Chiengmai to the care and protection of the Maha Uparat, the son-in-law of the king, charging him to assist, nourish, and protect them so that they shall suffer no trouble and hindrance in their work from persecutions like those through which they have passed since September 12th last.

"His Grace, moreover, is understood to have promised that he will certainly arrange to have those American citizens protected in Chiengmai according to the stipulations of the treaties, even though the present king should live and continue his reign.

"The Maha Uparat enjoys the reputation of being a mild and discreet prince. He received this his new title a few weeks since from His Majesty the Supreme King of Siam, by virtue of which he is constituted Second King of Chiengmai. I learn that His Grace the Regent has virtually committed the rule of that kingdom to him during the illness of the king, and has assured him that he is ultimately to become the king's successor to the throne.

"This I regard as good news, indeed, and too good to be held a day longer from the public. Who will not agree with me that the Siamese government is worthy of a great meed of praise for what it has done in the matter of the Chiengmai mission? But let us see to it that the King of Kings, as well, receives our highest praise for all these gratifying events of His providence."

While the Consul was pressing these claims, Prince Kāwilōrot, as was intimated in the last extract, became dangerously ill. He was stricken with almost instantaneous loss of consciousness, and complete paralysis of speech. Meanwhile we in Chiengmai, only five hundred miles away, were in profound ignorance of what was happening. If we had despatched a special messenger thither for news, it would have been three months before he could have returned with a reply. And the first news we received was not reassuring. Word came that the time was set for the Prince's return; that he had been promoted to higher honours, and had received higher titles; that he was returning with full power, and probably flushed with fresh victories. Of course, that did not necessarily mean very much. Siam understood perfectly the great trick of oriental statecraft, the giving of high-sounding titles, with, perhaps, a larger stipend, in compensation for the loss of real power. But it was a time of great anxiety for us. Revenge was a passion which that man seldom left ungratified. Would he come breathing out slaughter against the church and vengeance on us?

By and by there came a message stating that the Prince was ill, and directing that offerings be made for his recovery. Then came news that he was already on his way, and had sent orders for a hundred elephants to meet him at the landing station below the rapids. Some surmised that his illness was feigned in order to escape the lawsuits which were pressing him. About the middle of June we learned that he had reached the landing station, but was very seriously ill. It was still more urgently enjoined that his relatives and the monasteries in Chiengmai should "make merit" in his behalf, and propitiate the demons by generous offerings.

On the evening of June 29th, while riding through the streets of the city, some one called out to me, "The Prince is dead!" No news ever gave me such a shock. I stepped in to the residence of one of the princes, a nephew of Kāwilōrot, to get the particulars, but found him in a dreadful state of mind. Yes. The Prince was dead; and word had come that he (the nephew) was to go to Bangkok to bear the brunt of the lawsuits—to answer in his own name for transactions done by order of the dead Prince!

How soon the strongest prejudices fade and disappear in the presence of death! The anxious fears of his return that had haunted us, all dissolved into tender sympathy now that he was gone. We forgot his treachery and cruelty, and thought only of his interesting human qualities. We recalled his taking tea or dining with us, and even the dry jokes that he so much enjoyed. He was a tender father. He could be a warm, though a fickle and inconstant friend. In many respects he was a good ruler. He was absolute and tyrannical; but there was no petty thieving in his realm. And now that voice that had made thousands tremble was silent in death! No doubt it was with a sigh of relief that the Siamese government turned over the government of the North to one whom they could better trust.

But it would be a hard heart that could follow unmoved that long, weary homeward trip of the dying Prince. He was so weak that he could not endure the jarring caused by the use of the setting-poles. His boat had to be taken in tow of another. When the last lingering hope of life died out, his one desire was to reach home—to die in his own palace. The trip through the rapids he could not bear, and it was too slow for the dying man. Travel by elephant is both rough and slow. He is brought ashore, therefore, and borne on a litter as swiftly as relays of men can carry him. Over the mountains and up the valley of the Mê Ping, under burning sun and through driving rain, they hasten. At last, on the evening of June 28th, they halt on the left bank of the Mê Ping, with only that stream between him and his own country. "What land is this?" he asks. "Lampūn," is the reply. "Carry me across quickly!" He is obeyed, but sinks exhausted by the fatigue of crossing. He passes a restless night. His mind wanders. He dreams of being at home; of worshipping in his own palace. The morning comes. He is still alive; but so weak that, in spite of his eagerness to hasten on, at every few paces his bearers must halt, while attendants fan him or administer a cordial. At last fan and cordials fail. The litter is set down under the two golden umbrellas that screen it from the burning rays of the sun. The little group stand with bowed heads and hushed hearts while the spirit takes its flight, to appear before its Maker.—Almost, but not quite home, and with none of his immediate kin by him to see the end! The attendants cover the body with a cloth, and hasten on to the next station, a few miles below the city. The procession halted there at about the very time that the messenger reached Chiengmai with the news that he was dead.

Such, as I learned next day from the attending prince, were the last hours of His Highness Chao Kāwilōrot Suriyawong, Prince of Chiengmai. He died at ten o'clock in the morning of June 29th, 1870, in the seventieth year of his age, and in the sixteenth of his reign.

Next morning before breakfast I was sent for by the younger daughter of the Prince, to go to the residence of the nephew, whom I had left late in the evening before in such a distracted state of mind. How shocked was I on entering to find the prince cold and dead! The Princess wished to get my judgment whether he was really dead beyond all hope of resuscitation. But it required no skilled physician to answer that question. He had evidently died by a dose of opium administered by his own hands. The little cup from which it was taken was still by his bedside. Whether it was intentional suicide to escape the lawsuits of his deceased master, or was simply designed to ease the mental troubles of that night, they could tell as well as I. In either case, he slept the sleep that knows no waking till the summons of the last trump.

After breakfast I rode out to the encampment, only two or three miles away, where the body of the Prince was lying. The family and officers and friends were assembled to look for the last time on that noted face. The last act before placing the body in the coffin was to cover it throughout with gold-leaf, to give it the appearance of being a Buddha. But no gold-leaf could disguise that face. The family remained there a few days, partly for the much needed rest, but chiefly to await a day of good augury for carrying the remains to the city.

The day was well chosen for such a pageant as the country had not seen, to honour alike the departed, and to welcome the succeeding Prince. There was a long and imposing procession of soldiers, monks, and people marching to the wailing of the funeral dirge and to the slow, solemn beat of drums. Near the head of the line, on his elephant, was the son-in-law, Chao Intanon, soon to be Prince of Chiengmai. Not far behind came the body of the dead Prince, borne on a golden bier and accompanied by a large train of yellow-robed priests. Behind this was the vacant throne, and on it the royal crown, both testifying to the emptiness of human pomp and power. Then came one leading the horse His Highness used to ride; and next, his favourite elephant, its huge body covered with trappings of gold. After these came members of the Prince's family and other near relatives.

About ten o'clock the procession approached the city which, by inexorable custom, may never open its gates to receive the dead—not even though the dead were he whose word for so many years had been its law. What a comment on human glory and on the tyranny of superstitious custom! On reaching the South Gate, therefore, the procession turned to the right, and passed on outside the city wall to the East Gate. There, in the Prince's summer garden, beside the river, his remains lay in state until the great cremation ceremony a year later. Meantime a lamp was kept burning at the head and at the foot night and day. A prince was in constant attendance. Courses of monks chanted the requiem of the Buddhist ceremonial for the dead. At intervals during the whole night the beat of the drum resounded through the air, reminding the city that there lay all that remained of one of its greatest masters.

Prince Intanon, though not yet officially installed, assured me, as soon as I met him at the encampment, that we were to remain and build our houses and prosecute our work without let or hindrance. Other princes and officers were pleased to give the same assurance. With the Prince's party there came a large mail from friends in Bangkok, giving full particulars of the negotiations that were stopped by the sudden illness of the Prince, and clearing up the questions about which we were so much in doubt. The interposition of Providence had been so marked that we could only stand in awe before Him who had so wonderfully led us. For, after the utmost stretch of my own credulity in trying to trust the Prince, my final conviction is that, had he lived, he and the mission could not have existed in the same country. He could never have endured to see his people becoming Christians— Not that he cared so much for Buddhism; but it would have been a constant challenge to his autocratic rule.

In March, while the scenes of this tragic drama were slowly enacting in Bangkok, and while we were anxiously awaiting the dénouement, we had a pleasant episode of another kind. One morning we were surprised to learn from some natives that out on the plain, not far from the city, they had passed two white foreigners, a man and a woman, and that they were coming to our house. Sure enough, about ten o'clock, who should ride up but Rev. and Mrs. J. N. Cushing of the American Baptist Mission in Burma! What an unexpected pleasure! For three years we had seen but two white faces outside of our own little circle. Some of our latest news from home friends was eleven months old when we received it. What a social feast we did have!

They had started from Shwegyin, Burma, had made a tour west of the Salwin River, crossed over to Keng

Tung, come down by Chieng Sên and Chieng Rāi, and now called at Chiengmai on their way back to Burma. Their visit was a real godsend to us in the time of our troubles.

XII

THE NEW RÉGIME

ONE of the results of the change of government was that we were able to build permanent houses. For three years and more we had lived within basket-woven bamboo walls that a pocket-knife could pierce, neither secure nor wholesome nor favourable for our work. They bore silent but steady testimony that we ourselves did not regard our stay as permanent. The results of our manner of living were already seen in the impaired health of the members of the mission. My wife surely could never have lived another decade in the old sālā with bamboo walls and ceiling, where the dust from the borers in the wood constantly filled the air and poisoned the lungs. Mrs. Wilson bore up bravely for five years, until there was just ready for her reception the permanent house which she was never to enjoy. As soon as they could, the family started for the United States on furlough, all thoroughly broken down. After two years of rest Mr. Wilson alone was able to return to the field, leaving Mrs. Wilson behind. She never regained her health, and they never saw each other again. Her departure was a great loss to the mission. She was a gifted lady, a fine vocal and instrumental musician, and a consecrated missionary. She left one literary work in Lāo, the translation of Bunyan's *Pilgrim's Progress,* which has since been published.

But as matters then were, there was much perplexing work to be done before we were at all ready to begin building. I was favoured in getting a lot of first class teak logs delivered at a very cheap rate. Then the trouble began. The logs must be hauled up from the river by elephants to the lot where they are to be sawn. The log is raised and mounted on two strong trestles. A black line to guide the saw is struck on either side. Two sawyers stand facing each other across the log, grasping the handles of a long framed saw with horizontal blade. Then the operation begins. The saw is pushed and pulled back and forth till the cut is carried through to the end of the log. This operation is repeated for every stick of timber put into the house.

But we are already too fast. Where are the sawyers to come from? There were then no good sawyers among the Lāo. No one dared to learn for fear of being appropriated by the Prince, or of being compelled to work on public buildings. There were, however, three pairs of sawyers, debtors to the Prince, whom he had brought up from Rahêng for his own work. Whenever not needed by him or by some other person of rank, they were allowed to seek employment elsewhere. So, at odd times, I was able to secure their services. But if the Prince needed them, they must at once drop everything and go. Scores of times our sawyers were called away, often for weeks at a time, and at the busiest stage of the work.

And now for the carpenter. The Lāo dared not be known as carpenters for the same reason as that given above in the case of the sawyers. They would have been constantly requisitioned for government work. There was in the place only one Siamese carpenter reputed to be a good workman. In order to get him, I had to advance him three hundred rupees, professedly to pay a debt, but most likely to gamble with. He was to build by contract. But he had already received his money, or so much of it that he was quite independent. He soon slashed and spoiled more timber than his wages were worth. So, to keep him from ruining the whole, I had to get rid of him, even at some sacrifice. Just then a Siamo-Chinese turned up, who took the job by the day under my direction, to be assisted by some Christians whom we trained thus as apprentices. The house was built on the plan of the East Indian bungalow—raised ten feet from the ground on posts, with single walls and a veranda all round. Its large lofty rooms, screened on all sides by the verandas, make it still one of the most comfortable houses in the mission. It was more than eight years from the time of our arrival when we entered it; and even then it was not finished.

Although the new government was friendly, yet some of the ruling spirits were in their hearts as hostile as the deceased Prince had ever been, and without his more noble qualities. There were two in particular who soon began to show that their secret influence would be against the mission—and their open hostility, too, so far as they ventured to let it appear. One was the adopted son of the late Prince, and the other the new ruler's half-brother, who had been made Uparăt, or second in power, when the new Prince ascended the throne. Had these both lived, their combined influence would have been nearly as formidable as that of Kāwilōrot. Unfortunately, too, the actual business of the country was largely in their hands. Prince Intanon was not at all ambitious for power.

He liked nothing better than to work without care or responsibility in his own little workshop, making fancy elephant-saddles, and let his half-brother rule the country. During the following year the adopted son went down to Bangkok to receive the insignia of his new rank, but never returned. His death was even more sudden than that of his foster-father. He was taken with the cholera, and died in a few hours. This left the elder of the two avowed enemies of Christianity, and the higher in rank and power. To give an illustration of the kind of spirit we had to contend with in him, I will anticipate an incident of a few years later.

Two native Karens, ordained ministers, were sent by the American Baptist Mission to initiate in Lāo territory a work among the Karens, a hill-people scattered sparsely throughout all the mountain region between Siam and Burma. The native evangelists brought with them letters from the missionaries in Burma, requesting us to aid them in getting Lāo passports. We went with them to the new Prince, and he very graciously gave direction to his brother to see that passports were issued, stating not only that the visitors were to be protected and aided as travellers, but also that they were to be allowed to teach the new religion, and that people were allowed to embrace it without fear.

I was specially interested that they should succeed in the first village which they were to visit, for it was the one where I had vaccinated the whole population during the first year of our mission. Since I had failed to make Christians of them—partly, as I supposed, on account of my ignorance of their language, but more on account of the persecution which followed so soon after—I hoped that when the message was delivered in their own tongue, with official permission to embrace it, the whole village might accept the Gospel. What was the astonishment of the preachers that, instead of being received with the characteristic hospitality of their race, they hardly found common civility! At last they learned the reason. The Chao Uparāt had secretly despatched a special messenger with a letter under his own seal, forbidding any Karen subject to embrace the new religion. All who did so were to be reported to him. What that meant, or what he wished them to infer that it meant, was well understood.

Our readers, therefore, will not be surprised that we found it necessary to keep an eye on the Chao Uparāt, and to use considerable diplomacy in counteracting his schemes against the church. It was my policy in those days to keep up as close an acquaintance as possible with the members of the ruling family. It was the misfortune of all of them that they were ignorant;[1] and ignorance begets suspicion. Some of them were naturally suspicious of the missionaries. They could not understand what motive could induce men who were neither government officials nor merchants, to leave a great country and come to live in theirs.

Two objects were gained by keeping in contact with the rulers. They saw, then, with their own eyes, and heard with their own ears, what we were doing. In nearly every interview our one great work was magnified alike to prince, priest, and people. I have heretofore specially mentioned princesses, too, as well as princes, in this connection, because the Lāo have a

[1] This same Uparāt, whose word ruled the country, was unable to write his own orders.

proud pre-eminence among non-Christian races in the position accorded to woman. In the family, woman's authority is universally recognized. At the time we speak of it was much the same in the government also. The influence of women in affairs of state was doubtless greatly increased during the previous reign, when, there being no sons in the royal household, the daughters naturally became more prominent. They were trained to understand and to deal with public business.

I have already referred to the kindness of the elder daughter, now not, as in former reigns, the head-wife, but the only wife of the new ruler. By birth she was of higher rank than he; and she was in every way worthy of the high position she now assumed. Hers was, in fact, the strong intelligence and steady will that kept her more passive consort from errors into which he would otherwise have been led. At this particular juncture she was needed as a check against the Prince's more ambitious and less principled half-brother. She had a woman's instinct to discern a point, and a woman's revulsion against lawless acts, even when done by her own father. In honesty of purpose she and her consort were one, for his kindness of heart had drawn to him more dependents than any other prince in the land possessed. The murder of the Christians they both regarded as "worse than a crime—a blunder." For the present, however, there was no indication of the sinister forces which came into play later. All in authority seemed to be honestly carrying out the orders from Bangkok concerning the missionary work.

A year was spent in preparation for the ceremonies attending the cremation of the dead Prince. During the last three months of this time, everything else in the whole land yielded place to it. Not only was there requisition of men and materials throughout the province of Chiengmai; but all the neighbouring states furnished large levies of men under the personal direction of their princes or officers of rank. Such occasions offer exceptional opportunities for meeting people from all parts of the country, for forming lasting friendships, and for sending some knowledge of the Gospel to distant provinces. In after years I never made a tour on which I did not encounter friends whose acquaintance I had made at the great cremation festival.

The preparations were hastened somewhat because of the unsettled state of the country. Chao Fā Kōlan, the Ngīo freebooter of whom we have already heard, was still at his old tricks. Emboldened by the death of the Prince, and the confusion incident to the change of rulers, he had become more insolent than ever. Villages had been burned within less than a day's march from the city. Bands of men, euphemistically called an army, were levied and despatched to capture him; but long before they could reach him, he was safe within his stronghold in the mountains.

The dead Prince was born on a Sunday; therefore every important event of his life must take place on that day, even to the last dread summons, which is not under man's control—and beyond that, to the final disposition of his mortal remains. Sunday, therefore, was the first day of the ceremonies. On that day the body was removed from the summer garden to the "Mēn," where it was to lie in state to receive the homage of his relatives and subjects until the following Sunday. The morning of each day was

A CREMATION PROCESSION

devoted to "merit-making" of various kinds—feeding the monks, making offerings to them, and listening to the reading of the sacred books. The afternoons were largely spent in boxing games, a favourite amusement of the Lāo. The evenings were given up to gambling.

Everything went on according to programme until Thursday morning, when the festivities were rudely interrupted. Chao Fā Kōlan, the bandit chief, taking advantage of the occasion, made one of his sudden forays to within so short a distance of Chiengmai that he actually had posted on the city gates during the night an insolent manifesto to the effect that the assembled Princes need not trouble themselves further with the cremation of the dead Prince. He and his band would attend to that! The news produced a tremendous panic. The whole business of the cremation was incontinently stopped. A force was sent out after the marauder—with the usual result. Before the end of the week, however, the panic had sufficiently subsided to permit the ceremonies to be resumed. The cremation itself was carried out on the following Sunday as planned.

During all these years the demand for medical treatment, and the opportunity which its exercise brings, had been constantly growing. I made, for example, a second trip to Lampūn, this time at the call of the Chao Uparāt of that city. The poor man had consumption, and at first sent to me for some foreign medicine, thinking that would surely cure him. Judging from his symptoms as reported, I sent word that I could not cure him; that the soothing mixture which I sent was sent in hope that it might give him a few nights' rest; but that was all I could do. Presently he sent an elephant with a most urgent appeal that I come to see him. I was glad of the call, for it gave me the opportunity of directing a dying man to something even more urgently needed than medicine. I spent a few days with him, and visited all of the leading families and officials of the place, establishing most valuable and friendly relations with them.

Long before this time, both the demand for medical treatment and the responsibility involved far exceeded what any person without complete professional training could undertake to meet. We had urged upon our Board the claims of our mission for a physician. The following touching appeal, which appeared in the *Foreign Missionary* for March, 1870, was made by Mr. Wilson not long after the death of his son Frank. After sending an earnest appeal from Nān Inta for helpers, Mr. Wilson says:

"Of course Nān Inta's call for help includes in it a Christian physician. Who will respond? I am convinced there are many young men in the medical profession whose love for Jesus and whose sympathy with human sufferings are strong enough to bring them all the way to Chiengmai, if they will but yield themselves to this constraining influence. Christian physician, you are greatly needed here. The missionary's family needs you. This suffering people needs you. You were needed months since, when a voice so sweet and full of glee was changed to piteous shrieks of pain. You were not here to give relief; and if you now come, it will not greet you, for it is hushed in death. You are needed here *now*. A plaintive cry comes to me as I write. It is the voice of our dear babe, whose weak condition fills our hearts with deepest anxiety. May I not interpret this plaintive cry as addressed to you? It is the only way that M. has of saying to you, 'Come to Chiengmai.' When you arrive, she may be sleeping beside her little brother. But you will find others, both old and young, whose pains you may be able to soothe, and whose souls you may win from the way that leads to eternal death."

Great was our joy, therefore, when, in the summer of 1871, we learned that Dr. C. W. Vrooman, from Dr. Cuyler's church in Brooklyn, had responded to our appeal, and already was under appointment of our Board for Chiengmai. His arrival was delayed somewhat because it was thought unsafe for him to make the river trip during the height of the rainy season. So it was January 22d, 1872, before we welcomed him to Chiengmai. He came with high credentials as a physician and surgeon with experience both in private and in hospital practice. He began work on the day of his arrival. He found Nān Inta at the point of death from acute dysentery; and his first trophy was the saving of that precious life. Had he done nothing else, that alone would have been well worth while. One or two operations for vesical calculus gave him such a reputation that patients came crowding to him for relief. In his first report he writes:

"I was very glad to commence work as soon as I arrived in the field. The number was large of those who came to the brethren here for daily treatment; and such is the reputation which they have established for themselves as physicians, that the demand for our professional services is greater than we can properly meet. I am satisfied that the demand for a medical missionary here was not too strongly urged by the brethren in their earnest appeals to the Board.

"I have already had much professional work to do, and while I am ministering to physical ailments, Brother McGilvary, who is kindly my interpreter, has opportunity to break unto many the bread of life. . . . Two men have just left who came a long distance, hoping we could bring to life a brother who had died hours before."

XIII

EXPLORATION

NOT long after Dr. Vrooman's arrival it was decided to undertake our first extended tour. It was important to ascertain the size and population of our whole field; and this could be accomplished only by personal exploration. A journey for this purpose would, of course, afford abundant opportunity for preaching the Gospel; it would, besides, give the doctor a needed change, and would effectually advertise his work. Our objective was Lūang Prabāng, then one of the largest of the provinces of Siam, as it was also the most distant one. A journey to it seemed the most profitable that could be made during the time at our disposal, and the most comfortable as well, since a large stretch of it could be made by boat. It was already too late in the season to accomplish all that we desired; but "half a loaf is better than no bread." It might be years before a longer trip could be made. As a matter of fact, it was sixteen years before I visited Lūang Prabāng again.

The Prince gave us a passport, sending us as his guests to be entertained without expense; though, of course, we always paid our way. Our letter stated that we went as teachers of religion and as physicians for the sick. It was a virtual proclamation for all the sick to apply to us for treatment. This gave frequent occasion for retort that we did not remain long enough to comply with our letter. We could only reply by pointing to the clouds and the long journey ahead.

The party consisted of Dr. Vrooman, myself, a cook, a body-servant, and eight carriers, with a newly baptized convert as the only available assistant in the religious work. The elephants required for our transportation over the first stage of our journey—to Chieng Rāi—we had secured, for a wonder, without effort, and very cheaply. Their owner was anxious to get them out of the country to escape an epidemic which then was prevalent. The start was on April 15th, 1872, after a heavy storm which ushered in the rainy season. This was my first trip over the road to Chieng Rāi, afterwards so familiar to me. After leaving the plain of Chiengmai, the road ascends the valley of the Mê Kūang River, fording that stream no less than forty-nine times before it reaches the summit, 3100 feet above sea-level, the watershed between the Mê Ping and the Mê Kōng.[1] Thence it descends to the Mê Kok at Chieng Rāi. The owner of our elephants travelled

[1] In standard Siamese the vowel in the name of this great river is undoubtedly long o, and has been so since the days of the earliest Siamese writing. Such also seems to have been the understanding of the early travellers who first brought the name into European use, for Mekong is the uniform spelling of all the standard Atlases and Gazetteers which I have been able to consult. In the Lāo dialect, however, the vowel is that represented by *aw* in *lawn*. This is the pronunciation which Mr. J. McCarthy, Director of the Siamese Royal Survey Department, heard in the North, and transferred to the Map of Siam, which he compiled, as Me Kawng. This, however, Mr. R. W. Giblin, Mr. McCarthy's successor in office, recognized as an error, and assured me that it should be corrected in the new map which he hoped soon to publish. Mr. Giblin, however, has left the service, and the map, I fear, has not yet been issued. But since Siamese speech and the usage of geographical authorities are at one on this point, there can scarcely be question as to the proper form for use here.—Ed.

with us, and was unnecessarily tender to his beasts. In consequence we were ten days making this stage of the trip, which afterwards, with my own elephants, I used to make in less than six. On this trip I walked almost the whole distance.

At Chieng Rāi we were cordially received. The governor listened to the Gospel message, and, I believe, received it in faith, as we shall see later. Thence we took boat down the Më Kok to its junction with the Më Kōng. The sand-bar where we spent the Sabbath was covered with fresh tracks of large Bengal tigers.

Shortly after this we passed out of the Më Kok into the great Më Kōng, with reference to which I take the liberty of quoting from a recent work, *Five Years in Siam,* by H. Warrington Smyth, F.R.G.S.

"Few can regard the Me Kawng without feeling its peculiar fascination. That narrow streak connecting far countries with the distant ocean,—what scenes it knows, what stories it could tell! Gliding gently here, and thundering with fury there where it meets with opposition; always continuing its great work of disintegration of hard rocks and of transport of material; with infinite patience hewing down the mountain sides, and building up with them new countries in far climes where other tongues are spoken; it never stays its movement. How few men have seen its upper waters! What a lonely life altogether is that of the Me Kawng! From its cradle as the Gorgu River in the far Thibetan highlands, to its end in the stormy China Sea, it never sees a populous city or a noble building. For nearly three thousand miles it storms through solitudes, or wanders sullenly through jungle wastes. No wonder one sat by the hour listening to its tale. For though but dull to read of, the wide deep reality rolling before one had an intense interest for a lonely man.

"Rising in about 33° 17′ N. Lat. and 94° 25′ E. Long. in the greatest nursery of noble rivers in the world, where six huge brethren have so long concealed the secrets of their birth, it flows southeast through Chinese Thibetan territory to Chuande, where the tea caravan road from Lhasa and Thibet on the west, crosses it eastward towards Ta Chien Lu and China, over 10,000 feet above sea level."

Almost within sight from the mouth of the Mê Kok were the ruins of Chieng Sên, once the largest city in all this region. Its crumbling walls enclose an oblong area stretching some two miles along the river. Seventy years before our visit it had been taken by a combined army of Siamese and Lão. Its inhabitants were divided among the conquerors, and carried away into captivity. At the time of our visit, the city and the broad province of which it was the capital had been desolate for three-quarters of a century. Nothing remained but the dilapidated walls and crumbling ruins of old temples. Judging from its innumerable images of Buddha, its inhabitants must have been a very religious people. One wonders whence came all the bronze used in making them in those distant days. To me it was an unexpected pleasure to find myself in that old city, the ancestral home of so many of our parishioners. Little did I think then that twenty years later I should aid in organizing a church where we then stood. The Mê Kōng is here a mighty stream. It must be a magnificent sight in time of high water.

A short distance below the city we passed a village recently deserted because of the ravages of the tigers. The second day from Chieng Sên brought us to Chieng Kawng, one of the largest dependencies of the province of Nān. There we spent two very interesting and profitable days. I had met the governor in Chiengmai. He was delighted with my repeating rifle, and had us try it before him. There was also his son, who not long after was to succeed the father; but his story we shall come upon some twenty years later.

At this place we were fortunate in finding an empty trading-boat going to Lūang Prabāng, in which the governor engaged for us passage on very reasonable terms. We left Chieng Kawng on May 3d. The trip to Lūang Prabāng occupied five days, and was one of the memorable events of my life. In some respects the scenery is not so striking as that of the Mê Ping rapids. The breadth of the river makes the difference. You miss the narrow gorge with overhanging cliffs and the sudden bends closing in every outlet. But, on the other hand, you have an incomparably greater river and higher mountains. I quote again from Mr. Warrington Smyth the following description of one portion of the river scenery:

"The high peaks, towering 5,000 feet above the river, which give it such a sombre appearance, are generally of the very extensive limestone series. They present tremendous precipices on some of their sides, and their outlines are particularly bold. . . . Some miles above Lūang Prabāng the large and important tributaries of the Nam Ū and the Nam Seng enter the Mê Kawng. The clear transparent water of these tributaries forms a strong contrast to the brown sediment-laden water of the Mê Kawng. . . . In some of the rapids with sloping bottoms, the first jump over the edge is very pleasant; the fun then comes in the short roaring waves. Everybody on board is fully occupied; the men at the bow-oar canting her head this way and that, the helmsman helping from the other end to make her take its straight, the men at the oars pulling for all they are worth, and the rest bailing mightily, or shouting to any one who has time to listen. If the rapid is a bad one, the crews land to have a meal before tackling it, and stop to chew some betel and compare notes after it. So it is always a sociable event."

My travelling companion, Dr. Vrooman, thus gives his impressions.

"The current of the Cambodia is very swift, in places so much so that it was dangerous to navigate. The river is nearly a mile wide in places; and where the channel is narrow, it rushes along with frightful rapidity. No scenery is finer throughout the entire distance we travelled on it. Mountains rise from either bank to the height of three or four thousand feet. The river fills the bottom of a long, winding valley; and as we glided swiftly down it, there seemed to move by us the panorama of two half-erect hanging landscapes of woodland verdure and blossom. Only as we neared the city did we see rough and craggy mountain peaks and barren towering precipices."

Twenty-six years later I descended the Mê Ū River from Mûang Kwā to Lūang Prabāng, and then ascended it again. The perpendicular rock-cliffs at its junction with the Mê Kōng surpass any that I ever saw elsewhere.

Of greater interest to me, however, than roaring rapids and towering rocks were the evidences of numerous human habitations perched far above us on the mountain sides. Rarely can their houses or villages be seen; but in many places their clearings have denuded the mountains of all their larger growth. It was tantalizing not to be able to stop and visit these people in their homes. But my first opportunity to make extensive tours among them was not till some twenty years later. As for the Mê Kōng, my comment is: If I wished an exciting river trip, and had a comfortable boat, I should not expect to find a more enchanting stretch of three hundred miles anywhere else on the face of the earth.

Lūang Prabāng was then the most compactly built of all Siamese cities outside of Bangkok, which, in some respects, it resembled. It differs from the other Lāo cities in having no great rural population and extensive rice-plains near it. Its rice supply was then levied from the hill-tribes as a tribute or tax. The city has a fine situation at the foot of a steep hill some two hundred feet high, tipped, as usual, with a pagoda. The Nām Kêng there joins the Mê Kōng, dividing the city into two unequal portions. The view from the top of the hill is delightful. The inhabitants belong to a large branch of the Tai race, extending southward at least to Cambodia. They are called the Lāo Pung Khāo (White-bellied Lāo), as ours, because of their universal practice of tattooing the body, are called Lāo Pung Dam (Black-bellied).

The Prince of Lūang Prabāng was absent from the city hunting wild elephants, in which game his province abounds. The Chao Uparāt gave us a hospitable welcome. Behind the city is a noted cave in a mountain, which the natives think is the abode of the very fiercest evil spirits. No doubt the real spirits are the malarial germs or the poisonous gas which later we found to be the chief danger of the Chieng Dāo cave. It was in this cave that M. Mouhot, a noted French scientist, contracted the fever from which he died. The natives believed that his death was caused by his rashness in trespassing upon the domain of the spirits who preside over the cave. We were astonished at some sorts of fish displayed in the market, such as I never saw anywhere else. Mr. McCarthy tells of assisting at the capture of one, a plā buk, seven feet long, with a body-girth of four feet and two inches, and weighing one hundred and thirty pounds.

We remained in Lūang Prabāng six days, leaving it on May 14th. I was very loath to go so soon. The people were eager for books as well as for medicine. It was the one place where Siamese books were well understood. We could have disposed of basketfuls of the Scriptures, as Dr. Peoples did twenty-four years later. It is one of the anomalies of the twentieth century that when we finally were ready to establish a Christian mission, after the country had passed from non-Christian to Christian rulers, we could not get permission.

From Lūang Prabāng we again took boat to Tā Dūa, some sixty miles below. There we bade good-bye to the wonderful river, and turned our faces homeward. Our elephants were good travellers, the swiftest we had so far found. They gave us no chance to stroll on in advance, and rest till they should come up, as we had done before. They brought us to Nān in six days, four of which were spent in travel over high mountain ridges. Our road passed near the great salt wells; but we had no time for sight-seeing.

Two experiences on this portion of the trip will not be forgotten. One was a fall from my tall elephant. A flock of large birds in covert near us suddenly flew up with loud shrill cries. I was reclining in the howdah at the time, and raised myself up to look out under the hood, and, while suspended there in unstable equilibrium, another and louder cry close at hand made the beast give a sudden start backwards, which landed me in a puddle of water. Fortunately no further damage was done. Another annoyance, more serious, was the land-leeches which we often encountered when we dismounted to walk. The whole ground and every shrub and twig seemed covered with the tiny creatures. Sensitive to the least noise, each one was holding on by his tail, and waving his head back and forth to lay hold of any passing animal. We soon found that they had a special fondness for the *genus homo.* Do what we might, every hundred yards or so we had to stop to rub them off, while the blood ran profusely from their bites. We had none of the herbs which the Mūsô bind on their legs to keep them off.

On Saturday evening we reached Nān, the first place where I found friends since leaving Chieng Rāi. Chao Borirak, whom I had met in Chiengmai, nephew of the Nān Prince, and a few others, were soon on hand to give us welcome and to offer any aid we needed. The Prince was a venerable old man, with four sons—fine men, all of them. The country was well governed, though it long continued conservative as regards the adoption of foreign ways and the welcoming of foreign traders. I fell in love with Nān at first sight, and marked it for a future mission station.

On our departure from Nān, Chao Borirak accompanied us as far as Prê, bringing his own elephants—one of them a colt, which he rode astride like a horse—the only one, in fact, that I ever saw so used. At Prê we found our government letter not very effective. Rupees, however, were effective enough to prevent any long delay. The ruling authority in Prê has always seemed weak.

There was an amusing circumstance connected with an eclipse of the moon while we were there. Since the conversion of Nān Inta, I had taken pains to announce each eclipse as it was to occur. I did so in

INTERIOR OF A TEMPLE, PRÊ

Prê the day before it was due. The eclipse took place early in the night, and I expected to hear the city resound with the noise of every gun and firecracker in the place. But everything was as quiet as a funeral. It seemed to be regarded as *our* eclipse. The silence may have been intended to test our assertion that Rāhū would renounce his hold without the noise, or possibly they were unwilling to proclaim thus publicly the superior wisdom of the foreigner in predicting it. At any rate, they utterly ignored it, and let the monster have his will unmolested.

My associate had gained all that could have been expected from the tour; but an aching tooth was giving him great trouble, and we hurried on. We reached home on June 22d, just sixty-eight days out. We found neither family in very good health. The doctor's toothache drove him to such desperation that he insisted on my trying—all unpractised as I was—to extract the offending eyetooth. It broke. There was then nothing to do but to make the trip to Bangkok for the nearest professional help. By the time he returned, it began to be evident that he could not hope to remain long in the field.

Between Bangkok, Pechaburī, and Chiengmai, I had been fifteen years in the field; and my wife had been in the country from girlhood without change. We had both endured it remarkably well, considering that we had had the strain of starting two new stations. Before the end of the year, however, my wife had reached the limit of her strength, and it became necessary to hurry her out of the country. So, on the 3d of January, 1873, she was carried in a chair to the boat, and we embarked for the United States.

XIV

THE FIRST FURLOUGH

THE tour of the previous season had been so hasty and unsatisfactory, that I was very anxious, if possible, to duplicate the homeward stretch of it as far as Nān, then descend the Pitsanulōk Fork to the Mênam, and so follow my family to Bangkok. But would it be safe to leave my wife to make the river trip without me, when she was in such weak condition, and burdened with the care of four children, the youngest of whom was but two years old? I embarked and travelled with them as far as the landing for Lampūn—where we must separate, if I were to cross over to Nān—still uncertain as to whắt I ought to do. It was then Friday. We decided to stop there over Sunday, and see how matters looked on Monday morning. The quiet and rest of the boat were improving her condition somewhat; and her own bravery made up whatever was lacking there. I had secured a strong letter from the Prince, calling for the best of steersmen through the rapids, and for protection where the boat should stop for the night. So, with some anxiety, but with strong faith that the plan in itself so desirable would prosper, we separated —one party going by boat down the Mê Ping, and the other going afoot across country to Lampūn. For the present we leave the wife and children, to hear their report when we meet again.

My plan was to rely on getting elephants from point to point. Elephants are always very hard to get; so it seemed doubtful whether my confidence were faith or presumption. But I was remarkably favoured. At Lampūn there was not an elephant nearer than the forests, save two of the governor's own. I had trusted to his friendship, and it did not fail me. I got off in fine style next morning on the governor's two elephants, with a letter to all the governors on the route directing them to see that I was supplied with whatever I needed on the journey.

I felt strong in having with me, in the person of Nān Inta, so wise a teacher and such a living witness of the power of the Gospel. On our first visits it has usually seemed wise to spend much of the time in visiting and making known the Gospel privately to those of reputation, as we know one wise missionary did in old times. It is necessary to give the rulers a clear idea of the non-political nature of our work. In order to do this, we must show positively what our message is—not merely that we are religious teachers, but that, as such, we have a message different from all others, not antagonistic or hostile to them, but supplementing rather that which they offer.

In visiting among the princely families in the old city of Lakawn we met one most interesting case. It was that of an aged bedridden Princess high in rank, who received the Gospel with all readiness of mind. By nature, habit, and grace she had been very religious. She had in her day built temples and rest-houses, had feasted Buddhist monks, and had fasted times without number, in order to lay up a store of merit for the great future. She hoped sometimes that she had laid up a sufficient store; but the five and the eight commands were against her. She had killed animals; and the command is explicit, and condemns without a saviour. That the Creator of all had made these creatures for our use and benefit was a new idea. That of itself would remove much of the burden on her conscience. And as one after another of the great truths of revelation was opened up to her, particularly the doctrine of the incarnation and atonement of our divine-human Redeemer, it seemed as if the burden was lifted. Nān Inta was himself a living testimony that the Christian teaching can and does give instantaneous relief when simply believed. It is difficult to tell which was more touching, the sympathetic earnestness of the speaker, or the comfort it imparted to the hearer. The Princess begged us to come again and often. And neither of us found any other place so attractive.

After a week spent in Lakawn, we departed on our way to Nān. The next Sunday we spent in the forest. I look back with delightful memories to the occasional Sabbaths thus spent in the deep forest after a busy week with no rest and no privacy—a Sabbath in solitude, away from every noise, and even every song except the music of the wind and the song of birds! We always had service with our men; and then, under the shade of some cool spreading tree, or beside a flowing brook, one could be alone and yet not alone. No one more needs such retirement than a missionary, whose work is always a giving-out, with fewer external aids for resupply than others have.

The next Sunday we spent in Wieng Sā, the first of the numerous little outlying towns of Nān. On Monday we reached Nān itself, the limit of our tour in that direction. The country was well governed, the princes intelligent, and the common people friendly. But the special attraction that Nān had for me largely centred around one man, the Prince's nephew, Chao Borirak—the one that rode astride the young elephant to see us safe to Prê on our earlier trip, with whom we used to talk religion about the camp-fires till the small hours of the morning. We left him then apparently on the border land of Christianity, with strong hope that he soon would be ready to profess publicly the faith which he was almost ready to confess to us. His rank and connection would make him of great assistance in opening a station in Nān, which, next to Chiengmai, was the most important province in the Lāo region. Again he offered us a warm welcome, giving up his time to visiting with us the rulers and the monasteries, in one of which his son had long been an abbot. It seemed as if Nān Inta's experience would be all that was needed to settle his faith. At his request I asked and received permission from the Prince for him again to accompany us—with his young elephant foal and her mother—five days' journey to Tā It, where I was to take boat. Our walks by day and our talks by night are never to be forgotten. But the convenient season to make a public profession never came. He lived in hope of seeing a station in Nān, but died not long before the station was established.

At Tā It no boat was to be had either for sale or for hire. But my face was turned toward home, and I would have gone on a raft. I had to do the next thing —to take a small dug-out which the Prince got for me, and go on to Utaradit, the next town below. There I was able to purchase a boat, which I afterwards sold in Bangkok for what it cost me. Nān Inta was the steersman, and my four men rowed. Our longest stop was at Pitsanulōk, where the Siamese mission now has a station. On reaching Bangkok I was delighted to find that my family had made their long trip down the other river in safety, though not without great anxiety, and some threatened danger. Our oldest daughter had been quite ill on the way. Once they came perilously near falling a prey to a band of robbers. It was only by a clever ruse of the captain that they escaped. As soon as he caught sight of the suspicious-looking group of men on a sand-bar ahead, he had the gong loudly sounded. That and the waving American flag evidently made them think that this was the leading boat of some prince's flotilla. They incontinently fled into the forest. At the next stopping-place our boatmen learned that it was, indeed, a marauding band that had committed many depredations on passing boats. What a merciful preservation!

We spent a few weeks in Bangkok, resting and visiting in the home of my father-in-law, Dr. Bradley, of sainted memory. It proved to be the last time that we ever saw him. He lived only a few months after that.

In fifteen years the world had moved. Going round "the Cape," even in a good clipper ship like the *David Brown,* had become too slow. We took, instead, the steamship *Patroclus* from Singapore to London, via the Suez Canal. The Rev. Mr. Keyesberry, a missionary friend of Dr. Bradley's, had been waiting to find an escort to England for two young sons and a daughter. We gladly undertook that service, and so had a flock of seven young folks to look after!

We were barely under way when our own children broke out with the measles. The disease, fortunately, proved to be of a mild type, and our new charges were not hard to manage. So, on the whole, we got along very well. In London we had unexpected trouble because the friend who was to meet Alice Keyesberry at the dock failed to appear, and, strangely enough, we had received no memorandum of her destination. It cost us two days' search to discover her friends at the Walthamstow Mission School.

The boys I had promised to convoy as far as Edinburgh. So, leaving my family in London, I had the great pleasure of a visit to the beautiful Scotch capital. The day spent there was to me a memorable one. It was, however, a matter of great regret that, being so near the Highlands, I could not also visit the original home of my ancestors.

We arrived in New York on July 11th, 1873, after an absence of fifteen years. Under any circumstances fifteen years would work great changes. But that particular fifteen had included the Civil War. The changes in the South were heart-rending.

Though North Carolina was drawn late into the Confederacy, it is said that she furnished a larger number per capita of soldiers and had a larger number of casualties than any other state in the South. The havoc among my old schoolmates and pupils, and among my flock, was distressing. In many places, too, the sectional feeling was still bitter. The wisest of the people, however, were becoming fully reconciled to the results of the war. The largest slaveholder in my own section assured me that the freeing of his slaves had been a boon to him, and that he was clearing more from his old farm under free labour than he had done before with slaves.

Unfortunately in the churches the feeling was more bitter. My old associate, Dr. Mattoon, had accepted the presidency of Biddle Institute at Charlotte—now Biddle University (colored). For a time he was very coldly received except by such broad-minded men as his old Princeton classmate, and my friend, Dr. Charles Phillips. By virtue, however, of his noble Christian character and his conservative bearing, Dr. Mattoon overcame these prejudices, and lived to be welcomed in the largest churches in the state. I spent most of my furlough in North Carolina; and personally I received a welcome almost as warm as if I were a missionary of the Southern Board. Returned missionaries were not numerous then. It was not an uncommon thing for me to lecture in churches which had never before seen the face of a foreign missionary.

Soon after our arrival in the United States news came of the resignation of Dr. Vrooman; and my first duty was to find a successor. For myself, and even for my family, I could endure to return without one. But I could not face the distressing appeals from the sick whose ailments I was powerless to relieve. In my visits among friends in North Carolina I met a young medical graduate, Dr. M. A. Cheek, who received from warm friends of the mission flattering recommendations for the place. He himself was pleased with the opening, and would willingly accept it, if he could first take a graduate course in surgery. This was easily arranged, and he was ready to return with us the following summer.

The hardest thing to face was the parting with our children. But the bitterness of this pang was softened by the kindness of friends which opened the best of Christian homes and schools to receive them. We can never sufficiently express our gratitude for the kindness shown us in this matter by the late Mrs. E.

N. Grant and Miss Mitchell of the Statesville Female College, and to Mrs. McNeill, the widow of my old pastor.

These two great questions settled, we left North Carolina in March, 1874—my wife with the two younger children, to visit friends and relatives in the North; and I, as I hoped, to visit the churches and the seminaries in search of recruits. But a cold contracted on the trip north ran into a dangerous attack of pleuro-pneumonia, followed by a slow recovery. Thus I missed my visits to the seminaries and the meeting of the General Assembly in St. Louis.

The return to the field was by way of San Francisco, and we reached Bangkok on August 27th, 1874. On November 14th a son was given us to take the place of the children left behind. In December began our river journey to Chiengmai. The river was low, and we were a month and a day from Bangkok to Rahêng. There we found four missionaries of the Nova Scotia Baptist Board seeking to establish a station among the Karens of Siam. But they found their villages too small and too widely scattered to justify the establishment of a station. So they were returning to Burma. On Saturday night we all dined together, and had a sociable hour. On Sunday evening we drew up our boats side by side, and had a prayer-meeting that we shall long remember. There was something delightful in thus meeting and enjoying Christian fellowship on a sand-bar, and then passing on to our respective fields of work. Some of these men afterwards went to India, and started the Telegu mission, which has had phenomenal success.

There were still the rapids and four more weeks of travel before we could reach our Lāo home. But the home-coming at last was delightful. Our faithful old coolie, Lung In, with his wife, met us in a small boat three days' journey below Chiengmai, with fruit and fowls lest we should be in want. Then the tall figure of Nān Inta, with his face like a benediction!

It was February 7th, 1875, when at last we drew up alongside our own landing-place, and felt the warm handshake of old friends. Among the Lāo at last!—and no place that we had seen would we exchange for our Lāo home. For the first time since our arrival in 1867 we had a permanent house to enter!

XV

MÛANG KÊN AND CHIENG DĀO

DR. CHEEK'S arrival was a matter of great rejoicing. He was very young—only twenty-one, in fact, on the day he sailed from San Francisco. The trying drudgery that he and others of our early medical missionaries had to endure, is now in great measure obviated through the help of native assistants. The remainder of the year 1875 I devoted very largely to assisting in the medical work, interpreting, helping in operations, and caring for the souls of the numerous patients, without feeling the weight of responsibility for their physical condition, as I had done before. Dr. Cheek came out a single man; but, like others before him, he lost his heart on the way. Toward the end of that year he went down to Bangkok, and was married to Miss Sarah A. Bradley. He returned to Chiengmai just as Mr. Wilson was ready to start for the United States on his second furlough. The April communion was postponed a week that the newly-arrived and the departing missionaries might commune together before separating. It was Mrs. Wilson's last communion with us.

In May, 1876, Nān Inta was ordained our first ruling elder. The story has often been told that before his ordination the Confession of Faith was given him to read carefully, since he would be asked whether he subscribed to its doctrines. When he had finished the reading, he remarked that he saw nothing peculiar in its teachings. It was very much like what he had read in Paul's Epistles! In January Pā Kamun, the widow of Noi Sunya, was baptized. It was thus appropriately given to her to be the first woman received into the communion of the church. Two of her daughters, and Pā Peng, the wife of Nān Inta, soon followed. Lung In was elected the first deacon, but was too modest to be ordained to that office. Meanwhile he was becoming a most useful assistant in the hospital. Strange as it may seem, the office of hospital nurse is one of the most difficult to get a Lāo to fill. Lung In, however, was not above the most menial service for the sick. His real successor was not found until the present incumbent, Dr. Kêo, was trained. Dr. McKean's testimony is that it would be scarcely more difficult to procure a good surgeon than to fill Kêo's place as nurse and assistant among the hospital patients.

During the summer of 1876, in company with Nān Inta, I made a tour among the four nearest provinces to the north and west. The governor of Mûang Kên had long given promise of becoming a Christian, and now invited me to visit his people. On his frequent visits to Chiengmai on business, he always called on me, and no subject was so interesting to him as the subject of religion. Before the proclamation of toleration, while the common people were still afraid of making a public profession of Christianity, our most effective work was probably that with the higher class of officials, who stood in somewhat less fear of the known antagonism of the Chao Uparāt. They were, besides, a more interesting class than the common people, for they were better educated, were more accustomed in their daily duties to weigh arguments and decide on questions of evidence, and many of them had been trained in the religious order.

This governor of Mūang Kēn had learned enough of the tenets of Christianity to become unsettled and dissatisfied with the prospects of salvation offered by a purely ethical religion. He saw the weakness of the foundation on which he had been taught to rely, and the difference between the authors of the two religions. So he stood on the border land between the two, at the very gate, wishing to enter in, but with many obstacles in his way, and strong opposing influences to overcome.

My first objective, then, on this tour was Mūang Kēn. The governor had asked me to come and smooth the way for him by teaching his under-officials and his townsmen. Nān Inta was the living, concrete argument, and he put his whole heart into it. We had a few days of deeply interesting work. Few, however, saw the matter as the governor did. Most of them "would consider it." Some would go further and say that they worshipped Jesus under the name of their promised Buddha Metraya, yet to come.

From Mūang Kēn we went to Chieng Dāo, where we visited the great cave with its famous Buddhist shrine. Ever since Nān Inta became a Christian, he had been anxious to test the truth of some of the legends connected with the place—a thing he dared not do before. The cave is the abode of the great Lawa spirit, for fear of offending whom Prince Kāwilōrot was afraid to allow us to build to the north of the city bridge in Chiengmai. Chieng Dāo mountain, which rises above the cave, is seven thousand one hundred and sixty feet high—one of the highest peaks in all Siam, and visible from Chiengmai, some thirty-seven miles away. One of the sources of the Mê Ping River, twenty feet wide and knee-deep, flows bodily out from the cave. Since no animal is allowed to be killed in so sacred a place, the stream abounds in a great variety of beautiful fish waiting for the food which no visitor fails to give them. The scramble for it is as interesting to watch as the performance of the sea-lions at San Francisco.

The legend is that no one can cross the stream inside the cave and return alive; and that beyond the stream, under the crest of the mountain, there is an image of pure gold seven cubits high. One enters the cave at a little distance from the stream, and finds first a grand chamber which is a veritable temple, with arched dome, natural pulpit, and innumerable images of Buddha, large and small. This place is regarded as a most sacred shrine. Buddhist monks are always there performing their devotions. The chamber is so dark that they have to use tapers to see to read. The dim light and the long-drawn tones of the worshippers produce a very weird impression.

From the temple-chamber narrow passages lead off in different directions, till there is danger of losing one's way in the labyrinth. I followed Năn Inta and his sons to the stream, which is reached at some distance farther on. Being neither tall nor a swimmer, I stopped and sauntered about in the various rooms, waiting for my companions to verify or to disprove the legend. Needless to say, both parts of it were proved myths. My companions did return alive, and no golden image was found. The cave is too damp to make it safe for one to remain long in those distant passages. Farther on the tapers burned but very dimly; and one would not choose to be left there in pitch darkness. We could understand very well how the legend arose of Yaks that devour those that intrude into their dark caverns. There is no doubt of the presence of a deadly gas much more to be feared than the spirit of the great Lawa king, which is believed to have taken up his abode there. We all experienced more or less of the symptoms premonitory of malarial attack, and before we got back to the town Nān Inta was shaking with a genuine chill. A heroic dose, however, of Warburg's tincture with quinine soon set him to rights. In this case, then, as in many others, there is a foundation of truth at the bottom of the legend.

That night we had a great audience. It was generally known that we intended to explore the cave, and many, no doubt, came to see how we had fared. It was well that Nān Inta had so far recovered from his morning's chill as to be ready to join in bearing testimony not only to the falsity of the legend, but also to the truth of the Gospel. It was a bright moonlight night, and the people listened till very late, while we sang hymns, preached the Gospel, and pointed them to the better way. The result was seen years after in the founding of a church there.

All these provinces that we were now visiting, and others more distant still, were originally settled by refugees driven from the more southern districts by the persecution for witchcraft. Now they are important provinces. Since these people had been ruthlessly driven forth because of the spirits, I thought they would willingly accept any way of escape from their control. But they seemed, if anything, more superstitious and harder to reach than others. Having suffered once, as they supposed, from the malicious power of the spirits, they seemed even more than others to dread to incur their anger again by deserting them. But there were many hopeful exceptions.

Mûang Pāo was the next city visited. From the incidents of our stay there I select the cases of two persons who excited our deepest sympathy. One was an aged Buddhist monk, a Ngïo, who, with a younger companion, visited our tent daily. The monk was a venerable man, with striking features, serene countenance, earnest and intelligent. His long life had been spent in worship, meditation, and study. All this he soon told us with some quite natural pride. While not bold, he was not reticent, freely stating his own doctrines, hopes, and fears, and asking ours. To the question what were his hopes for a future life, he frankly said, "I don't know. How can I? I have tried to keep the commandments, have performed my devotions, have counted my beads. But whether I shall go up or down [indicating the directions with his finger] I do not know. I have done what my books tell me, but I have no light *here* [pointing to his heart]. Can the teacher's religion give me any light?"

The earnestness and the despondency of the man drew me to him. I asked, what of his failures and transgressions? "That," he said, "is the dark point. My books say that all my good deeds shall be rewarded, but the failures and transgressions must be punished before I can reach Nirvāna, the final emancipation of the soul by the extinction of all desire." "How long will that be?" we ask. He answered by giving a number that would baffle even astronomers, who are accustomed to deal in almost fabulous numbers.

"But is not that virtually endless?"

"Yes; but what shall we do? That is what our books say."

"But is there no room for pardon?"

"No. Buddha only points out the way that he followed himself. He reached the goal by the same almost endless journey. How shall we hope to do so by any shorter or different route?"

"But supposing there is a way—that there is a great sovereign of the universe, before all Buddhas and higher than all Buddhas, who has the right and the authority to grant full pardon through his own infinite merit, and his vicarious assumption of all our obligations and payment of all our debts. Would not that be a joyful message?"

"Yes; if true, it would be."

And so we argued till light seemed to gleam for once into his mind. But the image of the dear old man pointing up and then down with the sad confession, "I know not whither I shall go," is a vision that has saddened me many a time since.

The other case of special interest I state as it occurred, with no attempt at explanation of the dream involved in the story.—On the morning after our arrival, Nān Inta and I started out to visit monasteries or houses, wherever we might find listeners. I was dressed in white clothes, and Nān Inta had on a white jacket. We had made a number of calls, and were about to pass by a house in which we saw only an elderly woman and some children, presumably her grandchildren. We were surprised to see her come down from her house and run out after us, and prostrating herself with the customary salutation given to priests and princes, she begged us to stop and come in. We accepted her invitation, though surprised at her evident demonstrations of joy. Sitting down on the mat, we began to explain that we were teachers of religion, pointing out the sure way of happiness both in this life and in the life to come. Our message was one from the great God and Creator to all races and nations, inviting them to return from all other refuges, and He would give them an inheritance as His children in the life to come. She listened with marked interest as we explained to her our religion, and urged her to accept it. We were surprised at the explanation she gave of her intense interest.

Not long before our arrival she had a dream that two men dressed in white came to her to teach her. What they were to teach her she did not know; but when she saw us walking up the street she said, "There is the fulfilment of my dream!" She had watched us as we entered other houses, fearful lest we should omit hers. Now she was so glad we had come. It was at least a strange coincidence, for she affirmed that the dream was before she had ever heard of us. Whatever may have been the cause, it was a delight to instruct one who seemed to receive all that we said as a direct message to her. This at once attracted Nān Inta to her, and she listened to him with frequent exclamations of delight, while he, in his earnest manner, explained the Gospel message of pardon and life eternal through Him who liveth and was dead, and behold He is alive for evermore. She said her one great desire had been to escape from the punishment of her sins; but she never before had known that there was any other way but to suffer for them herself. She, too, was a Ngīo. We visited her frequently during the week of our stay in Mûang Pāo, and to the last she interpreted our coming as the fulfilment of her dream. This was the last that we knew either of her or of the aged monk. Before we visited the place again she was dead, and he had moved away.

In those days when the people were afraid to make a public profession of Christianity, it would have been a great gain to the mission if we could have had schools, and used them as a means of evangelizing the youth. A first attempt, indeed, had been made by Mr. Wilson with a few Burmese boys. A young Burmese who had been trained in Maulmein, and who spoke English, was employed to teach them under Mr. Wilson's oversight, in the hope that Lāo boys would presently join them. This hope was not realized, and the experiment was presently abandoned.

The first call for a Christian school was for the education of girls. In the first Christian families girls predominated. Mrs. McGilvary collected six or eight Christian girls, and devoted as much time to them as her strength and her family duties would permit. They were really private pupils, living on our premises and in our family. More wished to come than she could do justice to. Hence about this time an appeal was made for two single ladies to devote their whole time to the school. But it was not till four years later that Miss Edna E. Cole and Miss Mary Campbell of the Oxford Female Seminary, Ohio, reached Chiengmai. Very soon they had twenty pupils. From this small beginning has grown our large Girls' School. Two of Mrs. McGilvary's pupils were soon made assistants. These and others of the first group became fine women, who have left their mark on the church and the country.

Notwithstanding our disappointment in the delay

of the school for boys, it proved a wise arrangement that the Girls' School was started first. A mission church is sure to be greatly handicapped whose young men must either remain single—which they will not do —or be compelled to take ignorant non-Christian wives. Such are a dead-weight to the husband, and the children almost surely follow the mother. After marriage, the almost universal custom of the country has been that the husband lives with the wife's family. He becomes identified with it, and for the time a subordinate member of it, almost to the extent of becoming weaned from his own family. Where all the atmosphere of the family is strongly Buddhist, with daily offerings to the spirits and gala days at the temple, the current would be too strong for a father, with his secondary place in the family, to withstand. For a while it was feared that Christian girls would have difficulty in finding husbands. But, on the contrary, our educated girls become not only more intelligent, but more attractive in manners, dress, and character; and, therefore, have been much sought after. The homes become Christian homes, and the children are reared in a Christian atmosphere. The result is that, instead of the wife's dragging the husband down, she generally raises the husband up; and, as a general rule, the children early become Christians.

In August, 1876, our beloved Princess became very seriously ill. Dr. Cheek had been called upon to treat domestics in the family, but not the Prince or Princess. Hearing that she was in a critical condition under native doctors, and fearing the worst, I took the liberty of suggesting that they consult Dr. Cheek. They seemed pleased with the suggestion, and asked me to accompany him—which I did for one or two visits. His treatment was very successful, and soon she was convalescent.

About this same time we had an adventure with white ants which came near costing us our much-valued cabinet organ. It will serve to illustrate an experience formerly common enough, and still not unknown. One Wednesday evening before prayer-meeting Mrs. McGilvary sat down at the instrument to look over the tunes, when she found it full of white ants. Our house was built on higher ground, into which the creatures are driven when the lower grounds are filled with water from the annual floods. They do not attack the teak walls and floors of our houses, but, climbing up the posts, at last they stumbled upon the soft wood and leather inside the organ, and were just beginning their feast when our meeting broke in upon them. Had we not discovered them then, the instrument would have been completely wrecked before morning.

Once the white ants destroyed a trunkful of our children's clothes, once a box of "knock-down" chairs, and once they attacked my library—evidently not at all deterred by the learned discussions and deep thought of Dr. Joseph A. Alexander's *Commentary on Isaiah.* They had got through the margin, and would soon have digested the rest, had not an unexpected occasion for opening the library saved it.

XVI

SEEKERS AFTER GOD

ON New Year's Day, 1877, I went into the city to make some calls. The first was at the new palace. In the large reception hall I found the Princess, virtually alone. She was embroidering some fancy pillow-ends for the priests—a work in which she was an expert. Her maidens, some distance off, were sewing priests' robes. The Prince was in his little workshop not far off, turning ivory rounds for the railing of an elephant howdah, a favourite amusement with him.

The subject of religion was one that continually came up in all my interviews with the Princess; but hitherto she had apparently argued more for victory than from a desire to reach the truth. She was as keen as a lawyer to seize a point, and her quick wit made her a very enjoyable antagonist. Not only she and her domestics, but the whole country as well, had been preparing for a great occasion of merit-making in connection with the approaching dedication of a shrine. Whether the peculiar interest of this conversation was due to the fact that these matters had been running in her mind, or to some particular mood in which I found her, I never knew. Most likely it was both. A chance allusion to the great event which was in every one's mouth, at once brought up the question. Stopping her work and resting her arms on the embroidery frame, she asked, "Why is it that foreigners do not worship the Buddha or his images, and do not believe that merit is made thereby?"

She seemed to approach the question as a personal one for herself. If we were right and she were wrong, she would like to know it. We agreed on that point, and I encouraged her in her estimate of its paramount importance to every rational man or woman. If Buddhism does, indeed, lead to happiness in a future life, she was wise in diligently following its precepts; but if wrong, it would be a fatal mistake. Why do we not worship Buddha? Because he was only a man. We reverence his character, as we do that of other upright men who have tried to do good and to lead their fellow-men to better things. Gautama Buddha seems to have sought with all his soul for light—was willing to forsake a kingdom and to renounce all sensual and even intellectual pleasures in this life for the hope of escaping sin and its consequences in the next.

Why do we worship Jehovah-Jesus? Because He is our sovereign Lord. The Buddha groaned under his own load of guilt, and was oppressed by the sad and universal consequences of sin among men. The Christ challenged His enemies to convince Him of sin, and His enemies to this day have confessed that they find no sin in Him. Buddhists believe that Buddha reached Nirvāna after having himself passed through every form of being in the universe—having been in turn every animal in the seas, on the earth, and in the air. He did this by an inexorable law that he and every other being is subject to, and cannot evade. Our Jehovah-Jesus, as our Scriptures teach, is the only self-existent being in the universe, and Himself the cause of all other beings. An infinite Spirit and invisible, He manifested Himself to the world by descending from heaven, becoming man, taking on our nature in unison with His own holy nature, but with no taint of sin. He did this out of infinite love and pity for our race after it had sinned. He saw there was no other able to save, and He became our Saviour.

And take the teachings of the two systems—which is the more credible? The sacred books of the Princess teach that there is no Creator. Everything, as the Siamese say, "pen ēng"—comes to be of itself. All this complicated universe became what it is by a fortuitous concurrence of atoms, which atoms themselves had no creator. We come as honest seekers for truth. We look around, above, beneath. Everything seems to imply the contrivance of mind. The sun rises and sets with greater regularity than our clocks strike the hour of noon. The seasons follow each other with wonderful uniformity. Animals are born and die, plants and trees grow and decay, each after its kind, and in wonderful adjustment to the conditions about them. The eye is made for seeing, the ear for hearing, and the air for breathing. Light is necessary for work by day, and darkness for sleep by night. This city has its walls and gates; this palace has its beams, its roof, its doors and windows, and its different apartments, because it was so planned. The Princess gives her orders, and her servants in distant villages come at her summons. The Prince's command is obeyed throughout all his dominions. Subjects obey because they are under constituted authority. Even so we obey Jehovah and not Buddha, because we believe that He is the Creator and the sovereign Lord of the universe.

In His word—His letter to our race—He claims

to be Creator and Lord. We read His word, and then we look around for evidence as to whether this is really so. We find that evidence in earth and sea and sky. A letter comes from the King of Siam. How do we know that it is really his? It has his seal. Not otherwise "the heavens declare the glory of God, and the firmament showeth His handiwork." By faith, then, we believe that the worlds were made, as His word tells us. We read the account of that creation. What wonderful beings we are!—made in His image, endowed in our degrees with His own attributes, and with authority over the world in which He has placed us. He has given us dominion over all the beasts of the earth, the fowls of the air, and the fish of the sea. Every time that a Buddhist kills a fish or a fowl, he sins, because he breaks a command of his religion. Why not so for a Christian? Because these creatures were made for man's use, and were given to him. We partake with gratitude of the gifts our Father has provided for us. This one great truth, when received by Christians, relieves the conscience of one of the greatest burdens that the followers of Buddha must bear.

But if God made man in His image, why all this suffering that we see and feel? The best explanation ever given is that given in the Bible. Man was created holy, and was put on trial. He transgressed. A subject who disobeys the law of his sovereign incurs his displeasure. He suffers for it. We are suffering from this disobedience of our first parents by a law that we daily see exemplified. A man by extravagance or vice squanders his estate. His children are born penniless. The Prince of Wieng Chan rebelled against the King of Siam. His country was conquered and laid waste, and thousands of its inhabitants were made captive and deported. Thousands of the descendants of these captives are now serfs. Why are they so? Because of the errors or misfortunes of their ancestors. The Prince appoints a governor over a province, with the promise that if he is faithful, his children shall succeed him. Because of misdemeanor he is deposed. His descendants are born subjects and not rulers. We belong to a fallen race.

Somana Gautama belonged to the same race. He groaned under its pains and penalties. He saw a race sunk in misery. He saw its religion shamefully corrupt. He inaugurated one of purer morality. But he does not profess to be divine or a saviour. His religion does not offer a sufficient remedy. By asceticism and self-mortification it would extinguish all noble desire as well as the vicious instincts with which we are born. And then, after interminable cycles of transmigrations, we may hope to reach a state of unconscious sleep. Happiness and misery are inseparable things. We escape the one only by escaping the other. That is the dark prospect which makes Buddhism so pessimistic. To this the Princess assented, "That is so."

Now compare this with the religion of Jesus. The sovereign Father who loves His wandering, sinful children, in His infinite wisdom devised a plan that satisfies their needs and desires, "God so loved the world that He gave His only begotten Son, that whosoever believeth in Him should not perish, but have everlasting life." Our Maker became our Redeemer by emptying Himself of His glory and becoming man. He is Himself the greatest possible illustration of the love of God to the race. He came to reveal the Father. His holy life we have in His word. He set us the only perfect example, full of pity toward the miserable and the sinful.

Then, by a painful and shameful death, He became Himself a sacrifice for the sins of the world. He obeyed the law which we had broken, and which condemns us; and suffered in our stead the penalty due to us. He conquered death. He took away the sting of death by taking away sin. He arose from the dead, showing Himself for many days. He ascended to heaven before the eyes of His disciples. He has sent His servants and His word to offer a full and free pardon to all who will accept. He is now, and ever will be, our intercessor in heaven. He sends His Spirit to purify and fit us for an endless state of conscious existence which begins at death, and not cycles after. Millions of the best men and women the world has ever seen have given their testimony to the reality of this salvation by a triumphant death, with the assurance that all sin and all suffering were past. Jesus removed the curse, and brought to light the immortality which we had forfeited by sin. The missionary and his associates have left both parents and children that they might offer this to the Princess and to her people.

To all of this the Princess was mainly a most interested listener. She had asked to be taught. She put no captious questions. I have omitted an occasional assent that she gave, and an occasional difficulty or doubt—not all of which could be fully answered; as, for example, why an all-powerful God allowed the entrance of sin, and now allows wicked spirits to tempt us; or that other sad question, why the Gospel had not been sent to them, so that they might have known this from childhood—a question the burden of which should press on my readers as well as on the missionary.

At last, after a long pause, the Princess made a wonderful confession, the very words of which I can never forget:

"Tā chak wā dūi kwām ching, kā han wā paw krū ko tūk lêo." To speak the truth, I see that the father-teacher is right. "Kā chûa wā kong chak mī Pra Chao ton dai sāng lōk." I believe there surely must be some divine Lord who made the world. "Lê bat nī ko chûa tī paw krū atibāi dūi kān pon tōt dōi Pra Yēsū." And now I believe what the father-teacher has explained about escape from punishment through the Lord Jesus. And then, sadly—almost despairingly—she added, "Tê chak yīa cha dai?" But what shall I do?—I fear it will not be well to forsake "hīt paw hoi mê"—the customs of my father, the foot-prints of my mother.

We were sitting in the new brick palace—the first ever built in the country. In the hall was a large pier-glass with numerous other foreign articles, most of them bought in Bangkok, and brought up for offerings at the coming dedication of the shrine. I asked, "Princess, did your father or grandfather have a brick palace like this?" Somewhat surprised at the question, she replied, "No." "And I see the Princess riding down to the landing every day in a foreign carriage. Did your ancestors do that?" Before I could make the application, she blushed, perceiving that she was caught. I went on: "You do daily forsake old customs, and adopt new ones which your ancestors never knew. The whole method of government is changing. This foreign cloth, which your maidens are sewing for priests' robes, was all unknown to your forefathers. These things all come from lands where the people worship neither the Buddha nor the spirits. These are only some of the fruits that grow on the tree. Better still, plant the tree; for all good fruit grows on it." Just then our long conversation was interrupted by the entrance of the Prince, who had worked till he was tired. He asked what she and the teacher were talking about so long. She replied that we were discussing "bun lê bāp"—merit and sin.

The question often came up after this. She was in a position where it was, humanly speaking, almost impossible for her outwardly to forsake the customs of the country. But I have reason to know that on that morning she received truths which she never forgot. We have seen before that neither she nor her husband approved of her father's act in murdering the Christians. She continued a warm friend to the last, and so did the Prince.

On my way home that same forenoon I had another interesting talk with our dear old friend, the abbot of the Ūmōng monastery, who had been so true to us during our troubles. On the gate-posts, as I entered, were offerings of fruit, rice, betel, etc., to propitiate the spirits. This is in flat violation of one of the fundamental precepts of Buddhism, which declares that any one who makes offerings to spirits is outside of the pale, or, as we should say, is virtually excommunicate. Of course, my abbot friend exculpated himself from all complicity in the offerings. He himself neither worshipped nor feared the spirits. But his disciples and parishioners did, and he could not withstand them. He, too, never gave up the form of Buddhism, but he claimed that he worshipped Jesus daily as the great Creator and Benefactor of our race. His merit he believed to be infinitely greater than that of Buddha, whom he knew to be a man. The abbot was a man of broad mind, and a true and faithful friend. It is well that it is not for us to say how much of error is consistent with true discipleship, even in Christian lands. I know that his deep-rooted friendship for us was because we were teachers of a religion that offered hopes which Buddhism does not give. I have in mind many others, also, who believed our doctrine, though they were never enrolled in our church; and not a few that would urge others of their family and friends to take, as Christians, the open stand which, from various causes, they themselves were prevented from taking. But the Lord knoweth them that are His.

The great event of the year 1877 was the dedication of a Buddhist shrine recently rebuilt on Doi Sutēp, the noble mountain which is the pride and glory of Chiengmai. From the level of the plain, and at a distance of but four miles westward from the city, the mountain rises in a single sweep four thousand five hundred feet, forest-crowned to its very summit, seamed with rushing brooks, and embroidered with gleaming waterfalls. In the rainy season the play of cloud and vapor, of sunshine and storm about its mighty mass, forms an ever-changing picture of surpassing beauty and grandeur. The Siamese and the Lāo are very fond of an imposing setting and a commanding view for their temples and shrines—on bold promontories by sea or river, on high knolls and summits. The one on Doi Sutēp crowns a projecting shoulder or bastion of the mountain, some half-way up, and visible from all parts of the Chiengmai plain. Each reigning Prince has been desirous of doing something to beautify and enrich this shrine. To rebuild it was, therefore, an attractive idea to Prince Intanon at the beginning of his rule.

To do honour to the occasion, and to make merit thereby, all the northern states, as far east as Lūang

AN ABBOT PREACHING

Prabāng, sent their highest officials with costly offerings; and the government of Siam sent a special representative. For weeks and months previously the whole country had been placed under requisition to make preparations. Offerings were levied from every town, village, and monastery, and, I believe, from every household. Each guest of honour had a temporary house built for him at the foot of the mountain, with smaller shelters for persons of less rank. Nearly all the princes and nobles of Chiengmai joined the encampment at the base of the mountain, and thither, also, was the city market removed, so that our housekeepers had to send four miles to market!

I had intended to pitch a tent near the encampment, so as to be near the people for missionary work. But a rheumatic attack during the opening days of the festival prevented. Still, we had as many visitors at home as we could attend to, and under conditions more favourable for missionary work.

Such occasions are very attractive to the Lāo people. For the time being the prohibition against gambling is removed, and they make the most of it. It may seem a queer way of making merit, but the theory is that their merit earns them the right to a good time for once. Thousands of rupees change hands on such occasions. The mornings are given to making offerings, the afternoons to boxing and games, and the nights to theatricals and gambling. I was glad that I was prevented from pitching my tent in the midst of the noise and revelry. All those interested in religion were the more free to call and converse with us apart from the princes and the rabble. Officers and monks from a distance were always especially welcomed, and few of them in those days returned to their homes without calling on the foreign teacher.

I did not get off on a long tour that season, being unable to secure an elephant. It was better so, however, for early in May Dr. Cheek went to Bangkok to consult a physician, and went on thence as far as Hongkong. It was April 30th of the next year before he got back to Chiengmai. And the season proved to be one of the most unhealthy in the history of the mission. Worst of all, we had only six bottles of quinine to begin the season with. There was a rush for the quinine, and it seemed cruel to withhold it so long as any was left. The fever was of a violent type, and often fatal. Native doctors were helpless before the scourge. On looking about me for a substitute for quinine, I found that arsenic was the next best remedy, and that Fowler's Solution was the best form for administering it. But we had not a drop of the solution. We had, however, a bottle of arsenious acid, and a United States Dispensatory, so that I had to become pharmacist as well as doctor. I had all the ingredients save one, an unessential colouring matter. So I made it up by the quart. But it was not a medicine to be trusted in native hands. They were accustomed to take their own medicine by the potful, and had the theory that if a little is good, a great deal would be better.

XVII

THE RESIDENT COMMISSIONER

IN this same year, 1877, there occurred an event of utmost importance to the mission and to the whole country. We have seen that, up to the death of Prince Kāwilōrot, those Lāo provinces which are now a part of Siam had been virtually free states. The Siamese yoke had been very easy. They had never been conquered in war. Their original association with Siam had been a voluntary one, in order to escape the oppressive rule of Burma. Their location and their weakness made it a necessity that they should look to one of these rival kingdoms for protection against the other. At the same time, they added both dignity and strength to the one on which they leaned —they served it as a buffer against the other. Nature had connected the Lāo country more intimately with Siam. All its communication with the sea was through the Mĕnam Chao Prayā and its tributaries, while a range of lofty mountains separated it from Burma. In race and language too, they were Siamese, and not Burmese.

The relation had been mutually beneficial. Both parties recognized the advantages of the arrangement, and were satisfied. The balance of real advantage had been to the weaker states. Their chiefs, indeed, were required to make triennial visits to the Siamese capital, to present there a nominal tribute, and to renew their oath of allegiance. But with this exception they were virtually free. In his own country the Prince had absolute rule. The Siamese had never interfered with, or assumed control of, the internal affairs of the North Lāo states. It will be remembered that the sanction of the Siamese government to the establishment of the mission was given only after the Lāo Prince had given his.

It was probably an inevitable result that the stronger power should in time absorb the weaker. And the course of events had been tending that way. The forests of teak on the upper branches of the Mênam were too valuable to be concealed or to remain profitless. The world needed the timber, and was willing to pay for it. The country needed its value in money. The Burmese of Maulmein, who were British subjects, had skill in working out the timber, which the Lāo had not. With money and valuable presents they tempted the Lāo rulers, who formerly had absolute authority over the forests, to grant them concessions to cut the timber and market it in Bangkok. Both parties were avaricious, and both were probably crooked. Larger bribes sometimes induced a Lāo ruler to issue a second concession to work a forest already assigned to an earlier applicant. The result was a constant succession of lawsuits brought by British subjects against the Lāo. Since the Lāo states were dependencies of Siam, the Siamese government was often called upon to enforce judgment against them; while the Lāo felt that the Siamese suzerainty ought to shield them from such attack. Siam was now come to be in fact the buffer between the Lāo and the outside world. Instead of the pleasant relations which had hitherto existed between the two peoples, there was now constant friction.

Up to the time when Prince Kāwilōrot gave his public and official promise before the United States Consul and the representative of the Siamese government, in the little sālā at the landing-stage of Wat Chêng in Bangkok, no foreign power other than the English had had any claim on the Lāo or any contact with them. It was only the impolitic act of killing the Christians which brought the Lāo Prince into conflict with the representative of the United States government. The fact that it was the missionaries who were immediately concerned had nothing to do with the question. Had the agreement been made with American citizens in any other capacity or business, the obligation would have been the same. The Siamese government recognized the obligation, and, as we have seen, guaranteed the continuance of the mission. And that guarantee was an additional reason for having an official representative of Siam resident in Chiengmai.

Had the new Prince been as strong as he was mild and good, and had the Chao Uparāt been like him, it is possible that the old feudal relation might have continued another generation or two. No doubt the Siamese government thoroughly trusted the loyalty of the new Prince; but it did not regard him as a man sufficiently strong to hold the reins of power at that juncture. Moreover, all the business of ruling was largely given over to the Uparāt; and he in a number of ways had shown his opposition to our work and his jealousy of the English and of foreigners generally. When news reached us first that a High Commissioner was appointed, and then that he was on the way, there was great anxiety to know what stand he would take with reference to Christianity.

Prayā Tēp Worachun proved to be an admirable

selection for Commissioner. He had many of the qualities of a statesman. He was cool, calm, patient, and wise. Judging from the result, it is evident that his instructions were: to be conservative; to make no rash or premature move; and to uphold the royal authority conjointly with the old princely rule—peaceably, if possible, but firmly—till Siam could assume complete control. Meanwhile he was to follow the English plan of governing through the native rulers. He was willing to bide his time. Every new assumption of power on the part of Siam was reluctantly yielded by the Lāo. But everything conspired to favour the policy of Siam. The Lāo Prince was passive and unambitious. For the Uparāt no one felt the reverence or the fear that all had felt for the late Prince Kāwilōrot. The Commissioner's fairness and business integrity enabled him to maintain himself perfectly in his difficult position between the two branches of the Tai race, and amid the conflicting interests of the time.

In religion the new Commissioner was a stoic. His boast was that he needed no other religion than to be loyal to his king, and upright and just in his dealings with men. Virtue was its own reward, and vice was its own punishment. He accepted Gibbon's conclusion that all religions are alike good for the state, alike true for their adherents, and alike false for the philosopher. He encouraged Christianity because it taught a good morality and made good citizens. But he could see neither the possibility nor the necessity of an atonement for sin. On one point I should say we were in full accord. In his opposition to the spirit-worship of the Lāo he was almost rabid. He sympathized deeply with the poor people accused of witchcraft, who were driven out of the country.

During the absence of Dr. Cheek and Mr. Wilson with their families, I should have been utterly unable to cope with the situation, had it not been for my wife's clear business talent and tact in planning. The little girls, too, had begun to show somewhat of their mother's aptitude for work.

Meanwhile the fever scourge continued to spread and increase in violence. The progress of the disease was so rapid that often the person attacked would never rally at all. An interesting example of the way in which healing of the body sometimes opened the way to the healing of the soul, is seen in the case of Sên Kam, an officer who was in charge of all the irrigation works on the Doi Saket plain, and who one day was brought to my gate, as it was supposed, to die. The new medicine quickly checked his fever, and presently he began to study in Siamese the Shorter Catechism, Genesis, and the Gospel of John. In due time he returned home a believer. But his desertion from Buddhism caused such opposition in his province that his baptism was delayed. His family were so shaken that some of them wished to return to the old worship. But one young grand-daughter of twelve or thirteen years had begun to read our books and to attend our services. She refused to return to the monastery, and would run away from it to the chapel. She persevered until she brought back the whole family into the Christian fold.

In further illustration of the crowded experiences of this time, I may cite the following items from letters to our children, written during the latter half of the year 1877.

"Last week the King sent for your father to treat a prince who had had the fever for fifteen days. During his paroxysms his cries could be heard throughout the whole neighbourhood. In their extremity they sent for your father, and gave up the case to him with permission to remove all spirit-charms during the treatment. He is now out of danger." [MRS. McG.]

"For three weeks I have had a young prince in hospital who had attempted suicide by cutting his throat. He was a fearful sight. It did not seem possible that he could survive the night. I sewed up the wound, however, and now he is well, and apparently penitent." [D. McG.]

"We are well as usual, but engrossed in work. Your father is pressed beyond measure with the work of two men. On the return of Dr. Cheek's boats, we received forty ounces of quinine; but it is going at a fearful rate. The hospital is full of patients, and there are at least one hundred more to be prescribed for daily. If I did not drop everything else and help him, he could not possibly get through the day's work." [MRS. McG.]

"Soon the quinine was all gone, and our compound was becoming a veritable lazaretto. Most of the patients were anæmic and dropsical from long-standing fever. They came, because to remain at home was to die. Then a new complication arose. Unusual symptoms began to occur that I could not account for. One morning at breakfast we were called to see a little girl who had a hemorrhage. She had no cough and had no consumption. While I was looking up the symptoms and cause, your mother discovered that the bleeding was from the gums. That gave us the clue. It was scurvy. I found that we had at least thirty others whose gums were similarly diseased. We began at once to give them lime-juice, and prescribed vegetables, for the lack of which they were starving. It is the invariable custom of Lāo doctors in cases of fever to put the patient on a strict diet of boiled rice and dried fish. On such diet some of our patients had been living for two or three months. They might as well have been on an arctic voyage!"

[D. McG.]

"Day before yesterday we tried to have a picnic. A princess had promised us two elephants, but only one came. Your father took a horse. The three children and I rode the elephant. Our destination was the Doi Sutēp temple. About half the way up the mountain the elephant either concluded that there was no fun in going up alone, or, more probably, that he had an uncomfortable load, and refused to go any further. He turned out of the road, and tried to throw the driver from his neck. The children became alarmed, and we dismounted as best we could. The children refused to try riding him again; and since we had come largely for their pleasure, we had our lunch by a brook, and returned home on foot." [MRS. McG.]

"We had an interesting incident at our December communion. Just as I had announced the communion hymn, I saw Chao Borirak—the Nān prince, who had twice accompanied me with his elephant on my journeys, and for whose sake largely one of my trips to Nān had been taken—enter the room. As he had been the subject of much special prayer on our part, I could hardly command my voice sufficiently to proceed with the hymn. On my return from my furlough he had written that he would visit me at the first opportunity. His uncle, the Prince of Nān, had a grandson in danger of losing his sight from an accident. He had persuaded the Prince that possibly our medicine might help him. He brought a few presents from the Prince, and for himself had brought a gold ring with a native pearl from the Nān river. He is very anxious that I should move to Nān, but I tell him that he must wait for you. . . . With fever and death around us we have been wonderfully preserved from 'the pestilence that walketh in darkness, and the destruction that wasteth at noonday.' We have had our anxieties about the children. During the last hot season we were afraid that little Margaret would melt away, she was so thin." [D. McG.]

But the labours of the year were not in vain. During its progress Nān Suwan, who afterwards became the founder of the church in Chieng Sên, and four others who became influential ruling elders, were baptized. And with these was Pā Kawng, an aged slave of the Prince, who lived to be one of the Lāo saints.

XVIII

WITCHCRAFT

ON January 6th, 1878, two native converts were received into the church—Nān Sī Wichai, the fine scholar who had been Dr. Cheek's teacher, and the wife of a leading elder—and with them our own daughter Cornelia. This was the bright beginning of the year that brought in religious toleration.

One day in March, as I was sitting in my study, I was surprised to see a tall man, a stranger, with the bearing of an officer, enter. He pointed with both fingers to his ears, and asked if the teacher could say "Ephphatha," and open the ears of a deaf man as Jesus did. It was a strange introduction—to be accosted by a Lāo with a quotation from Scripture in the ancient Aramæan tongue! I judged by his accent that he was from Lakawn. In answer to my enquiry as to who he was, I learned that he was a Prayā, the highest rank among Lāo officials; that he had formerly been first in the Lakawn court, but was not then in office. But where had he received a Bible, and who had taught him?

I learned that some twenty years before this he had accompanied his Prince to Bangkok, and there had met Dr. Bradley, from whom he received a copy of the Old Testament History in Siamese, and the New Testament so far as it was then published. He had learned Siamese in order to be able to read and understand the contents of these books. He often wished that he had lived in the time of Christ. But, having no one to guide him, he had not learned to draw the lessons that the Bible story was designed to teach.

He had come to Chiengmai to get the assistance of the princes there in righting an unjust decision of the Lakawn court against him. He had heard, too, that there were teachers of a new religion; and he wished to know whether we taught as did Dr. Bradley and the books received from him. His position, his manners, his whole history, including his connection with my father-in-law, attracted me to him with uncommon force. Our first interview was long and very satisfactory. His questions were such as he had long wished to put to some one who could explain them. The truth had been securely lodged in his mind. It was most interesting to see how a single new thought would illuminate it all.

But what he had sown he was then reaping. While in power he doubtless had oppressed others. Once he had received "hush money" from murderers whom he should have prosecuted. If he had not taken it, he said they would have murdered him, too. His sins weighed upon his conscience. His most anxious question was whether Jesus could really save *all* men from *all* sins. When asked if Buddha could do so, he said that he never had seen any such promise in any of the scriptures. He would search again. He went to an abbot friend from whom he borrowed, as he said, "books by the armful." He looked them over with this one question in view: Is there hope of pardon offered to sinners? He went a second time for more. At his third coming the abbot, finding out what he was after, refused to lend to him further. But he confessed that his search was in vain. He argued with the monks, refuted them; and they cast him off. Upon his arrival the Chao Uparăt had promised his assistance in the lawsuit. When, however, he found that the Prayă was becoming a Christian, he dropped him. But he had found an intercessor greater than any earthly prince. For Him he was willing to face all opposition and to bear all reproach.

He was baptized on the 8th of May, just before returning home. The rains had already set in, and were likely greatly to impede his journey. Yet he reached Lakawn without encountering a shower. His account of it afterwards was, that whenever he saw the clouds threatening, he would wave his hands and pray that they might be dispersed. Lāo Christians have not become befogged with doubts as to the efficacy of prayer for temporal blessings. After his return to his home, his family all became believers, and others also whom he taught. At his invitation I went over to instruct them and to administer the sacraments. Two years later the number was sufficient to warrant their organization into a church, of which the Prayă was made the first elder.

Dr. Cheek's return at the end of April, 1878, took from my shoulders the care of the medical work—a very great burden. During his absence I had put up a hospital building of six rooms. This since then has been moved, and now forms the nucleus of the Chiengmai Hospital. The doctor soon found himself overwhelmed with practice. He was a fine surgeon and a good doctor, and had great influence both with princes and with people. Moreover, Mrs. Cheek's inheritance of the language—like my wife's—was a great advantage to them both. Only a few days after the doctor's arrival we lost our valuable hospital assistant, Lung In. One evening he complained of some trouble about the heart. He talked a few moments with his family, then said he felt better and would go to sleep—and in an instant was gone.

In 1878 Chieng Sên, the old abandoned city which I visited in 1872, became the theme of anxious consultation on the part of the government. The Lāo had taken away the inhabitants, but could not take away the land. It had become a rendezvous for robbers and lawless men from all quarters. The Western Shans from Burma were settling upon it. Siam evidently must repopulate the province, or lose it. It was finally agreed that one thousand descendants of the original captives should be drafted from Chiengmai, one thousand from Lakawn, and five hundred from Lampūn, and sent back to reoccupy the province. Chao Noi Inta, the highest in rank of the available descendants of the original captive princes, was commissioned as governor. The special interest this exodus has for our narrative lies in the fact that among these returned captives was the family of Nān Suwan, one of our best men, and already an elder of the church. At first Nān Suwan thought of buying himself off, as many did. But when it was pointed out to him that his going would be the means of starting a church there, he readily consented to go.

The governor was a warm friend of mine, and was urgent that we establish a mission and a church there before Buddhist temples could be built. The province was virgin soil. A great mortality usually attends the repeopling of deserted places and the clearing of the land. The governor was very anxious that we should

INTANON,
PRINCE OF CHIENGMAI

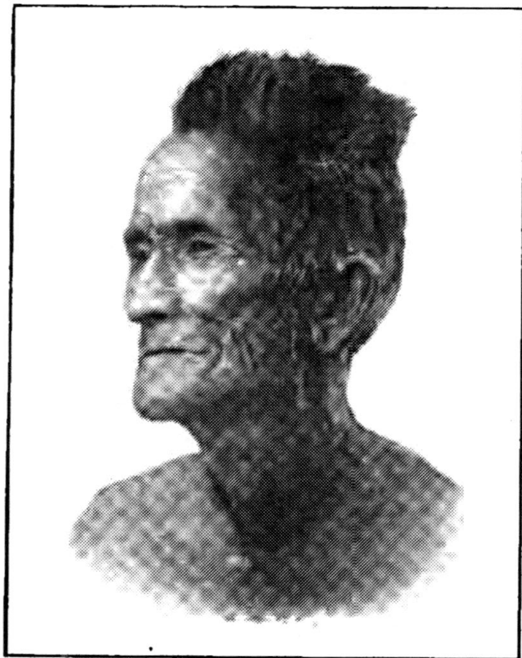

ELDER NĀN SUWAN

send a physician. Had we gone then with five hundred ounces of quinine, we should have had command of the situation. As it was, Nān Suwan was furnished with some quinine, which gave him the name of doctor. Broad-minded, hospitable, kindly, and thoroughly upright, there could have been no better selection. He became the real father of the Chieng Sên church. His family was a light in the city. His youngest daughter, Kūi Kêo, one of Mrs. McGilvary's first pupils, taught most of the early Christians there to read the Scriptures in Siamese. The elder himself became a great favourite with the governor, who used to say that the fact of his being governor, and, therefore, under authority, alone prevented him from uniting with the church. Another of the returning captives was Sên Yā Wichai, the first believer in Chiengmai. He settled on the western border of the Chieng Sên plain.

The Lāo as a race have been in bondage to the spirits. We have already had frequent occasion to refer to the slavish fear of them among all classes, from the highest to the lowest. No event in life, from birth to the last offices for the dead, could be undertaken without consulting or appeasing the presiding spirits of the clan, the household, or the country. Their anger is the fruitful cause of every disease and calamity that flesh is heir to.

In many ways this would seem a less elevating and ennobling cult than pure Buddhism. But really it has a much closer affinity with Christianity than has Buddhism, whether as scientifically held by the learned, or as embraced by the common people. Buddhism is too atheistic to bring it into comparison here with Christianity. It lacks the essential attribute of religion—a sense of dependence on some higher power. It belongs to a different order of thought. The spirit-cult, on the other hand, does recognize invisible powers whose good-will or ill-will brings prosperity or adversity. From this to one Great Spirit, who is sovereign over all, is but another step on the same line of ascent. So their spirit-offerings come nearer the idea of propitiation than do the offerings of Buddhism, which in some quite unaccountable manner are supposed to bring merit to the offerer.

A belief in witchcraft—that is, in the temporary or permanent residence of some evil spirit in men—has been confined to no one age or race. Its predominance among the northern Tai tribes is very remarkable in view of its inconsistency with Buddhism, which has long been the religion of the race. In the contest for supremacy, the spirit-cult, while it has not superseded Buddhism, has secured the stronger hold on the people. They worship Buddha and make offerings in his temples; but they fear and dread the power of the spirits to inflict present evil. It is safer to neglect Buddha than these. And the power of a malicious spirit is most dreaded when it has taken up its abode in a human habitation.

From the time of our first arrival in Chiengmai we were continually amazed to find what multitudes of people had been driven from their homes for supposed witchcraft. All the northern provinces and towns, as has already been mentioned, were largely peopled by that unfortunate class. Accusation of witchcraft had become one of the most dreaded means of oppression and persecution. It was a favourite way of getting rid of an envied rival or of a disagreeable neighbour. No family and no rank were safe from such attack.

Princes, even, had fallen under its ban. When once the suspicion of witchcraft was well started, the individual or the family was doomed. Our sympathies had often been aroused in behalf of these unfortunates; but no favourable opportunity had occurred for interference in any other way than by our teaching.

Finally, in August, 1878, the opportunity came. I had a request from a prince of some wealth and standing, that I would take under our protection Pă Sêng Bun and her family, accused of witchcraft. The woman was first the under-wife of the Prince's deceased father, who was a man of note in his day. She had two fine boys by a subsequent husband, and a niece nearly grown. This second husband was a widower, whose former wife was suspected of dealing in the occult art; and the theory was that the evil spirit came into her family through these sons. In that season of heavy rains and flooded streams, the whole family was to be driven off—some of them surely to die on the way. The patron said that he was helpless; that no one in the land, unless it were ourselves, could shield them from that fate. I told him that we were perfectly willing to risk the anger of the spirits, only we did not wish unnecessarily to offend the prejudices of the people. He was willing to assume all *legal* responsibility; for the rest, we might fight it out with the spirits as we pleased. After notifying the Siamese Commissioner of the situation, we brought the family to our place.

That very day their house was burned down; and not a tree or bush was left standing on the premises to furnish shelter to the spirits. But that did not stop the clamour. There was then in their village a great epidemic of fever. By common consent it was agreed that this had been caused by the evil spirit resident in the lads. With boyish curiosity they had twice or thrice gone back to visit the site of their old home, and, strange to say, after each visit a new case of sickness had occurred, which was, of course, attributed to their presence. It was vain to point out the utter ridiculousness of the idea, or to show that no sickness had occurred on our place since their arrival. That was easily explained. The spirit was afraid of our God, and did not dare to enter the premises. It took refuge in a large tree outside till the boys came out again, when it entered its former habitation and went with them.

Finally the patron prince sent word that we must give that family up. He could endure the odium no longer. When I refused, he threatened to take the matter into court. To this I replied that I was perfectly willing that the case be tried; but it should not be tried before a Lāo court, but before the Commissioner. If they could convince him that the sickness in the village was caused by a malicious spirit resident in that family, they should be sent off immediately. But, I added, it would be fair to make one condition. If the accusers failed, *they* should be driven off. This—as I knew it would do—put an end to the whole affair. We heard no more of it. It was a great victory in the demon controversy; and, later, as we shall see, it proved a boon to scores of helpless victims. Before the arrival of the Commissioner such an outcome would have been impossible. No Lāo court would have refused to expel persons so accused. The family of Pā Sêng Bun proved to be a treasure, becoming one of the most influential and valuable in the Chiengmai church.

XIX

THE EDICT OF RELIGIOUS TOLERATION

OUR narrative has now brought us to a point where an apparently trivial circumstance became the occasion of an event not only of utmost importance to us and to our work, but of far-reaching consequences to the country at large. Sometime near the middle of this year, 1878, the eldest daughter of Nān Inta was to be married to a Christian young man studying for the ministry. Both parties at that time were virtually members of our family. The expected bride was a pupil of Mrs. McGilvary's, and the groom was a private pupil of mine. The immediate family connections on both sides were Christians. Inasmuch as this was the first Christian marriage in the church, we had prepared to celebrate it with a little wedding feast. Besides the Christians, a few princes and a few special friends were invited, all anxious to see a Christian marriage-ceremony. Among the invited guests was Chao Tēpawong, Nān Inta's liege-lord, and brother of the Uparāt.

We learned that the family patriarch—known to be a violent opposer of Christianity—had threatened to prevent the marriage, unless we first paid to him, as tribal head of the family, the spirit-fee originally designed to furnish a feast for the spirits. It was a small sum—among common people not more than six rupees. That payment would legalize marriage without any further ceremony. In fact, the payment may be regarded as a distinctively religious act, since it recognizes the spirits as the guardians and protectors of the family. When one becomes a Christian, that allegiance is cast off. By an unwritten law or custom of the country, that fee belonged to the patriarch, and he decided to exact it or make trouble. I had explained the marriage ceremony to the princes and to the Commissioner. I knew that the latter recognized the justice of our position, and I assumed that the government would support us if the patriarch caused any trouble.

Sure enough, early in the morning the patriarch's loud voice was heard in our yard threatening dire punishment to the family if his demand were not granted. The bride's father became alarmed, and thought we must have some official backing, or he would surely get into trouble. The guests had arrived, and every one was on the *qui vive* to see which side was to win in the contest. I went to the liege-lord of the family for his sanction; but he said it was too big a question for him to pass upon. I must go to a higher authority. It had evidently become a question that could not be settled that morning. Old Adam would have said, "Marry them and trust to the justice of your cause. Let the old patriarch whistle!" But we teach our Christians to be obedient to the law, and we wished to avoid unnecessary trouble. So there was nothing to do but to swallow our mortification, apologize to our guests, invite them to partake of the feast, and seek legal sanction afterwards.

After dinner that same day Dr. Cheek and I called upon the Commissioner. We had failed, and were come to him for advice. His sympathies were easily enlisted, but he had no authority to interfere in local or tribal matters. He advised us to go to the Prince. We did so, meeting him and the Princess alone. Their position was like that of the Commissioner. They, too, sympathized with the young couple and with us. But it raised a new question for them, and they feared to give offence. The Princess said they had been criticised by our enemies for standing by us; but if the Chao Uparāt would give his sanction, no one else, they thought, would dare oppose. So we went next to the Uparāt; but there we ran against a stone wall. He inwardly laughed at our predicament. He had us just where he wanted us to be. If our young people could not marry, our work would be virtually stopped. He said that no one but the King of Siam had authority to interfere in such a question.

We returned home signally defeated. Next day I went alone to the Chao Uparāt, and argued the justice of our case. The parties had renounced their allegiance to the spirits. It was clearly unreasonable to require what we could not conscientiously submit to. I even begged him to come to our aid, since both the Commissioner and the Prince had said that they were sure that no one else would oppose his decision. If we were compelled, we must appeal to His Majesty the King of Siam, though we should be very reluctant to do so. Since marriage is a civil as well as a religious rite, I was sure His Majesty would admit the justice of our appeal. Either thinking that we would not make the appeal, or that the appeal would be in vain, he at last refused to discuss the question further. Little did he know, nor did we then, that he was doing the best possible thing for us.

I returned then to the Commissioner to report. The

conflict which, as we have seen, was probably inevitable between the royal authority represented by the Commissioner on the one hand, and the local rulers on the other, was becoming inevitable sooner than was anticipated. The Commissioner just then was himself having great trouble with officials who were restive under his authority. The Lakawn Princes had a difficulty among themselves, and had come to the Commissioner to have the case adjudicated. His decision had been unfavourable to one of the higher officials—probably the chief himself. Whoever it was, he had committed the unpardonable offence of departing to Lakawn without taking leave of the Commissioner, presumably intending to appeal to Bangkok. So that morning I found His Excellency indignant at the insult offered to him, and, through him, to his sovereign. The royal authority which he represented was challenged. Moreover, some of the acts of the Chao Uparăt had offended him. His impressions were confirmed and strengthened by the recital of our grievances. He advised me to write these all out in full, giving specifications that could be substantiated—and such were rapidly multiplying. For, provoked at Năn Inta and his family, and emboldened with his own success in stopping the wedding, the Chao Uparăt had summoned Năn Inta and had set him to watching his summer-house on the river—the work of a menial, such as Năn Inta had never yet been reduced to doing.

At last the moment had come when an appeal for religious toleration might be made with fair prospect of success. As the only way of avoiding continual interference in the future, the Commissioner himself advised that the appeal be made for religious toleration in general, rather than for freedom of

Christian marriage, which was only a single item. The Commissioner was busily engaged in writing out a report of his own grievances, to be sent to the King. He said that he would mention our case also in his report, and offered to forward my letter with his despatches.

I immediately dropped everything else, and addressed myself to writing that appeal unto Cæsar. In it I referred to the sanction of the Siamese government to the establishment of the mission, given after the interview with Prince Kăwilŏrot at Wat Chêng, and subsequently renewed on the appointment of his successor, Prince Intanon. I was very careful not only to exonerate the latter from all blame, but also highly to commend both him and his Princess for their uniform kindness, and for their sympathy in this particular emergency. But the act of the Chao Uparăt was, no doubt, only the beginning of what he would do if he were not restrained. It was evidently his intention to reduce to slavery a family that had always been free. In behalf of his loyal Christian subjects we begged His Majesty to guarantee to them the same privileges, civil and religious, which his other subjects enjoyed, among which surely was the right to be married according to the ceremony of their own religion. One request I put in with some misgiving—that the Christians might be exempted from compulsory work on the Sabbath; otherwise that point might always be used to create difficulty when the master was hostile. While thus making our appeal to man, importunate prayer was continually offered to Him who had been our help in times past.

It was very necessary that the appeal should go as the joint action of the mission as then constituted. I was aware that Dr. Cheek, the only other member of the mission then on the ground, did not enter heartily into the appeal. He was fearful that it would only make bad worse; that it would give offence to the Lāo rulers, and possibly to the Siamese as well. But as regards the Lāo, matters had already reached an extremity in the case of the one who really ruled the country. And as to the Siamese, our only human hope was in the King. So, when my paper was finished, I took it to Dr. Cheek, and read it over to him. He listened very attentively to the reading, and at its close I was delighted to hear him say, "That seems all right." After a few clerical alterations which he suggested, we both signed the paper. A summary of it was read to the Commissioner, and was afterwards enclosed by him with his despatches. Our appeal to the King of Siam had, of course, to be made through the United States Consul, Colonel Sickels. Our letter to the King was, therefore, sent unsealed under cover to the Consul, so that he might read it; and with it went a letter giving him a full account of all the particulars of the case, and urging him to use his influence, both personal and official, on our behalf. The whole was entrusted to a special messenger in a swift boat, with instructions to make all possible speed.

Having done our best, we waited prayerfully and hopefully. But the greatness of the issue involved made us anxious. The liberal policy of the young King was not then so well known as it became later. One could not be absolutely certain how even our Consul would regard it. We trusted, however, to the friendship of the Foreign Minister, who had invited me to Pechaburī, and who had always been our true friend. No one of all these persons concerned disappointed our expectations, or even our hopes.

Colonel Sickels acted with commendable despatch. He was favoured in securing an audience without the usual formalities. At that time His Majesty had a regular day each week when his subjects and others might approach him informally in his summer garden with petitions on urgent business. Our appeal was presented to him there. He was already aware of its nature through the Commissioner's despatches. Anxiety with regard to the political situation in the North no doubt prompted him to a decisive assertion of authority in this matter as well. His Majesy informed the Consul that his government had already reached a decision favourable to our request, and that full religious toleration was to be proclaimed.

The courier returned with unwonted speed, reaching Chiengmai on Sunday, September 29th. Late in the afternoon of that day the .Commissioner notified me of the arrival of despatches. Next morning I called upon him. He was radiant with joy. All his own requests had been granted, and enlarged powers had been given him, including power to make proclamation of religious toleration in all the Lāo states. He seemed as much delighted with our success as with his own. He said that he had already notified the princes and officials to call in the afternoon, and he would then inform them of the result. Of course, our hearts were overflowing with gratitude.

At the appointed hour the Prince, the Chao Uparāt, and all the high officials were assembled. When the order for the proclamation was made known, some of them made a final personal appeal to him to stay proceedings. They argued that unrestricted permission to become Christians would be the ruin of the country. To understand the force of this objection it must be remembered that among the Lāo, breach of the Seventh Commandment was punished, not by civil or criminal procedure, but by a "spirit-fine" paid to the patriarch of the woman's family. It was argued that if Christian young men should transgress with Lāo girls or women, under the new régime, no fine could be imposed, and there would be no redress whatever. The Commissioner then sent a messenger, asking me to come to the audience. The scene, as I entered, reminded me of that other notable audience with Prince Kāwilōrot and another Commissioner. The Commissioner stated their objection, and asked me what I had to say. I replied that the difficulty was purely an imaginary one. In the first place, it was a cardinal doctrine of the church to forbid such sins. In the second place, if a professed Christian violated his vows, he made himself amenable to the discipline of the church, and so put himself beyond its protection. The Commissioner said, "I have already so answered, but I wanted those who are present to hear it from the teacher himself." To this no reply was made. After a short pause the Commissioner broke the silence. With a gesture to the audience, he said that the business was ended. When he had leisure, the Edict would be issued. One after another the assembled princes and officials retired.

On my way home I noticed that the Chao Uparāt had stopped at his little sālā beside the river, the same that Nān Inta had been set to watch. To show that I had no personal grudge, I stopped to call on him. Rising, he gave me a more respectful welcome than usual, and ordered a foreign rug to be spread—the respectful way of receiving guests before the day of chairs. When I was seated he asked why I had made complaint against him to Bangkok—he was very sore at heart about it. I replied that I was sorry, indeed, to be obliged to do it. Did he not remember how I had told him that we could not submit to his decision; how I had even entreated him not to force us to appeal to the King? And I could not appeal without giving the facts as my ground for so doing. But now I hoped that bygones might be bygones, and that we might be friends.—The fact was that my letter had been translated in Bangkok, sent back to Chiengmai, and had been read at the audience before my arrival. But I never before had such a reception from the Uparāt.

The wording of the proclamation was left to the Commissioner. If he had been hostile, or even indifferent, its effect might easily have been neutralized by a little vagueness or ambiguity. But he was anxious to have the matter settled decisively. When I took my leave of him that morning, he promised to show me the draft of the proclamation before he should affix his seal. When I saw it, there were only a few verbal changes to suggest. It was a general permission to the Lāo to adopt any religion they pleased. I suggested that since it was specifically granted in the interest of Christians, it was desirable that Christianity be specifically named—which was done. At my request two extra copies of the proclamation were made with the official seals attached; one for deposit in our safe, and one that might be read to the people. The following is a literal translation of this famous document:

I Prayā Tēp Worachun, Representative of His Majesty the Supreme King of Siam in Chiengmai, Lampūn, and Lakawn, hereby make proclamation to the Princes, Rulers, and Officers of various grades, and to the common people in the cities and provinces named:—That His Majesty the King of Siam has been graciously pleased to send me a Royal Letter under the Royal Seal, to the effect that D. B. Sickels, Esqr., United States Consul, had communicated to the Foreign Minister of Siam a complaint signed by Rev. D. McGilvary and Dr. M. A. Cheek against certain parties for molesting the Christians and compelling them to observe their old religious customs. The Foreign Minister laid the subject before His Majesty, who most graciously listened to the said complaint, and gave the following Royal Command in reference to the same:—

That religious and civil duties do not come in conflict. That whoever wishes to embrace any religion after seeing that it is true and proper to be embraced, is allowed to do so without any restriction. That the responsibility for a right or a wrong choice rests on the individual making the choice. That there is nothing in the laws and customs of Siam, nor in its foreign treaties, to throw any restriction on the religious worship and service of any one.

To be more specific:—If any person or persons wish to embrace the Christian Religion, they are freely permitted to follow their own choice.

This Proclamation is to certify that from this time forth all persons are permitted to follow the dictates of their own conscience in all matters of religious belief and practice.

It is moreover strictly enjoined on Princes and Rulers, and on relatives and friends of those who wish to become Christians, that they throw no obstacles in their way, and that no one enforce any creed or work which their religion forbids them to hold or to do—such as the worship and feasting of demons, and working on the Sabbath day, except in the case of war and other great unavoidable works, which, however, must not be a mere pretence, but really important. Be it further observed that they are to have free and unobstructed observance of the Sabbath day. And no obstacle is to be thrown in the way of American citizens employing such persons as they may need, since such would be a breach of the treaty between the two countries.

Whenever this Proclamation is made known to the Princes

and Rulers and Officers and People, they are to beware and violate no precept contained therein.

Proclamation made on the Thirteenth Day of the Eleventh waxing Moon, in the Eleventh Year of His Majesty's Reign, October the Eighth, Eighteen Hundred and Seventy-Eight.

The Edict furnishes a second natural division in the history of the Lāo mission. Its first period was one of struggle for its very existence, culminating in positive prohibition to preach the gospel and virtual expulsion of the missionaries. That situation was abruptly brought to an end by the death of Prince Kāwilōrot and the appointment of his son-in-law, Prince Intanon. In our second period of struggle, the conclusion of which we have just witnessed, the conditions were in many respects similar to those of the first. Our chief antagonists in the two contests were alike in their love of absolute power, in their determination to break down all rival influences, and alike, therefore, in their settled hostility to our work. In neither case was their antagonism to Christianity primarily on religious grounds. But Kāwilōrot was of much more imposing personality and figure than the Uparāt.

Within his own realm Kāwilōrot was really "Lord of Life." He was absolute head both of church and of state. He brooked no rival and no contradiction in either. The highest positions in the religious hierarchy were bestowed or withdrawn at his pleasure. His own brothers-in-law languished in exile in Siam, because it was not thought safe for them to return and be within his reach. At home he had vanquished or terrified into submission all possible rivals. Even the court of Siam seemed inspired with a wholesome fear of meddling with him. The crime of the first Christians was the unpardonable one that they had dared to become such against the will of Kāwilōrot. But the time and place for such rulers had passed. Such attitude and temper suited neither a position under superior authority, nor the policy of a government striving to rise with the progress of the age. But he served his purpose in the world, and Providence used him.

Of his titular successor, Prince Intanon, and of his noble wife, I have already spoken. His real successor in the government of the land, and in his championship of the old régime of feudal autocracy, was the Chao Uparāt. But he had neither the commanding dignity of Kāwilōrot nor his interesting personality;—had little, in fact, of any of his qualities save his lodged and settled hatred of all innovation. For him we had none of a certain kind of respect which the late Prince inspired; and we were under no constraint of gratitude for favours. The only debt of gratitude the mission owed him was for being, by his lawless acts, the unwitting and unwilling cause of the proclamation of religious freedom.

But the crisis which he precipitated hastened likewise that centralization of government which Siam was waiting for. The tendency of the age is everywhere toward centralization. Strong central governments are everywhere taking the place of weak and scattered ones. Chiengmai itself and all the existing Lāo states have grown by the capture and absorption of their weaker, though by no means insignificant, neighbours. The authority and fear of Siam had long been felt indirectly in preventing those petty wars in which one weak state captured and enslaved another. That authority was now to be exerted more directly to bring to an end the era of arbitrary, personal, autocratic rule among its dependencies, and to establish in its place the more equal and stable reign of law. Feudalism with its "organized anarchy" was to give way to the Nation.

Such was the period at which we have arrived in this narrative of our life and work in the Lāo states. It is a wonderful thing to have lived through such a series of changes, and possibly to have been, under Providence, the means of bringing some of them about. We work for an end apparent to ourselves; but God's designs are deeper and broader than ours. "He maketh the wrath of man to praise Him." Of nations, as well as of individuals, is it true that

> "There's a divinity that shapes our ends,
> Rough-hew them how we will."

Among the Christians the Edict, of course, was greeted with an outburst of joy. To Nān Inta it was like life from the dead. It was in reality freedom from slavery. And no man made such efficient use of it as he did. With the sealed copy of the Edict in his hand, he returned to his village; and wherever he went he could assure the people, on the faith of his Sovereign, that a profession of the "Jesus-religion" meant neither the ruffian's club nor slavery. The effects of the Edict upon the church will be traced in its future growth as our story moves on. I may venture, however, to anticipate so much—that within two years' time two of our strongest village churches were organized; one of them in Nān Inta's own village. Neither of these churches could have existed had not the Uparāt's power been abridged.

To the country, the new authority conferred on the

High Commissioner at that time has resulted in a revolution as silent and as effectual as the change of the seasons. His new title, Pū Samret Rāchakān—he who fulfills the King's work—was used, I believe, for the first time in that proclamation; and it really marked the passing of the sceptre from the hands of the Princes of Chiengmai. The titular Chao Chiwit—Lord of Life—was allowed to retain his title and honours during his lifetime; but he has had no successor. The Lāo country has ceased to be either a feudal dependency or a separate "buffer-state." Silently—almost imperceptibly—it has become an integral portion of the consolidated Kingdom of Siam. Autocratic rule has everywhere ceased. And all these changes are directly in line with the civilization of the age.

XX

SCHOOLS—THE NINE YEARS' WANDERER

THE year 1879 opened auspiciously. In March a little variety was introduced into our secluded life by an official visit to Chiengmai of Major Street, the British Commissioner at Maulmein. He and his party arrived quite unexpectedly, spent a week in the city, and attended an English service at the mission on Sunday. We met them a number of times, both socially and at official dinners. They strengthened the position of the Commissioner, and did us all good. But at that time we were anxiously awaiting another arrival, in which we were more intimately concerned. Mr. Wilson, who had been for two and a half years absent on furlough, was daily expected, and with him were our long-looked-for teachers for the Girls' School.

The party was to arrive on April 9th. To please the three children and myself, on the afternoon of the 8th we four started down the river in a small boat to meet and welcome them. But the river was low, and we had not yet reached them when darkness came on and we were obliged to seek moorings. When, at last, we got ashore, we learned to our great joy that the mission boats were moored only a few hundred yards below, in the same bend of the river. We all walked down in the moonlight, and presently spied their lights close at hand. The young ladies had retired to read, but not to sleep. The meeting by moonlight at the river's brink was quite romantic. We talked till ten o'clock, though Mr. Wilson was so hoarse that he could scarcely speak. At daybreak our fleet was under way. We had a jolly breakfast together on board—our visitors at their little table, and we on the deck. We then visited hard again until noon; but it was two o'clock before we caught sight of the mission premises, with the native Christians all waiting to greet the arrivals, old and new.

The High Commissioner, a few days later, gave a dinner to the mission, saying in the note of invitation that it was in honour of the young ladies, for the boldness and piety that enabled them to leave their fathers and mothers, and come so far to teach his people. When notified of their arrival, the Princess sent down carriages and had us all up to call on her. She was delighted to welcome the young ladies, and was interested in the school.

The Siamese and the Lāo tongues are two closely related branches of the same linguistic stock. The idiom and the great body of common words are nearly the same in the two, differing, where they do differ, chiefly in accent and intonation. Siamese is, of course, the speech of the ruling race throughout the Siamese kingdom; and even at the time of which we are speaking it was easy to foresee that the local dialect of its northern provinces must eventually give way before it, especially for all official and literary purposes. The chief obstacle in the way of a speedy victory for the Siamese has been the fact that the Lāo is written in a wholly different character. Were the two alike in this respect, there is no doubt that the standard form of speech would take the place of the dialectal almost without notice.

Of necessity all teaching so far attempted had been in the Siamese. There was not a schoolbook in the Lāo character save the spelling tables. When these had been mastered, there was no reading-book in Lāo that could be put into the hands of the pupils; nor was there prospect of any such being printed for years to come. On the other hand, in the Siamese character there was a considerable Christian literature in print, both religious and general, already available for purposes of education. Our pupils, moreover, had all been girls; and almost no Lāo women at that time could read writing in any character. It was, therefore, not only much simpler, but quite as well for them on other accounts, to learn the Siamese character from the start.

Now, however, when we were arrived at the establishment of regular schools with a permanent organization and policy, the question could no longer be postponed, In which language shall instruction be given? It was not an easy question to decide. With regard to it there was difference of opinion among the missionaries, both old and new. On the one hand, it was urged, that since ours was a Lāo mission, the Lāo should, of course, be the language of the schools. On the other hand were pointed out the greater scope and availability of the Siamese, its assured supremacy, and the dwindling future of the Lāo throughout the territory of Siam. The matter at last was compromised by continuing the Siamese in the Girls' School, and adopting the Lāo for the boys.

Meantime it was desirable to have some portions of

the Scriptures in the Lāo character; and, to accomplish this, the first requisite was a font of Lāo type. To this end, on my first furlough in 1873, I went from North Carolina to New York, and not only spent some time, but was at some personal expense, in the effort to secure such a font. The American Bible Society voted a liberal sum for the purpose. But there turned out to be some mechanical difficulties to be overcome in making and using the type, which were beyond my skill to solve. So, lest the attempt should fail in my hands, I gave it up. And having accomplished nothing, I presented no bill of expense either to the Bible Society or to the Board.

There seemed, indeed, to be some fatality attending our efforts in this direction. Mr. Wilson, on the furlough from which he was but now returned, had gone further. He actually succeeded in getting a font of Lāo type. But the whole of it was lost, and never reached the mission.[1] It was not until Dr. Peoples' furlough in 1889 that we succeeded in getting our present type. Meanwhile we had used the Siamese Scriptures, with some present disadvantages, indeed, but with some advantages as well. Some of our first Christians were attracted to our religion by their desire to learn Siamese; and the Siamese Bible and catechism were our textbooks. And now, under Siamese rule, knowledge of the Siamese opens the way to promotion in the government service. Siamese alone is taught in the

[1] Mr. Wilson brought only a few specimens with him. He writes:—"The rest of the type was to be boxed up and sent to Mr. Cutter, and the boxes were to be put away in the store-room of the Mission Rooms at 23 Centre Street, and forwarded when called for. They must have been lost when the Board moved from 23 Centre Street to the Lenox property, and then to 156 Fifth Avenue.

government schools. Young monks are more eager to study Siamese than their own tongue.

But the important thing, after all, was that we had a school actually begun, and that there was teaching in *both* dialects. It was like a new beginning of our work under conditions more favourable than at the first. For twelve years it had been a hard, and, sometimes, an apparently hopeless struggle. But the history of missions affords many similar instances with even fewer visible results. In twelve years we had gathered forty converts into the church. Some of these were among the most useful we have ever had in the history of the mission. It is hard to estimate rightly the importance of work spent on the foundations of such an enterprise. But now, with that church organized, with the medical work well established, the evangelistic work strengthened, and the initial school, begun long before by Mrs. McGilvary, placed on a permanent basis, we could write in large letters on our altar, "Jehovah-Nissi"—Jehovah our banner.

In the early part of this year, 1879, twelve more persons were gathered into the church. One of them was Pā Sêng Bun, the poor woman accused of witchcraft, who, with so much difficulty, was saved from her persecutors. Another was Mûn C., who was a daily visitor when we were here on our first tour of exploration. And another was our own dear little Margaret. Somewhat later there came to our notice one of the most interesting of all the incidents in the chequered history of our mission. One morning, on returning from my work in the city, I was told that a man had been waiting to see me, and was then talking to Nān Inta. Stepping down to the house, where a number of persons had collected, I saw a handsome man of medium height, but of striking figure, larger and more portly than is usual among the Lāo, and thirty-three years old, as I learned.

Nān Tā, for that was the stranger's name, said that not long after our first arrival in Chiengmai, while he was yet a monk in the king's monastery, he had visited me, and was struck with those points in the teachings of Christianity which differentiate it from Buddhism. He received a copy of the Gospel of Matthew in Siamese, learned a few verses, and took the book home with him to the monastery. Afterwards he visited me occasionally to take a few further lessons in it. He was a protégé of Prince Kāwilōrot, who paid the expenses of his entering the monastic order. He thus became the Prince's "Luk kêo"[1] (*jewel-son*), in effect his adopted son. Not long after this he left the priesthood, married, and settled out in the country. But he paid us a few visits from time to time, always, as he said, to talk on religion and to study Siamese.

When the order for the murder of the Christians was given, a monk who was a friend of his met him in the streets, and asked whether he knew that his house was to be burned over his head, explaining that the Prince had nourished him as a son, and now he had apostatized and joined the foreign religion. Advising him to consider well and quickly, the priest hurried on. So it had become known in the palace that he was visiting us and studying the Jesus-religion. There was no time to be lost, not even to bid good-bye to his young wife. On that eventful Saturday afternoon, just before the

[1] A designation whose nearest parallel in English is, perhaps, *godson*.

flight of our servants, he stopped at our door; but seeing no one, he hastened on. On Sunday he secreted himself in a deserted monastery near the mountains. Next day he fell in with a company of traders, going to Chieng Rāi, six days' journey to the north, and travelled with them without making known what his errand was. At Chieng Rāi he learned that the Christians were put to death the day after he left. He was still within the Lāo realm, and might be arrested. He made his way, therefore, to Keng Tung, in Burmese territory, ten or fifteen days' journey still further to the north.

After remaining there some three years, he returned to Chieng Rāi, where he heard of the death of Kāwilōrot and the accession of Prince Intanon. Still in fear, he passed through the towns to the east of Chiengmai, venturing even as near as Lakawn. Then crossing the Mê Ping valley to the south of Chiengmai, he went beyond the Salwin into Burma, stopping awhile among the Red Karens, and then going on to Maulmein. Seeing there a foreigner's house, he enquired if anything was known concerning the missionaries in Zimme (Chiengmai). Nothing was known of them. Returning again to Siamese territory, he went to Rahêng, thinking that he would go on to Bangkok. There, however, he was told that the missionaries had gone back to the United States—information based, no doubt, on our departure on furlough.

During his long wanderings he had made friends as he could, and to support himself had sometimes turned peddler. In the haste of his flight from home he had taken nothing with him except his copy of the Gospel of Matthew in Siamese. He could not read it well, but he kept it as a kind of talisman, till it was now well worn. He had learned to pray daily. He never dared to return till he heard of the Edict of Toleration. He regarded it as a special providence that his wife, strange to say, had not married again. The child born after his flight he found grown to be a fine girl nine years old. He was delighted to find the missionaries again.

It was a thrilling story. This man did not have to become a Christian—he was one already. His first desire was to understand all that there was in his Gospel of Matthew. It was evident that he had been spared and kept for some wise purpose. And so it proved. Since I needed a teacher, and since he was a fine Buddhist scholar, I employed him as teacher, so that I might have him near me in order to teach him. He was an apt pupil, making rapid progress in knowledge, and growing in grace. His romantic history interested and attracted others. As a church member, as a ruling elder, and afterwards as an ordained minister, he was a power in the church till the day when he was taken up. Thousands heard the Gospel from his lips, and many were drawn by his words and by his life into the fold of Christ.

How wonderful are God's ways in leading His people! Doubtless the defection of this man was one of the things which alarmed Kāwilōrot. It may even have hastened the fate of the martyrs. But no doubt the Lord chose a wonderful way of saving to His church this most useful minister of the Gospel.

After long-continued weakness on the part of Mrs. McGilvary, an acute attack of pneumonia made a longer stay in the country impossible. My daughter Cornelia was taken ill at the same time. So, with but little preparation, on December 28th, 1879, both mother and daughter were carried in chairs to the boat, and we hastened out of the country. Stopping in Bangkok only a few days, we embarked for Hongkong. We met the China Sea in its worst mood. For three days and nights we did not see the captain's face; neither did he see sun, moon, or stars in that most dangerous tract of the sea. The skylight was fastened down, for the waves swept the vessel from stem to stern. We were good sailors; but we could not but pity the one hundred and twenty Chinese steerage passengers, allowed on deck only a few moments twice a day for a breath of air, after which they had almost to be forced back into their hole again. There was withal just enough of the spice of danger to make the sight of Victoria Peak at last doubly welcome.

By this time my family were all so much improved by the journey that there was question whether I should proceed with them, or should return to Chiengmai for another year's work. It was evident that, in order to regain her strength, Mrs. McGilvary would require a longer stay in the United States than one year. I could neither spare the time for so long a furlough for myself, nor could I expect the Board to grant it. The question was not an easy one; but we decided at last that my wife and children should continue their journey to the United States, and that I should return to Chiengmai alone.

During my few days' stay in Bangkok, through the kindness of our Consul, I had an audience with His Majesty the King. I desired to express to him in person my thanks for the Edict of Toleration. After some remarks addressed to the other gentlemen present, the King asked me if I were not, during the previous month, the bearer of despatches from his Commissioner in the North—showing that he did not overlook small matters, as a king might be expected to do. He enquired how I liked the Commissioner, whether I preached in Siamese or in Lāo, how many converts we had, etc., etc. It was a very pleasant interview.

As I ascended the river, it became plain that the water was too low to permit the latter stage of the trip to be made in my large boat. At Chiengmai I should find a house, but not a home. Before I could reach it, the touring season would be nearly over. The thought of stopping a season for work at Rahêng struck me favourably. The more I considered it, the more attractive it became. To be sure, I had not secured the sanction of the mission to that particular enterprise; but I had always been allowed to choose my own touring ground. An officer, Sên Utamā, offered me a site for a bamboo house gratis; and before I had announced my final decision, he and others began to cut bamboo on it to build the house. I had asked for guidance, and the question seemed to settle itself.

I cannot dwell on the interesting six months of the year 1880 spent there. Sên Utamā was interested from the first. By affliction he had been wonderfully prepared for, and seemed to be waiting for, the very consolation that the Gospel offered him. An ex-tax-collector, a Chinese of some influence, was in the same state of mind, and soon joined the other as an enquirer. My student, Noi Intachak, entered heartily into the work. Soon, with my cook and boy, we had the nucleus of quite an interesting congregation who attended worship twice a day. It was a delight to teach them.

The case of the Chinese was deeply interesting. He believed the Gospel plan of salvation, and was deeply anxious to be saved from his sin and its punishment. But there was one serious obstacle in the way of his making an open profession—he had two wives. The real wife—the one he had formally married—was childless. The one he had bought was younger, and had two lovable little children, both girls. I recall almost with tears the burning questionings we had over that situation. He seemed willing to make any self-sacrifice that duty required. But what was duty? Should he divorce one of them? If so, which one? "Of course, he must keep the real one," you will say. But what of the young mother and the helpless babes? The very mention of their being turned adrift, even with a dower, had produced a scene in the family. The poor woman felt quite unable to care for the children alone. The children were his children. It might easily have been the ruin both of mother and babes to put her away. My heart was not hard enough to advise that. Surely the man had not cut himself off from the hope of salvation by his past—by an error or sin of ignorance. The conditions of church-membership are faith and repentance. The sacraments of the church are baptism and the Lord's Supper. Shall we offer a man the pardon of his sin without its sacramental seals?—the glorious hope of endless fellowship in heaven, but not the communion of saints on earth? A precisely parallel case I had met before in the person of a native doctor at Mûang Awn. "What then," the reader will ask, "did you do?" Why, in each case I just did nothing. I followed the letter of the law, and baptized neither one. But "the letter killeth; the spirit maketh alive."

In due time Sên Utamā and a nephew of the Chinese were baptized. An interesting tour was made up the river. But the station in Chiengmai was feeling the pressure of the growing work. In July, 1880, the church of Bethlehem was organized, and there were promising openings in other districts. It was evident that the Board was not in a condition to consider a permanent station in Rahêng. It would have been an interesting field for permanent occupation; but for temporary work, I had been there as long a time as we could afford to spend in one place.

Just then Prayā Sīhanāt—the officer from Lakawn who, two years before, had greeted me with "Ephphatha"—invited me to return with him. His ears were not opened, but his heart was. He had taught the Christian faith to his wife and children and a few others, and among these was a fellow ex-officer. He wished with them to receive further and fuller instruction, and to be taken into the fellowship of the church. Without waiting to ascertain whether I could go, he was come with a boat to bring me. This seemed to me the guiding hand of providence, and I followed it.

Since a single boat cannot ascend the rapids without the help of another boat's crew, we made arrangements to join forces with another party, and make the trip together. The night before we were to start, the river, which had been steadily rising, became a flood so strong that my host dared not face it in his small craft. Our companions, however, did not wait for us, but went on as they had planned. We waited ten days for another party, as well as for the river to go down. Imagine my sensations, then, when, presently, we learned that the captain and owner of the principal boat in the flotilla with which we had planned to make the trip, was shot and killed, and his boat was plundered! A band of dacoits secreted themselves behind a cluster of trees where the channel runs close to the bank, shot the steersman at his oar, and then had the boat at their mercy. Since all foreigners are supposed to carry money, the attack may well have been intended for me. Earlier in that same year, while returning alone to Rahêng, I came near being entrapped by a similar band.

The visit to Lakawn was interesting and profitable. Ten days were spent with the new converts. While my friend, the Prayā, had been busy, the devil had not been idle. One of the princes had threatened to have one of his head men flogged if he joined the Christians. But before we left, a church was organized, with Prayā Sĭhanāt as elder.

From Lakawn I took elephants to Chiengmai, and spent the last Sunday of my trip with Nān Inta and the newly organized church of Bethlehem, named after Mr. Wilson's old church in Pennsylvania. Nān Inta was waiting for me where the road to his village turned off from the main route. On Christmas day following this, Mr. Wilson, Dr. Cheek, and Miss Cole organized yet another church at Mê Dawk Dêng, where Nān Suwan had been doing faithful work. In both these cases the persecution for supposed witchcraft had furnished a good nucleus for the church, which thereafter the Edict of Toleration protected from expulsion.

All the departments of our work, medical, educational, evangelistic, were prospering. Nān Tā, the long time wanderer, was becoming a power second only to Nān Inta, and destined ultimately to surpass him. Like him, he was a man of fine address and bearing, and a good Buddhist scholar; but he was much younger. Being, moreover, the son of a Prayā—the highest grade of Lāo officers—he had an influence with the nobility such as no other of our Christians had. In the church he began to show a capacity and power such as probably no other person has exercised.

Meanwhile Mr. Wilson was working on plans for a building for the Girls' High School. Already the school numbered forty-two pupils, but with no place in which to teach them save the teacher's house. The season had been very hard on Miss Campbell's health. She was very young, and had come direct to Chiengmai from the seminary without any period of rest, and with a constitution by no means robust. The mission voted her a trip to Bangkok for rest. Little did we think when we bade her good-bye that we should see her face no more.

Financially for me the year had been the hardest in my life. With all the economy we could use—and we did not spend a useless penny—it seemed impossible for me to keep my family going. When we left Chiengmai we had overdrawn our salary, and the amount had to be made up that year. This condition was one of the straws that helped to determine me to stop over in Rahêng. I could live more cheaply there; in fact, could hardly spend money there if I wished to. In only one matter had I been greatly disappointed in Rahêng; I hoped to be in somewhat closer communication with my family, about whom I still felt some anxiety. I was, indeed, nearer them in space, but it proved much further in time. The largest mail of the year passed on up to Chiengmai, and was sent back, reaching Rahêng just after I had left the place. It finally reached me in Chiengmai on the last day of the year 1880!

XXI

SECOND FURLOUGH

MY health had been such that I hoped I might safely forego my furlough, and have my wife and our youngest child return to Chiengmai alone. My wife, after finding a home for a while with her brother, Professor Bradley, in Oakland, had gone on in the spring to North Carolina. But she was not gaining much in strength, and plainly required another year. My own health was not so good as it was at the beginning of the year. Certain symptoms gave me anxiety, and decided me to delay my own furlough no longer. If it was to be taken at all, the sooner the better. So on March 12th, 1881, I started for the United States. The furlough which was now beginning ended twenty-three years of service in the general field of Siam, and fourteen years spent among the Lāo.

I had proceeded down the river but a few days, when a passing boat brought the astounding intelligence of the tragic death of our esteemed and youngest colabourer, Miss Mary Campbell. What words can express the shock I received! The news was confirmed a few days later by Dr. Cheek, whom I met on the river. At this distance it is unnecessary to enlarge on the particulars of the sad catastrophe. Indeed, it was all so sudden that there were few particulars to relate. Dr. Cheek had gone down to Bangkok on business soon after Miss Campbell left us, and now was returning with Miss Campbell under his escort. At the close of a hot day's run, the boats lay moored by a sand-bar for the night. They had had their evening meal and worship together. Dr. Cheek had taken his bath in the river, had examined the bar, and notified Miss Campbell how far it was safe to venture in taking hers. But somehow she ventured out too far —to a depth from which only angelic arms could receive her to a shore where there is no more death.

The brave effort of her Lāo maid, Kam Tip, and Dr. Cheek's unsuccessful search till long after life must have been extinct, were well known at the time. She had but just come to her chosen field of work, in the bloom of youth and in the full ardour of her first consecration, little thinking that her work was to be so soon and so sadly closed. Her last written words to a friend, with the ink on them scarcely dry before her death, were: "But I am not alone, for I have found in my dear Lāo girls, Bûk and Kam Tip, and in Nān Tā, my teacher, more company than I ever expected. I wish I could lend them to you long enough for you to know them."

It will be evident to all that in 1881 the working force of the mission was entirely inadequate for occupying and cultivating the broad and inviting field, now opened to us as never before. The medical work, constantly enlarging, occupied the physician's whole time. Mr. Wilson's physical condition, never very strong, confined his labours to the station and its immediate vicinity. The attention which these alone required would more than fill one man's time. The death of Miss Campbell made imperative an associate for Miss Cole. So, even if the trip to the United

States had not been rendered imperative by considerations of my own health, the best interests of the work itself seemed to demand that some one should go to seek reinforcement by direct and personal appeal to the church at home.

As for Mrs. McGilvary, after spending the spring of 1880 with her brother in Oakland, California, she came on with our younger son to Statesville, North Carolina, where she could be with our daughters, and not far from our elder son in Davidson College.

On my arrival in New York, I hastened on at once to North Carolina, where I spent the summer with my family and friends, lecturing from time to time in the churches. The fall of this year I spent in Texas and Arkansas, visiting relatives and friends who had migrated thither from the family nest in North Carolina. In Texas I attended the meeting of the Southern Synod, and both there and elsewhere I found many opportunities for presenting the cause of foreign missions; and everywhere I encountered warm reception and eager interest in the work among the Lão. In the winter I came north to visit the Theological Seminaries, and to enlist men for the Lão mission. On my way I stopped in Oxford, Ohio, where I met Miss Lizzie Westervelt (afterward Mrs. Stanley K. Phraner), then in her senior year in Miss Peabody's Seminary, and preparing for missionary work among the Lão, upon which she entered in the following year. This was the school which had given us Miss Mary Campbell and Miss Edna Cole a few years before.

While waiting for the Theological Seminaries to reopen after the Christmas recess, I was the guest of my wife's cousins at Castleton Corners, Staten Island. There I had the very pleasant experience of observing

DR. McGILVARY
1881

MRS. McGILVARY
1881

"Watch Night" with the Moravian Church, of which my friends were members. They called on the Lāo missionary for an account of his experience in the field. In that, of course, there was nothing remarkable. But near the close of the next year, when writing to the family, I alluded to the pleasant memory of Watch Night and sent my greetings to the church with a request to be remembered in their prayers. Instead of giving my message verbally, my friends read the letter itself, and it seemed to be appreciated. The result was that the Lāo letter came to be looked for regularly as a part of the watch service, and one was sent to them every year—if I were on the field—for seventeen years. It was a comfort to know that special prayer was always offered for us by that great missionary church as the old year was dying, and the new year was coming in.

The Professors at Princeton, Union, and Allegheny all gave their cordial endorsement and aid to me in my efforts to secure men. "We want you to get our best men," they said, and the Lord gave them to us. From Princeton came Chalmers Martin of the senior class. He had been chosen, however, for the Hebrew Fellowship, and was, therefore, delayed a year before entering upon his missionary work. Though his career in the Lāo field was a short one, he left a lasting mark there, as we shall see. Allegheny gave us Rev. S. C. Peoples, M.D., and his brother-in-law, Rev. J. H. Hearst. Dr. Peoples' bow still abides in strength. His double preparation both as a minister and as a physician, gave him unusual equipment for the work he has accomplished. Mr. Hearst, however, soon succumbed to the Chiengmai climate.

Union gave us that consecrated young man, Mc-

Laren, who chose the great city of Bangkok—a fitting field for him, since his broad sympathies were bounded by no one race or people. His career also was cut short within a few months by cholera, contracted while ministering to dying seamen in the harbour during a severe epidemic of the disease.

The Northwestern Woman's Board of Foreign Missions was then, as it has been since, a great centre of missionary enthusiasm. It had sent out Miss Cole and Miss Campbell; and now the sudden death of the latter had caused its interest and that of the Chicago churches to concentrate upon the Lāo mission. It was to this combination of circumstances that I was indebted for an invitation to attend its Annual Meeting in Minneapolis, and to speak there. Then the appointment of Dr. L. E. Wishard's daughter (afterwards Mrs. Dr. Fulton of Canton, China), and that of Miss Sadie Wirt (Mrs. Dr. S. C. Peoples), from his church in Chicago, gave me a pleasant visit in the Doctor's family both as I went up to Minneapolis and as I returned. On a Sunday at Lake Forest, between the Sunday School, the University, the Ladies' Seminary, and the church, the Lāo Mission had four hearings. At Minneapolis we learned that Miss Warner from the Northwestern Woman's Board, and Miss Griffin from the Southwestern, were also appointed to our mission, and Miss Linnell to Lower Siam. This completed our number, the largest reinforcement the mission has ever received at one time.

After the adjournment of the Northwestern Board, a Sunday was spent with the family and the church of Miss Mary Campbell. After that, appointments with other churches filled up my time till the meeting of the General Assembly in Springfield, Illinois, which I attended, though not as a delegate. Our Presbytery of North Laos had not then been organized, and Dr. E. P. Dunlap was the representative of the Presbytery of Siam. At that meeting it seemed to me that a golden opportunity was missed for drawing together in a closer union the Northern and the Southern branches of the Presbyterian Church. The outcome threw the Southern church, much more weakened by the war than the Northern, on its own resources. In proportion to its financial strength, it has developed into one of the strongest missionary churches in the land, both as regards the home work and the foreign. Meantime, with the growth of the country generally, the Northern Assembly is becoming too unwieldy a body for its best efficiency. I believe the time will come when there will be three Assemblies rather than one, with a triennial Assembly of all on a basis of representation agreed upon by the three—somewhat after the plan of the Methodist and the Episcopal churches; or, more nearly still, after the plan of the Pan-Presbyterian Council.

In duties and pleasures such as have just been described, the time slipped by till it was the 6th of June, 1882, before I again reached my family in Statesville. We were to start Lāo-ward about the middle of July. My furlough ended with a visit to my old charge at Union, to attend the dedication of a new church there, and to see my old friends once more.

We began to gather up our scattered forces at Chicago, where the Fifth Church gave to its pastor's daughter, and to the rest of us there present, a hearty farewell. The others of our large party joined us at different points on our route across the continent. Dr. Eugene P. Dunlap and his family, also returning from furlough, were the very last to join us, just in time to sail with us from San Francisco.

A missionary's vacation is very delightful, but the last day of it—the day that brings him back to his home and his work—is the best of it all. The small Bangkok steamers of those days could not furnish accommodation for our whole party at once. Some of us were, therefore, compelled to lie over at Canton—a circumstance which changed the ultimate location of one of our young ladies to the Canton mission, just as a previous successor to Miss Campbell had in a similar manner been changed to another station in China. But where there are young folks, such accidents will happen.

At Bangkok our United States Consul, General Partridge, arranged for us an audience with the King. His Majesty gave us a cordial reception, expressing his gratification at seeing so many American missionaries coming to his country; since he knew that they came to instruct his people, and to make them more intelligent and better citizens.

Reinforcements surely had not come too soon. Dr. Wilson, Mrs. Cheek, and Miss Cole were the only missionaries on the field when we returned; for Dr. Cheek was absent on business. It was now four years since the proclamation of religious toleration; and for the first time was there prospect of workers enough to make any use of the advantages it offered.

But had we relied too much on human aid? Were we too much elated in view of our present numbers, with Mr. Martin to follow the next year? After a short stay in Bangkok, we reached Chiengmai in the midst of one of those violent epidemics of fever by which the Lāo country was then, perhaps, more fre-

CHULALONGKORN,
KING OF SIAM, 1872-1910

quently visited than it is now. Mr. and Mrs. Hearst and Miss Warner were soon prostrated with the disease, and at one time, out of the whole mission, scarcely enough were left to care for the sick. Mr. and Mrs. Hearst soon decided to give up the struggle and withdraw from the field. Miss Warner continued longer, but ultimately she, too, retired with broken health. As already stated, Mr. McLaren died of cholera after a few hours' sickness in Bangkok. God was teaching us that it is "not by might nor by power, but by My Spirit, saith Jehovah."

Soon other complications arose. Smallpox was brought by pupils into the Girls' School, and, to our consternation, Miss Griffin fell a victim. She had been vaccinated in her childhood, but was not revaccinated on leaving home—which is always a wise precaution for those expecting to travel or to live in the East. Proper measures prevented further spread of the disease; and though our patient had a rather hard attack, yet she made good recovery.

During our absence, the church had sustained a great loss in the death of Nān Inta, our first convert and assistant. But his works do follow him, and his life will long continue to be a precious legacy to the Lāo church. He lived, however, until others were ready to take his place. Nān Sī Wichai, who long had been Dr. Cheek's teacher, was a strong character, and he was ordained as an elder. Nān Tā, also, who had wandered so far and so long after the persecution, was growing to be a power in the church, and afterwards had the honour of becoming the first ordained minister among the Lāo.

XXII

A SURVEYING EXPEDITION

ON the 26th of February, 1884, an East Indian appeared on our veranda with an unexpected note from my old guest and friend, Rev. Dr. J. N. Cushing of the American Baptist Shan Mission. The surprise and pleasure of a visit from him and Mrs. Cushing in the early and lonesome days of the mission have already been referred to. The note told us that he was now connected, as interpreter, with a surveying expedition under Holt S. Hallett, Esq., and that the party would arrive in Chiengmai on the following day. The railroad for which Mr. Hallett was surveying a route was part of a scheme, then on foot, to build a road from Maulmein to Chiengmai, there to connect with a road from Bangkok, through the Lāo country, to Chieng Sên, and, if successful, to be continued up to Yunnan, China. For some reason the scheme was not carried out, but the prospect of any road to connect our isolated field with the outside world was attractive to us.

The party arrived the next day; and since it would be very inconvenient for Mr. Hallett to be separated from Dr. Cushing, we found room in our house for Mr. Hallett also, and had a fine visit with both. They soon began to tempt me to join their expedition. All expenses were to be paid. They were not to travel on Sunday. Their intended route, through the towns and villages on the way to Chieng Rāi and Chieng Sěn, and southward again to Lakawn, was over ground I was anxious to travel once more. The trip would give me a long and profitable visit with my friend, Dr. Cushing. But, besides all personal considerations, it seemed right to give a little aid to an enterprise that would redound to the good of the country.

Our Chiengmai Prince, then quite old, was most incredulous as to the possibilities of the wonderful railroad. In his book, *A Thousand Miles on an Elephant in the Shan States,* Mr. Hallett has given an amusing account of his first interview with the Prince. He had great difficulty in understanding how a train could move faster than ponies, or how it could move at all without being drawn by some animal. And how could it ascend the hills? For it would surely slide down unless it were pulled up. "I explained to him that I had made three railways in England, therefore he might rely upon what I had said. Railways were made in various parts of the world over much more difficult hills than those lying between Zimme (Chiengmai) and Maulmein. . . . He seemed quite stupefied by the revelation. It might be so—it must be so, as I had seen it; but he could not understand how it could be. He was very old; he could not live much longer. He hoped we would be quick in setting about and constructing the line, as otherwise he would not have the pleasure of seeing it."

We started at last on March 3d, 1884, with four large riding elephants, four pack-elephants, and numerous carriers, making forty-one persons in all. The passport from the Siamese government, supplemented by one from the acting Commissioner, and the presence with us of a Lāo official of some rank, sent to see that

the orders were carried out, secured for us men and elephants and all necessary equipments, so far as the country could furnish them. The local officials were usually very kind, and as prompt as native officials ever were in those days. Mr. Hallett was very considerate in arranging to stop for the night and on Sundays near large villages and towns, where a little missionary work could be done. In the cities where there were Christians, we held regular services on Sundays. On these occasions our chief gave the influence of his presence, though, of course, he could not understand what was said.

On this trip we had a good opportunity for studying the characteristics of the elephant. He is very conscious of his dignity, and must be treated with the respect due to a king, and not with the familiarity of an equal. Yet one is amused at his timidity. I myself have seen one ready to stampede if a squirrel or a big rat ran across the road in front of him. Mr. Hallett says: "Elephants, though immense in size, are very timid, and easily startled. We had to take them off the path and turn their heads away into the jungles, whenever we heard the tinkling bells of an approaching caravan; and they will turn tail and run at the sight of an audacious little dog that thinks fit to bark at them."

On some of the stages of our march, when we had a mother-elephant in our company, we had the mischievous youngster along. Such are always an unceasing source of amusement. One of these seemed to have a special spite against Mr. Hallett's Madras boy, either because of his peculiar dress, or for some liberty he had taken with him. Mr. Hallett writes: "The little elephant was taking every chance he could get to hustle the men over as they forded the streams, and to souse them with water from his trunk. Portow, who had an overweening opinion of his own dignity, and was bent on setting up as an oracle, was, unfortunately, the butt of the boys, but was likewise the sport of the baby-elephant. Many a time have I seen him hustled over by the youngster, who seemed to have picked him out as his playmate. Slyly and softly stealing up behind, he would suddenly increase his pace, and, with a quick shuffle or a sudden lurch, shoulder him sprawling to the ground. Portow, during this part of the journey, behaved like a hunted man, ever looking behind to see whether the dreadful infant was behind."

My friend, Dr. Cushing, who had been put in charge of the train, and our prince-guide, both believed in the oriental idea of making an impression by as imposing a pageant as possible. On nearing Chieng Răi, they marshalled us in procession, so that we entered the city in state, with ten armed men leading the way. Possibly it had its desired effect, for a warm welcome was given us, and every aid was granted.

In the eleven years since my first visit there with Dr. Vrooman, the city had grown in size. The fertility of its soil and the large extent of its arable land were sure to attract still larger population from the south. In addition to these natural advantages, it had then another strong claim for a mission station. While all the other Lăo states, through their rulers, submitted to the introduction of Christianity rather than welcomed it, Chieng Răi and Chieng Sĕn were exceptions. The rulers of both desired the presence of the missionaries.

The Sunday spent there was a welcome day of rest.

The week had been a strenuous one. In the morning we held a public service—the first ever held there. Mr. Hallett and our prince-guide attended, and curiosity collected quite a congregation. After tiffin, Dr. Cushing and I spent several hours—the first quiet ones we had had—reading in the monastery grounds at the great bend of the river.

That evening I met the governor at home and, save for the presence of his wife, alone. His intelligent enquiries as to the truths and teachings of our religion showed that he had already thought much on the subject. Krū Nān Tă and he were not very distant relatives, and had had many conversations on the subject. His regard for our mission and his earnest desire for a mission station, as well as the protection he afterwards gave the Christians when they were wronged, had, I believe, a deeper foundation than an intellectual interest, or even a personal friendship for us.

Our next stage was Chieng Sĕn. There Nān Suwan, our ruling elder, and his family gave us a warm welcome. He met us at the city gate, hardly hoping there would be a missionary in the expedition, which, rumour told him, was coming. His house stood on the bank of the river, just where Dr. Vrooman and I landed thirteen years before, when the only occupants were wild beasts. The new settlers had been so busy providing housing and sustenance for themselves, that only one monastery building had been roofed, and only a portion of its images stored under shelter. Our old friend the governor had only a bamboo residence. Nān Suwan had made friends by the help of the quinine with which he had been supplied, and he had the best house in the city. It served, also, as a chapel, in which, with grateful hearts, we worshipped on Sunday.

The governor was even more insistent in his demand for a mission station than the governor of Chieng Râi had been. He even offered to send down elephants to move us up, if we would come. His was not the deep religious nature of the Chieng Rāi governor. He possibly believed that in their sphere all religions were alike good. He urged, as he had done before, that we might even then forestall the monasteries and preoccupy the field. Nothing would have pleased me more, had it been possible, than to accept the cordial invitation. It was true, as the governor said, "The people must and will have some religion. If you do not give them Christianity, they must take Buddhism." It was only necessity that could resist such a plea. But half a loaf is better than no bread. If we were not ready to start a regular station in Chieng Sên, we must somehow work the field as best we could. That consideration determined my long tours in the dry seasons of the years that followed.

Up to this time I had never been properly equipped and outfitted for such tours. One outcome of this trip was a great improvement in my means of transportation for the future. An application made long before this to the Board for an elephant, had been received as a huge joke. But now it happened that in the assignment of elephants for our upward trip, a large *sadaw*—a male without tusks—had fallen to me. He proved to be an exceptionally fine beast belonging to an estate about to be divided. He must be sold, and was held at a very cheap figure. With the help of a contribution by Mr. Hallett, and the hire paid for its use, I was able to purchase it. The deputy governor gave me a good howdah for it. I was as proud of my new acquisition as ever a boy was of a new toy. But since few elephants will travel well alone, I now needed a mate for him. Before long I was fortunate enough to get a cheap and equally good female. I was then prepared for my long tours. I could cross streams in safety, and be protected from rain, even if my journey were prolonged beyond the limits of the dry season.

On our return journey, in Mûang Payao, we came in contact with the worst epidemic of smallpox that I have ever seen. We met it at every turn in the street. With difficulty could we keep parents with children, all broken out with the disease, in their arms, from crowding round us in our sālā. We had hardly taken our seats on the rugs spread for us at the governor's official reception of Mr. Hallett, when we discovered cases of smallpox all about us. Dr. Cushing was nervously afraid of it, and retired. I had to remain an hour as interpreter. Imagine our consternation on reaching the next station to find that the Doctor showed unmistakable signs of having contracted the dreadful disease, although he had been vaccinated in his youth. What a discovery to be made on a journey, and four days from home! On consultation it was thought best to hasten on to Chiengmai, a thing which our mode of travel made possible. Mr. and Mrs. Chalmers Martin had arrived during our absence, and had taken up their quarters in our house. It was, therefore, impossible to take our sick friend in. We did the next best thing, and gave him a new bamboo house on our hospital lot, where Dr. Peoples carefully watched over him till he made a rapid recovery, and was able to return home in a boat as far as Bangkok, and thence by sea *via* Singapore. It was a sad close, however, to our pleasant visit together, and to our otherwise interesting and profitable tour.

I returned from Chieng Sên, as we have seen, with an elephant of my own. On reaching home I found awaiting me the best pony I ever had. It was sent to me as a present from the governor of Mê Hawng Sawn, near the Salwin River. I had never been to Mê Hawng Sawn, and had but a very limited acquaintance with the governor. According to my uniform custom in those days, on his official visits to Chiengmai, I had twice called upon him as the governor of a neighbouring province. On both occasions we had conversation on the different merits of the two religions. On one of these visits he had brought down some ponies to sell, and on my asking the price of one he said, "I am very sorry that I have sold all my gentle ones. There is only one left. If you can use him, I shall be glad to give him to you." It is a McGilvary trait not to be timid about horses, and I said, "I will try him." So the pony was sent down to my house; but he proved rather too much for my horsemanship. The first time I mounted him, he threw me and sprained my wrist. It was the unanimous vote of the family that he be returned with thanks. The governor sent back word that he was very sorry; but never mind; when he reached home he would see to it that I had a good pony—a message which, I am sorry to say, I took as a good oriental compliment. I had even forgotten all about the matter, when, on my return from this trip, I found the pony in my stable. He was a most valuable and timely present.

But we are not quite done with Mr. Hallett's survey. He made a short excursion without an interpreter to the hot springs. But his final trip was to be to Mûang Fāng, six days to the north and west of the route previously taken, and distant some eighty-three miles from Chiengmai. His object was to see if there were not an easier route to Chieng Rāi down the valleys of the Mê Fāng and the Mê Kok. The trip strongly appealed both to Mr. Martin and to me, and we gladly accepted Mr. Hallett's invitation to accompany him.

Mûang Fāng was an ancient city captured and destroyed by the Burmese in 1717; so that it lay in ruins nearly two hundred years before it was repeopled. Besides Mûang Fāng, we visited, either in going or returning, four other cities—Chieng Dāo, Mûang Ngāi, Mûang Pāo, and Mûang Kên. Not far to the south of Mûang Fāng we visited the cave of Top Tao, noted in the Buddhist legends of Northern Siam. Mr. Hallett thus describes our experiences there:

"Inside was a lofty cavern lighted by a natural skylight. On a raised platform in the cave was a great reclining image of Buddha some thirty feet long, and around it a number of figures representing his disciples. Numerous small wooden and stone images of Buddha had been placed by pious pilgrims about the platforms. Pillows, mattresses, robes, yellow drapery, flags, water-bottles, rice-bowls, fans, dolls, images of temples, doll's houses for the spirits, and all sorts of trumpery, were lying together with fresh and faded flowers that had been offered to the images, and were strewn in front of them. A steep ladder led up to niches near the roof of the cave, in which images were enshrined.

"My companions, full of ardor, determined to explore the inner recesses of the cave, and accordingly lighted their torches and proceeded further into the bowels of the earth, whilst I enjoyed a quiet smoke amongst the gods. Down they went, creeping through low, narrow passages, over rocks, and along ledges, with chasms and pits lining their path as the cave expanded—bottomless as far as they could judge by the faint light of their torches, but really not more than twenty or thirty feet deep—until they could get no further, and had to return, having proceeded about the eighth of a mile."

That night brought us to the Mê Fāng River. The narrative proceeds:

"Here we spent the most unpleasant night we had yet spent, as we were troubled with rain, heat, and mosquitoes. We were told that game was plentiful. Wild cattle larger than buffaloes come in droves from the hills to graze in the plain, while the rhinoceros and the elephant roam about the plains.

"At our next stopping place, after we had settled ourselves in an empty house, a villager came to inform us that the house belonged to the Chief of Mûang Fāng, and that anybody that slept in it would have his head cut off. As rain was threatening, we determined to risk the penalty, and we were soon glad that we had done so, as the rain poured down in torrents."

There is a small deer called tamnê, which twenty years ago was very abundant in all the northern provinces. They are not found in the very tall grass of the river-bottoms, but in grass about waist-high thickly covering the higher plains. They have their beds in this grass by day, and graze at night. They are lower than the grass, and never leap so as to show the body, but glide smoothly along as if swimming, discovering their presence only through the parting and waving of the grass. Sometimes you get right upon them before they will run.

One Saturday we got Mr. Hallett interested in some survey or calculations not requiring the aid of an interpreter, and Mr. Martin and I had our first deer-hunt.

We took six of our elephants, and, going out about an hour's ride or more from the city, we formed in open order abreast, about forty yards apart, and in perfect silence moved forward over the plain. The hunter thus starts his own game. He sits on the back, or, better still, on the neck of his elephant, with gun cocked, ready for a shot at the first noise or movement in the grass. We started about a dozen of the deer, and emptied many cartridges, but came back to camp with no meat—much to Mr. Hallett's disgust.

Mûang Fāng, like Chieng Sên, was rich in images of all sizes and materials. I never saw finer bronze ones. It was a favourite field from which Siamese princes and officials could get a supply otherwise unattainable in those days. Of course, *they* have a right to them. But when a German traveller undertook a wholesale speculation in the images of Buddha, it was quite another matter, and he got into serious difficulty with the government.

Soon after our return to Chiengmai, Mr. Hallett left us for Bangkok. From his long residence in Burma and from his close connection with the mission and missionaries during his expedition among what he calls the Shan States, he understood the methods and results of missionary work better than most visitors who have written upon the subject. The kind words of the dedication of his book, though often quoted, may well conclude this chapter.

"To the American Missionaries in Burma and Siam and the Shan States I dedicate this book, as a mark of the high esteem in which I hold the noble work the American Baptist Mission and the American Presbyterian Mission are accomplishing in civilizing and Christianizing the people of Indo-China."

XXIII

EVANGELISTIC TRAINING

ON our return from the surveying expedition in the summer of 1884, we found F. B. Gould, Esq., our first British Vice-Consul, already established in Chiengmai. It was an important event for the country; since a British official in any place is a guarantee that at least the outward forms of law and justice will be observed. In one important sense, too, it marked a new era for the mission, or, at least, for the missionaries.

Those who have not tried can hardly imagine the privation of living eighteen years without a mail system of any kind. Our only dependence so far was on catching chance trading boats to and from Bangkok. These were always an uncertain quantity; in very low water they almost ceased to travel. Some boatmen preferred not to be responsible for the mail, not knowing what it might contain. In the great city of Bangkok, and even in Chiengmai, it required a constant effort to keep ourselves informed of the departures of boats. The consequence was that an absence of news from children, friends, and the outside world generally, for three or four months at a time, was very common. Sometimes the interval was as much as eight months. Add to this the time of the long river trip, and our news sometimes would be nearly a year old when it reached us. Mr. Wilson's family and mine had schooled ourselves to these conditions; but to those who had been accustomed to a daily mail, they must have been almost unendurable.

The new Vice-Consul came, determined by all means to get some regular communication established, if it were only a monthly one. We were only too glad to do whatever we could to that end. It was a matter of pride to both parties that we arranged at once for a regular and most successful semi-monthly mail overland to Maulmein. I furnished a reliable Christian man for chief contractor, and good men for carriers. Since Mr. Gould had as yet no authority from his government to incur any expense, the arrangement was wholly a private affair, with the understanding that all who availed themselves of it should pay a quarterly assessment for the maintenance of the line. But in a short time the British government assumed the whole expense. Mr. Gould promised to get the staff exempt from corvée, or compulsory government service. He had to use his official authority for that.

The Lāo government had absolutely no interest in a mail, whether weekly or yearly; but the Siamese looked rather askance at having in their own country a mail service over which they had no control. It seemed to be in some way a reflection on their national pride. There is little doubt that our private enterprise hastened the weekly government mail from Bangkok, which was started the next year. And since the Maulmein route is quicker by two weeks than the one by Bangkok, the Siamese government has of late maintained both, the two meeting at Rahêng, and giving us a very creditable and regular mail service.

In the spring of 1884 the mission sustained a great

loss in the death of Princess Tipa Kĕsawn, Prince Intanon's consort, whom we were in the habit of calling "the Queen." Placed as she was, she could not well have avoided the making of priests' garments, and the going through with the form of making offerings to the spirits. But I seriously doubt whether she had any expectation of laying up thereby a store of merit for the future. One thing we do know, that in her last sickness she turned no anxious look to any of these things, at a time when thoughtful Buddhists are always most diligent in their efforts. Dr. Peoples of our mission attended her in her last illness, and the case was submitted entirely to him. Mrs. McGilvary and I were both with her the day before she died. Mrs. McGilvary was with her at her death, and remained to see the body dressed for the coffin. We missed her very much as a friend, and the whole country missed her as a balance-wheel for her husband.

On the arrival of the reinforcement in 1883, a Presbytery was organized of the four ministers, Wilson, Peoples, Hearst, and McGilvary. I was then full of the idea of a theological training-class. My experience of the accumulated power added to the missionary's efforts by having such assistants as Nān Inta, Nān Suwan, and Noi Intachak, raised in my mind the question, Why not increase the number? Having had no schools, we had, of course, no body of young men educated on Christian lines whom we might train for the ministry; and we could not have such for years to come. But we had in our churches mature men of deeply religious nature, earnest students of Buddhism, and carefully educated in all the learning of their race. And a man so trained has many compensations for his lack of training in our elementary schools. He knows the sacred books of his own people, their strength and their weakness. He understands the thoughts, the needs, and the difficulties of a Buddhist enquirer, and the mode of argument by which these difficulties are to be met, as no young man of his own race, and as no foreign teacher can do. The training needed to make such a man an efficient preacher of the Gospel, is training in the Christian Scriptures, together with practical experience in evangelistic work under efficient direction.

I was at that time giving regular instruction to Noi Intachak, one of the finest young men I have ever known in that country, and very anxious to become a minister.[1] To Nān Tā, afterwards our efficient minister, I was giving instruction less regularly, as it was possible for him to take it. But it would have been both easier and more profitable to teach a class of six or eight. By qualifying such a group of young men to work, and then working with them and through them, I believed that my own efficiency could be quadrupled, or even sextupled, as it was doubled when I had Nān Inta to work with.

With these thoughts and this experience impressed on my mind, and in order that my plan, if adopted, might have the ecclésiastical sanction of the Presbytery as well as the corporate sanction of the mission, I had urged the organization of the Presbytery just as soon as we had the minimum quorum required. In order to give the discussion its proper outlook and perspective, I noticed, also, in the paper which I read before the Presbytery, the necessity of a general edu-

[1] Our hopes for his future career, alas, were cut short by his untimely death in the following year.

cation for all our Christians, and of High Schools for both sexes; while I sketched more in detail the nature and the methods of special instruction intended for those in training to become evangelists and ministers.

The training proposed for this last group was intended primarily to equip the most capable and most promising individuals among the converts for filling well their places as lay officers and leaders in the churches, and for engaging intelligently in evangelistic work. But beyond this it was thought that it would ultimately furnish a body of picked men from whom again the best might be chosen as candidates for further instruction leading up to the ministerial office. The course was to be flexible enough to permit occasional attendance with profit on the part of men whose household duties or whose business would not permit them to attend regularly. Its special feature was actual and constant practice in evangelistic work under the direction and supervision of the Principal, and with him as his assistants on his tours.

In view of the poverty of the Lāo generally, and in order to make it possible for these men to maintain their families while occupied with this training, it was further proposed that they should receive a moderate allowance of, perhaps, eight rupees per month of actual service, or about three dollars of our money. This seemed not unreasonable, since in Christian lands it is thought a wise provision to assist students in their preparation for the ministry; and since what is required to support one European missionary family, would support half a dozen fairly educated native ministers or ten good native evangelists.

The Presbytery took hold of the scheme with much ardour, and at once began to organize it into shape, but on far too large a scale, and with far too formidable and too foreign apparatus. A regular "Board of Education" was created, with rules and regulations better suited to American conditions than to those of the Lāo churches. A committee was further appointed to examine all applicants for the course, much after the manner of receiving candidates for the ministry under the care of a Presbytery. Their "motives for seeking the ministry" were to be enquired into, while as yet it was not at all known whether they would desire to become ministers. The allowance in each case was to be the absolute minimum which it was supposed would suffice for the maintenance of the student after he had provided all that he could himself. Noi Intachak, for example, was allowed the maximum of eight rupees a month, while Noi Chai—one of the best Buddhist scholars in the country, a young man with a family, living ten miles away in the country—was allowed five rupees, on the ground that he was not very poor; while yet another was allowed but three.

After this ordeal—which was thought to be a good test of their sincerity—the rest of the six or eight candidates for instruction declined to commit themselves. None of them understood exactly what the Board of Education was about. I myself was greatly disappointed at the outcome. After a week of listless study, Noi Chai begged to be allowed to withdraw, and the whole thing was disbanded. My hopeful private class was killed by too much "red tape," and with it all possibility of a training-class for four years to come. I was again set free for long tours and my favourite evangelistic work.

I continued to teach Noi Intachak till his lamented death, and I devoted what spare time I could to teaching the long-time wanderer, Nān Tā, who had become our best evangelist. There seems to have been some fatality connected with all our efforts to establish a theological training-school. When the next attempt was made, under Mr. Dodd's direction, with a large and interesting class enthusiastically taught, through some cause or combination of causes—for it would be difficult to specify any single one as alone determinative—it was allowed to slip out of our hands. Possibly a leading cause in this case was the same that was operative in the other. At a time when the mission was pressing the idea of self-support to its breaking point, an allowance probably too scanty was offered in the evangelistic work to the men who had been trained for it. The whole question in the Lāo field, as it doubtless is in others, is a difficult one. As wages in other departments rise, and the demand for competent men becomes more pressing both in governmental and in private business, the question will become more difficult still. While on the one hand there is the danger of making a mercenary ministry, on the other hand we must remember that, the world over, educated labour now costs more, but is not, therefore, necessarily dearer. The same penny-wise and pound-foolish policy has lost us the strength of some of the best men in our church, our schools, our hospitals, and our printing-press, because more lucrative positions are offered elsewhere. But we must remember first of all that theological schools, like all others, are not made, but grow; and, second, that the law of competition prevails here, too, as well as elsewhere. It is easy to say that it ought not to do so, as between the ministry and other professions, or between the missionary work and other more lucrative callings. But to a certain extent the same law does hold, and it is a fact to be reckoned with.

In May, 1884, H. R. H. Prince Krommamûn Bijit, a brother of the King of Siam, arrived and took up his residence in Chiengmai—probably to give prestige to the High Commissioner, and possibly to smooth the road of the new British Consul. It was an open secret that the Prince of Chiengmai could see no need whatever for a British Resident, and at times he was not slow to make his views known. For a while the relations between the two were somewhat strained. Yet it was of the utmost importance that the relations between England and Siam should remain cordial. At the same time it was a part of the plan of Siam, since fully carried out, to assume complete control of the government in the northern states. What was of more special interest to us was, as we shall see, not only that Prince Bijit was personally friendly, but that he brought with him substantial evidence of the good will of His Majesty and of the Siamese government toward our work.

It was in this year that our first attempt at establishing a mountain sanitarium was made. It was designed to furnish a refuge from the great heat of the plain, to be a retreat for invalids, and a place where new missionaries might more safely become acclimatized, and still be studying the language. But as a matter of fact, new missionaries are put to work so promptly that it is about as hard for them to withdraw from the battle as it is for the older ones. Since we kept no watchman on the premises, the sanitarium was afterwards burned down—possibly by forest fires. Later a better and more convenient situation was found nearer the city, so near that a man can ride up in the evening, spend the night there with his family, and return in the morning to his work for the day. It is in a delightful situation beside a cool brook, but is too low for the best results as a health resort.

At the Annual Meeting in December, the importance of opening a new station in Lakawn was discussed. The baptism of the officer from that city, and the organization of a church there, have already been mentioned. The officer was constant in his appeals for the establishment of a station there, with a missionary in residence. Although Mr. Wilson was soon to start with his family for the United States on a furlough, there would still be left in Chiengmai—if I were sent to Lakawn—two ministers and two physicians, even if these were but three men in all. Besides, there were beginning to be some good native assistants in Chiengmai. No one had expressed a desire to open a new station, and no one had been sounded in regard to the matter. So I determined to make now the visit to Lakawn which I had planned for the previous fall, but had been unable to accomplish. My wife and our little son Norwood were to accompany me. When our preparations were well advanced, what was our delight to find that Dr. and Mrs. Peoples wished to accompany us, if they could obtain elephants. When this was mentioned to Prince Bijit, he not only volunteered the elephants, but informed us that he had authority from His Majesty to see that we had a lot for our station there, and, furthermore, that, in passing through Lakawn, he had already secured for us one of the most desirable lots in the place. In addition to this, His Majesty had sent by him two thousand rupees as a contribution toward the new station and a hospital. Who could fail to see that the guiding hand of the Lord was in it! Before this I had written to our United States Consul to get permission to secure a lot there, but had never once thought of a contribution, much less of one so liberal. Mrs. McGilvary thus reports our trip in a letter to our daughter:

"Lakawn, January 30th, 1885. We reached Lampūn on Friday. I curtained off one end of the sālā just north of the city, and Mrs. Peoples did the same at the other end, leaving the space between and the veranda for callers. There we spent the Sabbath. Your father preached twice to very attentive audiences. We were impressed with the favourable prospect for mission work, and hope to make a longer visit to the place soon. We left on Monday, and reached this place on Thursday noon, and lodged in a public sālā just opposite the beautiful lot which the Prince has given us for a station. It is in a fine site, one of the best in the city. We called on the Chief this morning, and all seemed pleased at the prospect of having a mission station here. It is not yet settled who is to open it. We are willing to come, and so are Dr. and Mrs. Peoples."

As may well be imagined, we returned to Chiengmai with grateful hearts for the many providences that had favoured us. The new station was assured. We had not then thought of keeping two physicians for Chiengmai. Dr. Cheek had charge of the medical work. Dr. Peoples, naturally, preferred a field where he would have ample scope both for his medical profession and for the itinerating work of which he was equally fond. His double profession and other qualifications fitted him as no one else could be fitted for opening the new station. On my wife's account I was very willing to yield him the pleasure—for such

PRESBYTERY, RETURNING FROM MEETING IN LAKAWN

to me it has always been—of breaking new ground. Mrs. McGilvary had already had the labour and self-denial of opening two stations, one of which was a new mission. The importance of Lakawn as the next station could not be challenged. Dr. and Mrs. Peoples themselves were pleased with the place and the prospect of the new field. So they were unanimously appointed and set apart to the new and important work.

XXIV

STRUGGLE WITH THE POWERS OF DARKNESS

THE belief in witchcraft was still prevalent everywhere, and this year brought us striking illustrations of its cruel power. An elderly man with his wife and family, living in one of the outlying villages, was accused of witchcraft. The pair of elephants which he owned and used had belonged to a man suspected of harbouring a malicious spirit; and it was thought that the demon had followed these elephants into the family of their new master. The family was promptly ostracized; but by driving off her husband with his elephants, the wife might avoid expulsion, and might save for herself and her daughters the comfortable home. I endeavoured in vain to prevent this outcome. "I am much more afraid of the spirits," said the wife, "than of bears and tigers." The husband could no longer face the universal odium which he encountered, and so was driven forth. But the spirits served the old man a good turn—they drove him into the Christian religion, which he lives to adorn, and they gave him two good elephants. The family afterwards applied for one of them. As a matter of equity he gave up one, and lived comfortably with a Christian son on the proceeds of the sale of the other.

Then there was a great epidemic of fever in Bān Pĕn in the neighbouring province of Lampūn. Few homes were left without sad hearts and vacant places through the death of one or more members. The destroyer must be some demon which had taken up its abode in a human habitation, and was preying on the inhabitants of the village. The family of one of the most prosperous men in the village was finally selected as the one which must be the abode of the destroyer. As they could hardly decide in which particular member of it the demon resided, they regarded all with equal suspicion, and proceeded to wreak their vengeance to the uttermost upon them all.

First, according to the usual custom, anonymous letters were dropped at the gate, warning the family to flee, or dire would be the consequences. When threats failed, armed with an order from the court, the whole village appeared on the scene and compelled the family to flee for their lives. No sooner were they out of the way than their two large teak dwelling-houses, with rice-bins, outhouses, etc., were torn down and scattered piecemeal over the lot. Not even a tree or shrub was left on the place. To gain a breathing-spell, the family moved into a bamboo shed hastily extemporized on the banks of the Mê Ping, some two miles distant from what had been their home. By some accident they were directed to our mission. They had learned that the King's edict protected the Christians, and, above all, that the Christian religion protected them from all fear of evil spirits. And so they came to see if it were true, and if there were any refuge for them.

Whatever was to be done for them in the way of earthly succor, must evidently be done quickly. Their neighbours in their temporary refuge would doubtless soon drive them away again. At the earnest entreaty of the man I took one of the elders, and went down to look into the case for myself. It was heartrending. Whatever they had been able to snatch from the wreck of a well-to-do home—beds, bedding, furniture, kitchen utensils—was heaped up in a pile that covered the whole floor-space of their shack. The great-grandmother, helpless in her dotage, and the little children, were lying here and there wherever a smoother spot could be found. Their case seemed almost hopeless as far as human aid was concerned. Nān Chaiwana had himself appealed for aid both to the court and to the governor, and had been told that there was nothing they could do for him. The court was committed against him. The governor, however, was personally friendly to us, and had shown no ill will towards the man. It was barely possible that something might be accomplished there. We all had worship together amid the confusion of their hut—the first Christian service they had ever attended. They assured us of their joyful acceptance of the Gospel, and pledged obedience to all its teachings. We promised to do whatever we could in their behalf, and returned home.

Next day Mr. Martin and I went down to Lampūn to call on the governor. He was not at home, but in the ricefields several miles out in the country. We followed him there. He received us kindly, but said, "Were I to make proclamation to protect that family, it would be impossible to enforce it. Nearly everybody in that neighbourhood believes that the bodies or ashes of fathers, mothers, brothers, sisters, or children are in that graveyard, sent there by the demon in that family. If you can devise some plan to protect them, you are welcome to try it; but if they return to that village, I cannot be responsible for the results."

When told that they had now renounced the spirits, and put themselves under the Great Spirit, he said, "That is all very well, but how am I to convince the others that *they* are safe?" We then begged that he would give the place over to us. We wanted a place for preaching. We would put up one of the houses and establish a Christian family in it, with medicine to cure their fevers. I would oversee it, but would ask the family to help in the work. To this he readily consented. We trusted his promise, and we returned encouraged.

A few evenings later I arrived on the scene with our elder and some other Christians, and pitched tent at the edge of the ricefield, a hundred yards from the deserted lot, to engage in a contest with the destroying demon. It was, moreover, a crucial contest as between Christianity and demonism. Our whole future work in that province, and, to a large extent, throughout the land, depended on the result. Soon curiosity brought to our tent the head man and a large number of the villagers. We spent the evening in preaching to them. When asked what we proposed to do with the situation, we explained that we had come to take possession of the house and lot—the governor had given it over to the mission for a station. It was now the property of the Christians, over whom the spirits had no power. It was to be dedicated to the Lord's work, and we even asked their aid.

Next morning we began work, bringing in some of the men of the outcast family to assist in identifying and reassembling the scattered timbers of the house. With much difficulty bone was joined to bone, and timber to timber. In a few days some of the villagers offered to be hired to help. One or two women of the family came over to cook for the workmen. Before long one house was set up, roofed, and floored; whereupon we moved up into it, and invited the neighbours to attend its dedication that evening. The evening was spent in song and prayer and praise. Many came up into the house. More listened from the ground below. We had given quinine to the fever patients, who were glad to get well by the help of Christian medicine. Meanwhile the epidemic subsided, and the worst fears of the people were allayed.

When it became necessary for me to return to Chiengmai, I left the elder to furnish moral support to the poor outcasts, who, little by little, came back to their home, and became the Christian family which we had promised to establish there. To save the land from being utterly lost to him, Nān Chaiwana had mortgaged it to one of the princes for the trifling sum of one hundred rupees. Not trusting to the prince's unselfishness, I took Nān Chaiwana's own money, paid the mortgage, and with some regret the prince released the property to me. Thus was it all restored to the family. Mr. Martin and I visited the station as often as we could. It became an interesting centre for our work, and ultimately grew into the Bethel church.

While I was engaged in this work, a strange thing was doing on the other side of the Mê Ping. One day a man came in from the "Big Tamarind Tree Village" to tell us that his whole village had become Christians, and were building a chapel. When it was finished, he would invite us to come down and indoctrinate the people in the teachings of our religion. This was something new, and, of course, most interesting. In due time the man came to Chiengmai to inform us that the chapel was finished, and we were invited to go down, take possession, dedicate it, and teach the people.

On the following Friday, Mr. Martin and I took boat and went to the village landing, where we separated, he going east to receive and baptize the converts in the "new home of the teachers," as the house at Bān Pên long was called; and I to dedicate the new chapel at the "Big Tamarind Tree Village." I found the chapel there all right, and the whole village assembled to welcome the teacher; and, apparently, like the audience that Peter found in the house of Cornelius, ready "to hear words whereby they might be saved." The chapel was built mostly of bamboo, but so new and neat that I complimented the villagers, and expressed my great delight. After our reception, I invited them up into the chapel for worship, and began by announcing a hymn, and inviting them to join in learning to sing it; expecting, with my assistant and other Christians who had accompanied me, to spend the time in teaching them what Christianity is; presuming that their reception of it was a foregone conclusion.

But somehow things did not seem to run smoothly. I was conscious of being in a wrong atmosphere. The leader of the movement seemed ill at ease. None entered in with the accustomed zeal of new converts. My assistant noticed the same thing, and whispered in my ear that something was wrong. They were whispering to him, "Where is the money?" "What money?" "Why, the fifty or one hundred rupees that we were told would surely be forthcoming to every family that aided in the building, and that entered the new religion. The foreigners are rich, and, of course, will be delighted to distribute money freely." The leader, of course, expected the lion's share. It had all been a mere business venture on his part—or, rather, a swindle! This was on Saturday. On Monday morning Mr. Martin and I met at the boat according to agreement, he to report a good day and the baptism of ten adults along with as many children, and the reception of a number of catechumens; and I to confess how I had been sold.

In the summer of 1885 a most interesting work was started in some villages to the southwest of the city. Our indefatigable Nān Tā had visited that region, and many had professed their faith. Mr. Martin and I both responded to the call, and made a number of visits there. Two chapels were built by the enquirers, one at Lawng Kum, and one at Chāng Kam. I quote the following account of this work from the New York *Observer:*

"June 9th, 1885.—I have just returned from the villages referred to in my last letter. I found twenty-two families of professed believers at Lawng Kum Chapel, which with the aid of a few dollars from elsewhere they had succeeded in building. Among them are at least six persons who give good evidence of a change of heart, and the rest are interesting enquirers. Ten miles from there, at Chāng Kam, I visited by invitation another company who had renounced Buddhism, and who call themselves Christians. On arriving there a roll of thirty-five families was handed me. Most of them had attended worship at times in the chapel at Chiengmai, and a few of them are no doubt true Christians. Here also we secured a native house for a chapel. They contributed a part of the small sum needed, while in this case, as in the other, their contribution was supplemented from the monthly contributions of the church in Chiengmai. Deputations have been sent also from places still further away, representing in one case twenty, and in another case twelve families enrolled by themselves, with others only waiting for the arrival of a teacher.

"It is probably premature to predict what will be the result of all this. The simultaneousness of the movement in villages thirty or forty miles apart is remarkable. It shows a longing for something they have not. To turn this awakening to most account, we need more help, both native and foreign. Mr. Martin enters into the work with all his zeal, and has contributed no little toward keeping up the interest."

Our expectations in regard to the work at Lawng Kum were disappointed mainly by removals of families to other places. The chapel in Chăng Kam was burned down by incendiaries, but was soon replaced, and the village has continued to be one of our most important out-stations. Its people have recently [1910] built a new and large chapel, and will soon be organized into a church. One zealous man in Mê Āo led first his own family and then his neighbours into the faith, till they, too, have now a chapel built of teak, with a band of faithful workers to worship in it.

Our first visits to these new places were intensely interesting. It seemed as if the Gospel would be embraced by whole villages. But the burning of the chapel tells a tale of a strong adverse influence. Opposition usually drives off the timid and the merely curious. The lines, then, are sharply drawn, and the Christian society really finds itself.

During the last week of the year I spent a few days at the village of Mê Dawk Dêng to hold a communion service there, and incidentally to give my family and the teachers of the Girls' School a much-needed outing. It was at the height of the rice-harvest, and, one evening, we all greatly enjoyed the sight of a regular rice-threshing "bee" at the farm of one of our elders. The "bee" is always at night. The bundles of rice from the harvest-field are piled up so as to form a wall five feet high around a space of some twenty-five feet square, with an opening for entrance at one corner. In the centre of this square is a horizontal frame of bamboo poles, against which the bundles of rice-heads are forcibly struck. The grain falls to the ground below, and the straw is tossed outside. In those days the whole plain at rice-harvest was lighted up by bonfires of the burning straw—a glorious sight as I have watched it from Doi Sutēp.

We pitched our tent near by to enjoy the scene. The men and boys do the threshing, while the women and girls do the cooking for the feast with which the work ends. The village maidens are always on hand to encourage their beaux in their work by passing to them water or betel-nut, and to serve the viands at the feast. It reminded me much of the husking bees I had seen as a lad in the South seventy years ago. How near of kin is all the world!

We had a delightful communion service on the Sabbath. Seven adults and six children were baptized. On Monday morning we returned home refreshed and better prepared for the work before us.

The year had been one of marked progress. The Girls' School had been strengthened by the arrival of Miss Lizzie Westervelt. The new station at Lakawn had been opened, and Dr. and Mrs. Peoples had been installed there. More new work had been opened in the neighbourhood of Chiengmai and Lampūn than in any one year of the history of the mission. One hun-

MARKET SCENE IN CHIENGMAI

IN THE HARVEST FIELD

dred and two adults were added to the communion roll, and about as many children were baptized. Our new "witchcraft-house" at Bān Pên, with its hospitable family, afforded a comfortable prophet's chamber for the missionaries and a chapel for worship. The Bethel church was afterwards organized in it. That family became highly respected, and has furnished some of the most influential members of our church. The work in Nawng Fān, seven miles south of Chiengmai—Nān Inta's village—had steadily grown. It still continues to be one of our best out-stations, and will, during the present year [1910] be organized into a church.

XXV

CHRISTIAN COMMUNITIES PLANTED

THE year 1886 opened auspiciously. But Mr. Martin had brought malaria in his system from his old home; and the Lāo country is a better place for contracting the infection than for eradicating it. He worked indefatigably, but seldom with a blood-temperature down to the normal. In January he accepted an invitation from Mr. Gould, the British Vice-Consul, to accompany him on a tour of inspection through the northern provinces, hoping that the change might prove beneficial. It afforded, moreover, opportunity for some missionary work in places seldom or never visited. He was the first to visit the Mūsô villages high up among the mountains. He baptized a few converts in Chieng Sĕn, and reported an interest there that should be followed up.

About this same time Krū Nān Tā—for such, though not yet ordained, I shall in future call him—returned from Chieng Rāi with a most encouraging report of developments there. Later a deputation of seven men, with Tāo Tĕpasing as their leader, came to us from the village of Mê Kawn in the Chieng Rāi province, earnestly entreating a visit from the missionary. In their number was Pū King from Chieng Rāi, who had been a notorious bandit, robber, and murderer. He had now submitted to the government, and was given a place as public executioner and as doer of other jobs from which only a lawless man would not shrink. Before meeting Krū Nān Tā, he had gone so deep in sin that no hope was left him, and he became hardened in despair. But his conscience was ill at ease. Hearing rumours of the Christian religion, he determined that if it could give him hope of pardon, he would seek it at any cost. He and his wife walked one hundred and ten miles to see if it were really true that Jesus could save even him. Our good friend the governor encouraged his coming, and said, "If the Christian religion can make a good man out of Pū King, I shall have no more doubts of its truth and power." And we have no doubt that it did that very thing.

In a few days Krū Nān Tā and I returned with the party. Elder Āi Tū of Chieng Rāi,[1] with his family, accompanied us. We thus had quite a little congregation to worship nightly about the camp-fire, and every one of the party was either a Christian or an enquirer. This was my third trip to the north, and the first of those annual trips that have made that road so familiar to me.

The little colony of Christians at Wieng Pā Pāo was prospering. One of them was the man whom his wife had driven off, elephants and all, for witchcraft. Nān Tā reported the governor of the place as a believer. He had ceased to make offerings in temples, and he ridiculed the idols. He received us most hospitably, and desired to have a mission station there. Afterwards, however, through policy and the influence of a Burmese son-in-law, he resumed his old worship; though to the last in his heart of hearts, I think, he believed our teachings to be true. In the case of subordinate officials, the final step of joining the church is terribly hard to take.

[1] Afterwards Prayā Pakdī.

At Salī Toi, " Grandma " Pan had been praying day and night for our coming. She lived some distance away from the road, and feared that we might pass her by. She was overjoyed to see us, and we had to check the homage she offered us. The poor woman was sadly in need of support. She was the only Christian in the place, and was surrounded by hostile neighbours who absolutely rebelled against her establishing herself in the place. Her family had renounced the spirits, and therefore her "patriarch," to whom she could rightly look for protection, became her chief accuser. He went to the governor of Chieng Rāi for an order forbidding her to settle there. But he had his thirty-mile walk for his trouble. The governor told him that the family was not to be interfered with. How could he forbid those whom the King's edict allowed?

Having failed with the governor, they tried to draw away the daughter-in-law. But she said she would stick by her husband and his family. Their religion should be her religion, and their God should be her God. The villagers then notified the family that it would be held responsible for the value of any buffalo or elephant that might die in the village. The theory was that the demons would take vengeance on the village for allowing the trespass of an enemy on their domains. But all their efforts to shake the poor woman's faith were futile.

At Mê Kawn village, from which the delegation had chiefly come, of course we were received with a warm welcome. On the recent visit of Nān Tā, when the leading supporters of the temple became Christians, the less religious families also deserted it. I even saw oxen sheltered from the rain under its roof. A club-footed man, Noi Tāliya by name, a good scholar in

Ngio, Burmese, and Lāo, had been the life of the temple. And it is the earnest Buddhist that makes the earnest Christian. His son first heard the Gospel, and, coming home, explained it to his father. Calling his family together, the father said to them, "There are the spirit shrines. Any one may have them who wishes to continue their worship." No one making a bid for them, a bonfire was made, and the once valued treasures all vanished in smoke. When he went to Chieng Rāi to announce his conversion to the governor and to the Uparāt, he said that he prayed all the way that he might answer their questions discreetly and wisely. He did not know that the governor had no more confidence in his deserted idols and spirits than he himself had.

On the evening of our arrival, the largest house in the village was filled to overflowing till late in the night. Before Sunday the people had extemporized a chapel which afterwards became the foundation of the Mê Kawn church. Two Sundays were spent in teaching these people before we moved on to Chieng Rāi, leaving the new disciples under the oversight of Noi Tāliya.

On reaching Chieng Rāi we were invited by the governor to take up our quarters in his old residence, which we did. It was a better house than his present one, but there had been two deaths in it, and it was pronounced unlucky. He knew we were not afraid of ill luck. On the contrary, it was very good luck that we got it, for the rains were now falling daily. The governor and Nān Tā were near relatives and very intimate friends withal. His interest in us was as teachers of the only religion that ever afforded him a ray of hope. But on this trip Pū King, the reformed bandit, and his family, were the centre of our interest there. And it was not long before he, too, like Saul of Tarsus, became a striking illustration of the grace of God.

A few hours beyond Chieng Rāi on the road to Chieng Sên, was the home of Āi Tū. His was the first Christian family in the province. He had built—in part that it might furnish a guest-chamber for the missionary on his visits, and in part that it might serve as a chapel for worship—the largest house in all that neighbourhood. When we arrived, he had already vacated it for us, and had moved his family down into a shed. A number of families had begun to attend worship, and to keep the Sabbath; but were frightened away by that ridiculously stale story that missionaries were making Christians in order to carry them off in their ships to feed the Yaks! Strange that such a palpable absurdity should deceive any one; yet we have known whole villages to be frightened away by it.

At Chieng Sên, in the home of Nān Suwan, we were at once aware of being in a Christian atmosphere—in a consecrated Christian family. That family was a city set upon a hill—a leaven in the new city and province. It alone had given Christianity a good name. The governor was free to say that if Christianity made such men as Nān Suwan, he would like to see the whole country Christian. The influence of the Girls' School in Chiengmai was strongly reflected in his daughter, Kuī Kêo. She taught no regular school other than her Sunday School; but from time to time during the week she taught the neighbours. Young men who began by trying to ridicule her out of her religion, now treated her with the greatest respect. We were told that rude young fellows singing vulgar songs would lower their voices when passing by the house.

We crossed the river in a small boat to spend a few days in teaching four new families of Christians on the eastern side. One of the men was Tāo Rāt, the village officer, and another was his son, Noi Chai. The latter became an influential ruling elder, and, like Nān Suwan, one of the pillars of the church.

From Chieng Sên we crossed the broad prairie-like plain westward to Bān Tam. The officer of the village was Sên Yā Wichai—mentioned in the early part of this narrative as the very first believer in Chiengmai. The journey was one of the worst for elephants that I ever made. Heavy rains had soaked the ground so that at every step it seemed almost impossible for them to pull their huge feet out of their tracks. The Sên lived only a quarter of a mile from a remarkable feature of the mountain ridge. The Mê Tam, the largest river in the plain, flows bodily out from under the mountain, much as does one of the sources of the Mê Ping at Chieng Dāo.

It was a great pleasure to spend a Sunday with our now venerable Christian and his family. It was a family of officers, his three sons all being either of the grade of Tāo or of Sên—which shows the esteem in which the family was held. But, unfortunately, their official position made it more difficult for the sons to follow the example of their father.

On Sunday night the rain came down in torrents, reminding us that it was better for us to be at home. We started homeward early the next morning. Our route skirted the beautiful mountain range, crossing brooks and the larger streams of the Mê Tam and the Mê Chan. Already the road had become almost impassable except for elephants and natives unencumbered with shoes or trousers.

We have already spoken of the great mortality incurred in the attempt to people these new Lāo states. Occasionally the straggling remnant of a family might be seen returning. One poor little boy awakened my deepest sympathy. All of his family had died except himself and his brother, a monk, who were trying to save themselves by flight back to their old home in the province of Chiengmai. After I passed them I began to wonder whether the pale, weary-faced, and exhausted travellers would ever reach the rest they sought. Then I began to think that here I was enacting again the old tale of the priest and the Levite who passed by on the other side. At last I could stand it no longer. I stopped and waited for them to come up. I offered the pitiful little skeleton of a boy a seat with me on the back of the elephant. At first he somewhat distrusted my motive, wondering what I wanted to do with him; but he was too weary to refuse. When he revived, he proved to be a veritable little chatterbox, and good company. I kept him nearly a week, till we entered the Chiengmai plain at Doi Saket. Only four years ago, eleven children out of five Christian families who had settled in Wieng Pā Pāo, died during the first year.

Returning through Chieng Rāi, we revisited the new families of Christians in that province. In the city the governor's wife asked us to have worship in their new house, to which they reverently listened. When we ended she said, "Why, they pray for everybody!" Pū King, the executioner, was holding on with a death-grip to the hope of salvation for the chief of sinners. The case of the apostle himself, and of the penitent thief, greatly encouraged him. Nān Tā also was greatly rejoiced that his brother Sên Kat became a believer on this tour.

On my return I found Mr. Martin but little, if at all, improved, by his trip. He was so thoroughly discouraged that he felt that he could not face another hot season. He remained with us till the end of the rainy season, and then, with his family, left Siam for the United States. I never had felt so thoroughly crushed as I was at his departure. During three whole years we had lived in the same house, and worked together hand in hand in the evangelistic work, of which he was very fond.

Dr. Cheek already had severed his official connection with the mission, and had gone into business of his own. But he kindly gave his professional service to the missionaries, and was ready to perform pressing surgical operations for the natives who came to the hospital.

I have often wondered whether all foreign missions have as many and as rapid alternations of sunshine and shadow, as the Lāo mission. Our medical work was once more at a standstill; and by the departure of Mr. Martin, the evangelistic work again was crippled. But at Hong Kong Mr. Martin met Rev. and Mrs. D. G. Collins, Dr. and Mrs. A. M. Cary, and Rev. W. C. Dodd, on their way out for the Lāo mission, with Rev. W. G. McClure for Lower Siam. Mrs. Cary had become so exhausted by continual sea-sickness during the whole voyage, that, on her arrival in Bangkok, many thought her unable to endure the long river trip of six or seven weeks. Mr. McClure offered to exchange fields with the Carys; but Mrs. Cary, with true pluck, said that she had been appointed to the Lão mission, and to the Lão she would go. But, alas! it was to be otherwise. She became worse soon after leaving Bangkok. On Sunday, January 16th, 1887, a mile above Rahêng, she became unconscious, and shortly after gently passed into her everlasting rest.

It was still a month's journey to their destination. There was nothing to be done but to lay the body to rest in the grounds of a monastery. Who can portray that parting scene, or adequately sympathize with the bereaved husband and sister (Mrs. Collins), or with the other members of the party, as they performed the last sad offices, and then resumed their lonesome journey!

When the party reached Chiengmai on the 17th of February, they found there only the McGilvarys, Miss Griffin, and Miss Westervelt. Miss Cole had gone to Bangkok. But the Girls' School was flourishing under the direction of the two ladies last mentioned. Former pupils of the school were then doing good service in three different provinces as teachers. But the arrival of the new forces made possible for the first time a Boys' High School. Circumstances now were much more favourable than they were when Mr. Wilson made the attempt in the earlier days of the mission. We now had Christian patrons, and there was a growing desire in the land for education. Buddhist pupils were willing and anxious to attend our school. Mr. Collins preferred the educational work. As soon as he acquired the language sufficiently well, he was put in charge of the school for boys, and it was soon crowded with pupils.

Mr. Dodd's preference was along the line of a Training School for Christian workers. Happily, the taste

GIRLS' SCHOOL IN CHIENGMAI
1892

and preference of both these men were along the lines of greatest need. Meanwhile Mr. Dodd entered into the evangelistic work also with a zeal that has never abated. As newcomers see things with different eyes, it is always interesting to get their first impressions. Mr. Dodd's first experience is thus given in a letter to the Board of June 9th, 1887:

"On Friday, June 3d, Rev. D. McGilvary of the Lāo mission left Chiengmai by boat for a tour southward, taking attendants and all necessary equipments, accompanied by a raw recruit, and three efficient native helpers. We arrived at our first station about the middle of the afternoon, and before bed-time held religious conversation with as many enquirers as time would permit. Our audience chamber was the house of one of our newly-received members. Our 'outward and ordinary means' of attracting an audience was a watch, two mariner's compasses, a magnifying glass, a stereoscope with an assortment of views, and a violin. The raw recruit played the violin, and thus called the audience together. We used both the other attractions to hold them and to gain their confidence and interest; and afterwards Dr. McGilvary easily and naturally drew them into religious conversation. Soon the conversation became a monologue of instruction in the religion of the great God. The violin was no longer needed to arouse or sustain an interest. Every day, and late into the evening, the Doctor and the three assistants conversed; sometimes to quite an audience, sometimes to individual enquirers.

"The religious attitude of the people was a revelation to the newly-arrived missionary, and doubtless would be to most of God's people in the United States. Nearly all of these people had heard of the 'religion of the great God,' but knew nothing about it, since the district had never before been visited by a missionary. . . . But their receptivity was marvellous. . . . Without exception these Buddhists confessed at the outset, or were soon brought to concede, the immeasurable superiority of Christianity. Many said, 'It is of no use to argue. Your books tell the beginnings of things; ours do not.' On one occasion when Dr. McGilvary had finished reading and explaining the first chapter of Genesis, one of his auditors remarked to his fellows, 'There is more real information on that one page than in all Buddha's writings.' The sense of sin is universal, so too is the insufficiency of the works of merit. Many sad souls confessed that they had long been dreading the penalty for sins for which they feared that 'merit-making' could not atone.

"The results we cannot measure. We were absent two weeks. Religious service or conversations were held in more than twenty different homes, and in some of these several times. Audiences varied from a single enquirer to fifty. Thus hundreds heard the gospel for the first time. Many who seemed above the suspicion of hypocrisy professed to believe and accept what they heard. . . . One principal reason for this tour just now, was to baptize in his own home and among his subjects the chief officer of the district. Himself, his wife, and his whole family were baptized—a most interesting household. The abbot of one village monastery professes to accept Christianity. For some time he has been sending his parishioners, including his own sister, for instruction. There is another district officer of the same rank as our newly-baptized convert, a constant visitor and deeply interested. This is a specimen tour, neither better nor worse than the average taken these days. For the last two years, although most of the time there have been but two ordained missionaries in the field, over ninety accessions have been made to the First Church."—*Church at Home and Abroad,* May, 1888.

Before the short trip reported by Mr. Dodd, I had taken a longer one to the northern provinces, going over the same ground which Mr. Martin and I had travelled the season before. This time I baptized thirty-six adults and thirty-two non-communing members. The communion was administered eight times. I married two couples and ordained one elder. Each Sunday was spent in villages where there were already Christians. This encouraging success was the harvest of seed sown on former tours, but gathered largely through God's blessing on the work of faithful elders. Both in Chieng Rāi and in Chieng Sên we might then have organized churches with a goodly number of members communing and non-communing, and with very good material for officers. Nān Suwan at Chieng Sên, like myself, never had the gift of fluent speech, but his reputation for sterling integrity has left a mark that eloquence might envy. And Āi Tū at Nāng Lê bids fair to be another power in the province of Chieng Rāi. Both of them are strongly aided by their daughters, the first-fruits of our Girls' School.

During the year 1887 the whole number of adult accessions was one hundred and seven; and one hundred and eleven non-communing members were added to the roll, making two hundred and eighteen additions to our little flock, exclusive of Lakawn. As I now look back over these years, it is plain to me that the great lack of the mission all the way through has been the lack of well-trained native helpers; and for this lack the mission itself is largely to blame. Those who are eager to accomplish the evangelization of the world within the present generation, should first of all lay hold of the present generation of Christians in every mission field. Fill *these* with enthusiasm, qualify them, and send them forth, and we have a lever that will lift the world.

From the Report of the Board in the same number of *The Church at Home and Abroad* cited above, we quote the following:

"Dr. and Mrs. Peoples are still left alone in Lakawn, the utmost picket of the foreign missionary line. Mrs. Peoples has not one lady for a companion; and the doctor is dangerously burdened, bearing all alone the labour of teaching and healing. For more than two years they have been waiting for help. No station under the care of the Foreign Board calls so loudly for reinforcements as this. Again and again we thought we had found a Christian couple for Lakawn; but in each case we have been disappointed. Single men could have been sent, but it is very much to be desired that the new missionary going there should be married. Dr. Peoples' medical work has won for him increasing friendliness throughout the city. . . . Mrs. McGilvary has revised the Lāo version of Matthew's Gospel, and has translated for the first time about half of the book of Acts. The Scriptures have had considerable circulation among the Lāo, but only in the Siamese tongue. . . . Dr. Cary had no sooner reached the field than through the assistance of Dr. McGilvary and Norwood McGilvary, a young lad, acting as interpreters, he was able to begin work with regular hours for receiving patients, and for surgical practice. . . . Mr. Collins has made a beginning in the much-needed school for boys.

"Only one other mission now under the care of our Presbyterian Church has during the last year shown as much growth, in proportion to the missionary force employed, as the Lāo mission. . . . It is never out of place to remind our Presbyterian Church that it is to her alone that God has committed the evangelization of the Lāo tribes."

XXVI

A FOOTHOLD IN LAMPŪN

AT a meeting of the Presbytery shortly before the opening of the year 1888, a committee consisting of Dr. Peoples, Mr. Dodd, and myself, was appointed to organize two churches, one in Chieng Sên and one in Chieng Răi, if the way were found open to do so. We also arranged that Mrs. McGilvary should accompany our son Norwood as far as Bangkok on his way to the United States. And both expeditions were to start on the same day, Monday, February 7th.

To ease somewhat the strain of such a parting, I took an earlier leave, and went on Saturday with Mr. Dodd to spend Sunday with the church at Mê Dawk Dêng. That evening we performed a marriage ceremony in the church. The next day thirteen adults were received into the church—nine by baptism and four who were children of the church. On Monday Mrs. McGilvary and I exchanged our last good-byes by note, and both parties got off on Tuesday morning. Dr. and Mrs. Peoples, starting from Lakawn, made the first stage of their journey separately from us to a rendezvous at the Christian village of Mê Kawn, twelve miles south of Chieng Răi.

At our next Christian village another wedding was waiting for us, but the course of true love did not run smooth. The bride belonged to a well-to-do Christian family; but no member of it could read the Scriptures. They, therefore, "redeemed" a Christian family for four hundred rupees, in order to secure the services of the son as a sort of Levite in the family, and to teach the eldest daughter to read. Naturally, the two young people fell in love with each other. That was a contingency the mother had not planned for, and a difficulty arose. She asked, "If I take Nān ——— for a son-in-law, where do my four hundred rupees come in?" It was all in vain to tell her that she got her pay in a good son-in-law. She said he was hers already till his debt was paid. At last she so far relented as to allow the ceremony to take place, but she would not see it performed. We invited the father and the rest of the family and the neighbours into our tent, where, to their great joy, the two were made man and wife. The implacable mother lived to see that she had not made a bad bargain, after all.

At Mê Kawn we were joined by Dr. and Mrs. Peoples, and we had a good Sabbath with the little flock there. Our club-footed man had looked after it well, and he became later a good elder and a fine disciplinarian. About this time I was taken with a severe attack of indigestion, from which I did not recover for many months—the only continued sickness from which I have suffered in all my connection with the Lāo mission.

On reaching Chieng Rāi, we found our good friend the governor mourning the death of his wife, the same who, when we last saw her, invited us to worship in her house. It was a pleasure to point the bereaved man to the divine Comforter, and we are fain to believe that our words were not in vain. He was still anxious to have the mission station established, which we, unfortunately, could not yet promise. The Chao Uparāt invited Dr. Peoples to lecture with his magic lantern, and to have worship in his residence, where we had a crowded audience. We did not organize a church in Chieng Rāi, however, partly because the two Christian villages, equidistant from the city north and south, could not agree on the best place of meeting. But we found the way open in Chieng Sên, and did organize a church there, in Nān Suwan's house, on the very bank of the Mê Kōng, and with one-half of its members living on the other shore.

Dr. Peoples had left a large practice in Lakawn, and was obliged to return. Mr. Dodd returned with them to Lakawn, and thence to Chiengmai. I had come untrammelled, to remain as long as duty called. It seemed very desirable to follow up the impressions already made on that community. But I was not well, and a week's delay found me no better. Thinking that a change might be beneficial, I crossed the plain to Sên Yā Wichai's home at the foot of the mountains. It was a hard day's ride, and I became worse on the way. On reaching my destination I could hardly stand, Resting there on my back a few days without improvement, it seemed my first duty to get to a physician as soon as possible, or, at least, make the effort to do so. Most of the way I could stop at night either with or near Christian families. This I did, and so reached Chiengmai on April 14th.

During my absence the building of the Boys' High School was completed; and the school was opened under the direction of Mr. Collins on March 19th, with an enrollment of forty-five boys, nearly all children of Christian parents. In June Dr. Wilson reached Chiengmai on his return from the United States; and with him came Miss Fleeson, destined with the Doctor to join the Peoples at Lakawn, and Miss Belle Eakin (now Mrs. Dodd), for the Girls' School in Chiengmai. Miss Griffin was already gone on her furlough.

The building for the Girls' School had long been in process of construction. Builders and plans had been several times changed, till at last Dr. Cheek took the contract, and finished it in the summer of 1888. It has served its purpose admirably these many years, and we then thought it would do for all time. But though the lot then seemed amply large, it proves now entirely too small for the needs of the school. Moreover, it is impossible to enlarge it. On its south side runs the most travelled road in the country; while on the east the land is owned by a wealthy official, who would not sell at any price.

Our congregations had grown till a church building became a necessity even more urgent than a schoolhouse. The first mission dwelling-house was planned in part with reference to such need, its largest room long being used for Sunday worship. Then a small temporary chapel took its place. After that a larger teak double dwelling was bought. That, however, would not hold more than two hundred persons—not more than half of our largest congregations at the present day. Then for a time we worshipped in the unfinished building for the Girls' School. When, at last, that was finished, it was needed for its original purpose, and we again must move. It was then decided that we must have a church, and one worthy of our cause—such as would attract rather than repel both rulers and people. So one Sunday afternoon we held a meeting of the congregation to take steps for building it. We were delighted to see the interest manifested in the enterprise. Pā Kawng, an aged slave of the Prince, laid down a silver rupee, which was all the money she possessed—and it was the very first money received toward the building. The church was completed by the end of this year.

We had continued evidence of the friendship of Prince Intanon, and even of his growing interest in our work. One Sunday, in answer to an invitation given by Mrs. Cheek, he attended our communion service, conducted that day by Mr. Wilson. Although he arrived an hour and a half too soon, he remained all through the long service, and bowed as he took his leave, just when the communion cups were about to be passed. On the day of our daughter's marriage in Statesville, North Carolina, he and the High Commissioner attended a reception given in honour of the event. The Prince had known her as a child, and seemed much interested. "Is it this very night that the marriage takes place?" he asked. The reception was a very pleasant affair. Though my wife was still in Bangkok, Miss Fleeson and Miss Eakin entered with all their hearts into the thing, and, with the assistance of Mr. Dodd and Mr. Collins, carried it through in splendid shape. After refreshments we had charades and other games. It was amusing to see the look of surprise on the face of the Prince when the charades were played.—"What are they doing?" "What does that mean?" "I don't understand." But the game was quite too recondite to be explained to him. So, after the first charade, His Highness and his party took their leave, assuring us that they had enjoyed the evening very much.

Dr. Wilson and Miss Fleeson presently journeyed on to their post at Lakawn. The governor there gave the mission a very desirable plot of ground for the new buildings which would be required, saying, "I am glad to have you come. It would be a shame, when you come to live in our country, if the government did not do something to make you comfortable."

Scarcely less important than the opening of the new station in Lakawn, was the opening of permanent work in Lampūn, the largest and most important substation of Chiengmai. Lampūn is a little gem of a walled city in the same great plain as Chiengmai, and only eighteen miles distant to the south. From the first settlement of the country, however, it has been a separate state, yet governed by a branch of the same ruling race.

We have seen that the new governor of Lampūn was friendly to the mission and the missionaries. The opening of the work in Bān Pên and other important villages near it, rendered it almost essential to have a footing in Lampūn itself. After some negotiation we secured a suitable lot, the grounds of the second governor recently deceased. We purchased from the family the land with the old residence and the stockade. But presently the family became alarmed lest they had been too hasty in selling it to foreigners, and brought back the money, begging us to restore the land. They brought, also, a message from the governor, saying that he wanted the residence and the stockade himself, but would *give* us the rest of the land. It was to our interest to keep on good terms with him, and we agreed to the arrangement. We got what we wanted, a good station, and we retained, and probably increased the governor's friendship.

To make possession sure, I purchased a newly-built house which had come to be regarded as unlucky, be-

REV. JONATHAN WILSON, D.D.
1898

cause the owner's wife had suddenly died in it. Having arranged to have the house moved and set up on the lot, I was about to return to Chiengmai, thinking that there was nothing more to do, when I was sent for by the chief executive officer of the Court. He said that the governor, indeed, had given us the place, but the Court wished to make one proviso. He begged that I would sign a paper promising in few words that if the government at any time should need it, we would give it up. The governor was growing old, and they themselves would be held responsible. I saw at once that such a step would put it in the power of any one to oust us. A need might be feigned, and yet we should be powerless to withstand it. I was perfectly dumfounded. My first thought was to go directly to the governor. But presently I bethought me of the terms on which H. R. H. Prince Bijit, the brother of His Majesty, had given to the mission the fine lot for its hospital. The lot was given in perpetuity on condition that it be used for medical and missionary purposes only. As long as it was so used, it was ours. But it could not be sold, or used for other purposes, without forfeiture to the Prince. The thought came to me as an inspiration. I told the officer of that written deed. "Very well," said he. "If you have such a paper as that, show it to me, and I will give you one like it for this lot."

The difficulty was solved. A swift footman was despatched to Chiengmai asking Mr. Martin to send me at once a copy of the Prince's deed of gift. Next morning it came, and I took it immediately to the Court. The officer's surprise was evident. He took it and read it carefully through. His word was given. After a moment's thought he said, "That is all right. It will relieve me of all responsibility." Then he called up his clerk to copy its terms and execute the new deed. The land was ours to use as long as we should use it for the purposes specified; and that I hoped would be until the millennium! With a light heart I was soon aboard my boat and homeward bound.

When the house had been removed and set up on the lot, Mr. Collins and I went down and spent a week there, with interested audiences every night. It at once became an important out-station of the Chiengmai mission. In the meantime Mr. Dodd had already collected some twenty students for his training-class, but without any quarters for them in Chiengmai. Later Mr. and Mrs. Dodd were put in charge of the station, and the Training School was moved over to Lampūn. When the Lampūn church was organized, its charter members numbered nearly two hundred. It is now the mother of two other churches. Scarcity of men in the mission, openings in other places, and other causes have prevented the Lampūn station from being continuously manned. But now, with such efficient workers there as Mr. and Mrs. Freeman, it has an important future before it, as a sub-station of Chiengmai.

Meanwhile my own sickness had continued, with several relapses. A minor surgical operation had so delayed my recovery that Dr. Cary now advised a change and rest in a boat trip to Bangkok. After the departure of our son to the United States, my wife had remained in Bangkok for a visit, and was soon to return. The telegraph line which the Siamese government had recently completed, enabled me to wire to her to wait for me to come and bring her back. Dr. Cary himself, who had never recovered from the shock occasioned by the tragic death of Mrs. Cary, and who was never well during his whole stay in the mission, decided to accompany me as far as Rahêng.

At Pāknam Pō I left my boat, and took passage for Bangkok by river steamer, thus saving seven days. After remaining in Bangkok only three nights, my wife and I took passage in the same steamer on her return trip, and rejoined our boat at the forks. The water was at its best stage, and we passed up some of the rapids without knowing that they were there. But my trouble had not left me. A low diet and long illness had left me thin and weak. The round trip occupied only two months. Our last Sunday was at Pāk Bawng, two days below Chiengmai. There we held a communion service with the Christian families, and a new family was baptized.

Three miles to the east is Bān Pên, the village which has figured in a previous chapter. The Christians there had long been asking for a visit, which my own sickness and want of time on the part of others rendered it impossible to make. On Monday morning I decided to take the risk and visit it. With some misgivings I saw my wife's boat move off and leave me—burning, so to speak, my bridges behind me. The whole country was flooded. Discarding shoes and stockings, I made my way on foot, weak as I was, through water, across ditches, or along the narrow ridges of rice-fields, and finally reached Bān Pên in safety.

And what a week I spent in that neighbourhood! At Nawng Sīu, a village two miles distant from Bān Pên, there were six families of professed believers whom Dr. Dodd and I had visited the season before—almost swimming at times to reach them in their scattered homes. Their admission was postponed at that time until they should have had further instruction. To these I specially addressed myself. During the week our faithful elder, Nān Tā, came down to assist me in the work. On Friday evening the session met at Nawng Sĭu to examine and instruct these new converts, and again on Saturday morning, closing finally at two o'clock in the afternoon with baptism and the Lord's Supper. On counting up the numbers, it was found that twenty adults and seventeen children had been baptized. Among them was an aged couple with their children, grandchildren, and great-grandchildren. It was a memorable sight. The Sabbath was spent at Bān Pên, where seven more adults and one child were baptized. On Monday I made my way back to the boat as I had come, and reached home on Tuesday. And now for the strange part of the story. *I reached home well.* My week's wading in the water, and the hard work, had done what medicine and doctors and a long boat trip had failed to accomplish!

But a new disappointment awaited me. Before I reached home, Dr. Cary had resigned. His short career is one of the mysteries to be explained in the great beyond. A consecrated physician, he had given his life to the Lāo people. Crushed by his tragic bereavement on the way out, and with a constitution never strong, he contended manfully for two years against the debilitating effects of a malarial climate. But at last he had to give up the fight. His work had been successful. "He saved others; himself he could not save!"

His departure threw on me again the oversight of the medical work. But this time most of the dispensing of medicine to the natives fell on Chanta, a protégé of my own, who had had good training under two physicians. Meanwhile Dr. Cheek looked after the mission families, and, as already stated, was always ready to respond to an urgent call in the hospital. My time was largely given, therefore, to the evangelistic work, to instructing Nān Tā and other elders, and to teaching enquirers and others to read in Siamese, first the Shorter Catechism, and then a Gospel.

The growth of the Chiengmai church, though not phenomenal, was very healthy and very uniform throughout the year. There were accessions every month save one, amounting in all to one hundred and sixty souls. At the end of the year Miss I. A. Griffin returned from furlough, and served a very useful term until 1896, when she retired greatly missed. At Lakawn, Rev. Hugh Taylor and his wife began a twenty years' course of evangelistic work carried on with indefatigable zeal, while Miss Fleeson was no less zealous and successful in laying the foundation of a Girls' School, destined to be a power in that province.

XXVII

A PRISONER OF JESUS CHRIST

WE have had frequent occasion gratefully to record the good will of the Siamese government, and of its commissioners and representatives, towards our mission. In all its history the only exception to this uniform friendliness was in the case of the Commissioner who, in 1889, succeeded Prayā Tēp Worachun. The Boys' School was on an old deserted monastery-site given by the Prince to Dr. Peoples for a medical or a mission compound. An old ruined chēdi or pagoda was still standing on it. Such lots, deserted by the monks, were then regarded as abodes of the spirits, and on such the natives dared not live. In preparing for the school buildings, the débris about the foot of the chēdi had been dug away. One of the early acts of the new Commissioner was to send a written notice to the mission that it was improper to use old Buddhist shrines for purposes other than those for which they were originally built; and he gave us notice that we were to have three months in which to find other quarters. But as no other lot was offered in its place, we remained quiet, and that was the last we heard of it.

Another incident, occurring soon after, was more serious, and gave us a great deal of anxiety; for it came near costing the life of one of our best native assistants. A deputation from some twelve or fifteen families in Chieng Dāo came to us with a request that a native assistant be sent up to teach them. Krū Nān Tā went up, and they became believers, but required much further instruction. We selected Noi Siri, the most prudent of our elders, for the task. We charged him specially, inasmuch as it was in a province new to our work, to use great caution and give no just cause of offence to the rulers or to others. He remained there a month, and then was recalled by the illness of his wife. He stopped at the mission to report progress, giving a good account of the conduct and diligence of the new Christians.

Great was our surprise, then, in a few hours to learn that Noi Siri had been arrested, put in heavy irons, and thrown into prison on a charge of treason against the government. Mr. Collins, Mr. Dodd, and I called upon the Commissioner to enquire the cause of his arrest. The Commissioner replied, Yes; he had him arrested on the grave charge of disloyalty in teaching the converts that they were exempt from government work. Such teaching was treason; and if the charge were true, the penalty was death. It was not, therefore, a bailable offence. At the same time, he said, no specifications had been forwarded. He would summon the accusers, and the man should have a fair trial, and should have the privilege of producing any witnesses he pleased in his defence. That was, of course, all that we could ask, save to beg that the trial be hastened as far as possible—to which he consented. Krū Nān Tā was allowed to see the prisoner in his cell. From him he learned that so far was the accusation from being true, that he had taught the Christians that they were *not* exempt from government work; and that, furthermore, no call had been made on them for service while he was there. We sent immediately for all the Christian men to come down.

After some delay the prisoner was called into court and examined. According to Siamese custom, his examination was taken down in writing.

"Are you Noi Siri, who has been teaching in Chieng Dāo?"

"Yes."

"When did you go there to teach?"

"On the fourth of the third waning moon."

"Have you taught that Christians are exempt from public service?"

"No. On the contrary, I taught that, as Siamese subjects, Christians are to pay their taxes and perform all the duties of other subjects."

The testimony of the governor of Chieng Dāo, his accuser, was then taken in his presence. Among the questions asked him were these:

"Can you state any particular time and place when the Christians were called to do government work and refused?"

"Yes. I called a man or two, and they did not obey."

"When was that call made?"

"On the fourth day of the third waxing moon."

This was the only specification which the governor gave. The date, it will be noted, was fifteen days earlier than that of Noi Siri's arrival in Chieng Dāo. If the statement were true, it might have subjected the persons who were summoned to trial and punishment for disloyalty; but it absolutely cleared Noi Siri. An upright judge would have dismissed the case. The Christian witnesses were in attendance to testify as to the nature of the instruction they received; but were not given the opportunity to do so. The accused man was remanded to prison. We waited, but nothing was done. We called once more on the Commissioner; but were told that the case had been referred to Bangkok, and he must wait for a reply. We waited again. At last we made a written appeal on his behalf, and in answer were told that the case was one with their own subjects, and we had nothing to do with it. Meantime Noi Siri had become quite ill, and all that we could do was to get him transferred from his dungeon to the common prison.

Eight months after this, when Mr. Dodd went down to Bangkok to be married to Miss Eakin, he made, through the United States Minister, an appeal to the Prince Minister of the North, who promised an immediate order for his release. As soon as we were assured of that, we went to the resident Prince in Chiengmai, H. R. H. Prince Sonapandit, who promised that the order should be issued at once. The next day we called on the Commissioner to remind him of the Prince's promise; but he and the Judge had just gone out for a stroll in the city. It was then Saturday afternoon. Next day was our communion service, and I was determined to have Noi Siri present. To do this I had to follow those men up at once. I was a fast walker, and, when necessary, could run. My race after them was the ludicrous sequel of the case. Two high officials closing their office and escaping, in order to keep their victim in chains another night, pursued by swifter feet, and overtaken in the street! The Judge acknowledged that the Prince had given the order. He would attend to it to-morrow. Since to-morrow would be Sunday, I need not come. But I knew that we should not see Noi Siri in time for our worship unless I went for him. So on Sunday morning I called once more on the Judge, who again said that I need not wait; but I had to tell him that I would not return till I saw his release. So the prisoner was called, and I saw the fetters taken off from his ankles.

The second bell was ringing when I entered the church; but Noi Siri was with me. The congregation rose and sang the long metre doxology. There were not many dry eyes in the room. Mr. Dodd preached from the text, "And we know that all things work together for good to them that love God." Among the converts who then stood up to make a public profession of faith was Nāng Su, a daughter of Noi Siri—and this happy coincidence was no planning of ours.

Noi Siri's faith had been tried by fire, and he had come forth from the furnace as pure gold. In addition to his own imprisonment and distress, his wife had been for months very low with sickness, and one of his grandchildren had died during the interval. But from his prison cell he had written to his family not to let their faith be shaken either by his trials or by their own. During the eight months and ten days of his imprisonment, one hundred and thirty-three persons—his daughter closing the list—were received into church membership. A European in employ of the government, who had cognizance of the whole case, afterwards said to me, "It might be well to get the Commissioner to imprison a few more Christians!" A history of the case was afterwards published by our Board in a leaflet entitled, "The Laos Prisoner."

Before the close of the year there was an event which for the time came near to overthrowing the government.

A new tax, levied chiefly on areca trees, caused much exasperation throughout the country. As usual, the tax was farmed out to Chinese for collection. The local officers in various districts formed a coalition to resist to the uttermost the collection of the tax. Of course, this could not be allowed, since the collectors were the agents of the government. The resistance was centred chiefly in the districts to the eastward of the city, where Prayă Păp, who had some reputation as a soldier, went so far as to gather a considerable force of the insurgents within a few miles of Chieng-mai. A day even was set for their attack on the city. If they had made a dash then, they could easily have taken it, for the sympathy of the people was wholly with them, and the government was unprepared.

Our house was only two hundred yards away from the Chinese distillery, which was the objective of the insurgents. The residence of the Commissioner and that of the Siamese Prince Sonapandit were nearly opposite us on the other side of the river. Our position was further compromised by the fact that the wives and children of a number of influential Chinese had almost forcibly taken refuge in our compound. In any case, we should have been in a position of great danger from the guns on the other side of the river aimed at the distillery. We were strongly advised to take refuge in the British Consulate, whose shelter was kindly offered us. But the whole population in our neighbourhood was watching us. If we stirred, there would have been a general stampede.

Fortunately for themselves and for the country, the courage of the common people failed. One after another they deserted the leader, till at last he also fled.

He was caught, however, and with seven other leaders was executed. This was the end of the matter in Chiengmai; but certain parties of the insurgents, escaping northwards, became roving bands of marauders that for some time disturbed the peace of the frontier towns. The rebellion never had any chance of ultimate success; but had the attack on the city been actually made, the immediate consequences would have been direful, and untold calamity would have been entailed on the whole country.

The arrival of Dr. McKean at the close of the year marked an era in our medical work. He was accompanied by our daughter, Miss Cornelia H. McGilvary, now Mrs. William Harris Jun. It was the pleasant duty of Mrs. McGilvary to escort the party up from Bangkok. The appointment of our daughter was no less a surprise than a delight to us. During her school days she always said that she would not become a missionary. When the question came up for final settlement, she fought it out in her own mind alone, and reached her own decision. The Lāo language, which, during her ten years' absence, she seemed to have lost entirely, came back to her very soon and with little effort.

It has been Dr. McKean's privilege to continue the work begun by able physicians, and to carry it to a higher degree of efficiency. He has combined, as most of our physicians have done, the two great objects of the medical missionary, the medical and the evangelistic, making the former a means to the latter. While the professional and the charitable features of the work have not been minimized, but rather magnified, no minister has more loved to preach the Gospel, or has been more successful in it. At the same time it may be that the great work now enlisting his sympathy and his strenuous efforts—the establishment of a leper colony and hospital, and the amelioration of the condition of that unfortunate class—may be the one with which his name will be most intimately associated.

XXVIII

CIRCUIT TOUR WITH MY DAUGHTER, 1890

I HAD been appointed by Presbytery to organize in Chieng Răi the church which was not found ready for organization on my previous visit. I had planned for a tour longer than usual, to include the eastern provinces as far as Năn, as well as the northern ones, and expected to take with me native assistants only. But upon the arrival of our reinforcement, I was no less surprised than delighted to find that my daughter desired to accompany me; and so it was arranged.

Starting on February 5th, we spent the first Sunday in Lakawn. Here we met another surprise. Mr. Taylor had spent his first year in that annoying work for the new missionary, the building of a house. He was anxious to get out among the people, but feared he was not sufficiently versed in the language to make profitable a tour alone. He and Mrs. Taylor would join us if they could get elephants—a matter which was easily arranged. Mr. Taylor proved to be an efficient helper. My daughter had a delightful companion, and it was a great pleasure to initiate the new missionaries into the evangelistic work which Dr. and Mrs. Taylor since then have carried on so successfully for twenty years. It is still their delight—may they live to carry it on for many years to come!

One of the chief diversions of the trip thenceforward

was afforded by the pranks of an uncommonly mischievous baby-elephant which accompanied its mother. On one occasion a footman coming towards us stepped out of the trail and stood beside a large tree to let us pass. The mischievous creature saw his opportunity, and before the man knew what was up, he found himself fast pinioned between the elephant's head and the tree trunk. The frightened man extricated himself with loud outcry, while the beholders were convulsed with laughter. Our own men were constantly the victims of his pranks; so that, one day, I told them that there would be no trouble if they would only leave the creature alone—adding, by way of clinching my advice, "You see, he never troubles me." Just then, to the great delight of all, he made straight for me, and if there had been a tree behind me I should have been in the same unpleasant position in which the footman found himself.

Mr. Taylor's account of the earlier portion of the trip is as follows:

"We left Lakawn on the 12th of February with Dr. McGilvary and his daughter, and in four days reached Mûang Prê. Our tents were pitched by the road just outside the city gate. The advent of four foreigners, two of whom were women, created quite a stir; and we were all kept abundantly busy in visiting and being visited. Mrs. Taylor and Miss McGilvary were the first white ladies to visit the place; and of course, much to their own discomfort, were the centre of attraction. . . .

"The people of Prê seemed very ready to listen to the Gospel; so plenty of auditors were found everywhere. On Sabbath, the 16th, the first convert in Prê was baptized. He is a blind man, Noi Wong by name, who came to Lakawn to have Dr. Peoples operate on his eyes; but as nothing could be done for him, he returned home carrying in his heart some of the teachings there received, and in his hand a manuscript copy of a small catechism I was able to spare him. From his answers before the session, it was evident that he had used his brother's eyes well in having it read to him.

"On Wednesday we started on for Nān, and arrived there the following Tuesday. We received a very cordial welcome from the officials of that city, who sent a man to put in order a rest-house for us, and another to conduct our elephants to a place for food and water. Next day, after the court closed, some of the officials came to visit us. After wading through the crowds on the first and second verandas, and finally planting himself cross-legged in the middle of the thronged reception-room, their Chief said they thought we would be lonesome; so they had come to visit us. No idea could have been more comical to us; but he was seriously in earnest, and explained that he had never known the people to visit with other foreigners who had come to their city. They would not, however, listen well when the subject of religion was broached, and with one or two exceptions would not attend any of our services."

The morning after our arrival in Nān, my daughter met in the market-place a daughter of the Prince, and, before she was aware, found herself escorted into the palace. Her newly recovered language stood her in good stead, and she had a pleasant talk with the Prince and his daughters and wives. Next day he sent word that he would be pleased to give our party an audience. He was of venerable age, and second only to our Chiengmai Prince in his influence at the court of Bangkok. He expressed his pleasure at our visit to his country. He was too old to embrace a new religion. We might teach his children and grandchildren. What they would do he did not know.

At Nān the Taylors left us, returning to their station, while we journeyed on. Our next stage was

Chieng Kawng, one hundred and fifty miles to the northwest. We usually stopped for the night at large villages, or sometimes in small towns. But once we spent two days in the forest, where bears, tigers, and wild elephants abound. The first evening we just missed the sight of three tigers. Our men had gone on ahead to select a camping-place for the night, and saw a mother with two cubs crossing the road. Next morning one of my elephants, that had been hobbled and turned loose, was not on hand. It was nothing unusual for one of them to be a little belated, so we loaded up the others and prepared for starting. But when an hour had passed, and then two hours, and the elephant still did not come, we unloaded them and waited a long weary day and an anxious night. Early next morning, however, the driver appeared. That was a relief, but still there was no elephant. He had followed her trail over the mountain ridge, down gorges, and across knolls, till, tired and hungry, he had retraced his steps. Night overtook him, and, crouched under a tree, he had caught snatches of sleep while keeping watch for tigers. For two nights and a day he had not tasted food. With an elephant's instinct, the beast was making her way towards her old range in Chieng Răi, many days distant. It was a relief to know that she had not joined a large wild herd, in which case her capture would be practically impossible.

We could not remain indefinitely in the forest. So giving the driver food, a gun, and two carriers for company, with instructions not to return till the elephant was found, we moved on five or six miles to the next village, Băn Kĕm. This was the noon of Wednesday. Our detention seemed providential. We found the place fever-stricken. Our medicines at once made us friends. Our tent was crowded with visitors, so that I had little time to think of the lost elephant. The people seemed hungry for the Gospel. Three substantial men in the village, on the night before we left, professed a sincere and cordial acceptance of Jesus as their Saviour.

On Saturday, shortly after midday, there was a shout, "Here comes Lung Noi with the elephant!" I was both glad and sorry to hear it. Had I been alone, I should have remained longer. But we had lost so much time, that every one was eager to depart. I promised if possible to come again, but the time never came.

Chieng Kawng was our next point, a place I had visited with Dr. Vrooman seventeen years before. The young lad who then was so much interested in my repeating rifle was now governor, and came running out, bareheaded and barefooted, to welcome us. In the interval I had met him from time to time in Chiengmai, and he always begged that I would make him another visit. I had been better than my word—I had come at last, and brought my daughter, too. His brother, the second governor, had seen us in time to don his audience dress, and he appeared more like a white man than any one we had seen since the Taylors left us. He was ready to start on an expedition to Mûang Sing, five days northward beyond the Mê Kōng. The Prince of Nān had received permission from the King of Siam to repeople that old province. Hence this expedition. The leader had three hundred men, and gave me a cordial invitation to go as chaplain and physician! After this, while the work was well under way, the territory was turned over to France as the result of the long and troubled negotiations over the boundary between Siam and French Indo-China.

The wives of both the governors could scarcely be content with my daughter's short stay. They would surely become Christians, if she would remain one month to teach them. All I could do was to promise once more to come again if possible. The promised visit was made two years later, but then the "Nāi" was not along.

From there the only travelled route to Chieng Sĕn was by Chieng Rāi, both hot and circuitous. The alternative was a blind, untravelled track through the forest, made over forty years before, when Siam sent its last unfortunate expedition against Keng Tung. Here was a tempting chance to test the old proverb, Where there's a will, there's a way. The governor procured a noted hunter to guide us. Every carrier and driver and servant in the party carried his bush knife, and all promised to aid if we only would take the cooler road. It was, however, literally making in the forest "a highway for our God," over which several missionary tours have since been made. In the denser parts of the forest, we could force our way only by cutting away branches and small trees, and at times felling clumps of bamboo.

We had a cool place for rest and worship on Sunday. Our hunter had not promised to keep the Sabbath, and we were on his old hunting-grounds, where game of all kinds abounded. At dawn he was off with his gun, and we saw no more of him till sunset, when he appeared smiling, with some choice cuts of beef hanging from the barrel of his gun. He had found and followed, all day, a herd of wild cattle—the Kating—and succeeded in killing one of them near our road, a mile or more ahead of our camp. Though killed on Sunday, we ate it and asked no questions for conscience' sake. It was surely the most delicious beef we ever tasted. We should have had a mutiny the next day, had we proposed to pass on without stopping to save the meat. And what a huge creature it was. It must have weighed nearly a ton. Our men extemporized frames over the fire, and were busy cutting up the meat and drying it until late at night. Next day each man went loaded with it to his utmost capacity. What we could not carry away, the guide stored in the fork of a tree against his return.

The journey through the forest was shorter and far more comfortable than would have been the regular route. When next I travelled it, it had become a public highway. And as long as I continued to journey that way, it was known as the "Teacher's Road."

Chieng Sĕn was the limit of our trip. Before reaching it, we began to hear rumours of war—that the city was blockaded, no one being permitted to enter or depart. The country population had been called in to defend the city, etc., etc. We were advised to return, but kept on. At the gate the guard admitted us without difficulty.

The disturbance was the aftermath of the previous year's tax-rebellion, which, as we supposed, was completely ended before we left home. But a portion of the insurgents had fled to Keng Tung, and, gathering there a larger force, came south again as far as Mûang Făng, where they were either captured or again scattered. It was the fear that this lawless band, on its retreat northward, might attack and plunder the city, that caused the confusion. But the fugitives would have been fools to linger about two weeks after their defeat, when they knew that both the army behind them and the country in front of them would be on the alert for their capture. The governor was delighted to see us, and we were able in some degree to allay his fears. We were there, too, to speak a word of comfort to our own flock, who, like the rest, had been called in to protect the city. The panic gradually subsided, and the people returned to their homes. Owing in part to the unsettled condition of the country, we did not remain long in Chieng Sên; but long enough to visit in their homes every Christian family save one, and to have a delightful communion season with the church on Sunday.

Our special commission on this tour was to organize a church in Chieng Răi, where our next Sunday was spent. Our governor friend was disappointed that we had not come to take possession of the fine lot on the bank of the Mê Kok which he had given us. At his suggestion a house on it was purchased from his son at a nominal price, with the promise that we would urge the mission to occupy it the next year. On April 13th, the three sections of the church assembled by invitation at Mê Kawn. The obstacles which prevented the organization before were now removed. Fifty-one communicants and thirty-two non-communing members were enrolled, two ruling elders were elected and ordained, and the new church started with fair prospects.

We reached home on April 29th, after an absence of eighty-one days. We found all well, and the work prospering along all the lines. It was none too soon, however. We were just in time to escape the rise of the streams. At our last encampment on the Mê

Kūang we had a great storm of wind and rain, with trees and branches falling about us. The trip was a long one for my daughter; but her presence greatly enhanced the importance of the tour. On my subsequent tours through that region the first question always was, "Did you bring the Nāi?" and the second, "Why not?"

On our return we were surprised to find Dr. McKean in a new and comfortable teak house, toward the erection of which neither axe nor saw nor plane had been used when we left. The saw-mill could deliver at once whatever was needed. But *my* house had been seven years in building!

By this time nearly all the Lāo cities of Siam had been visited by missionaries. In two of them—Chiengmai and Lakawn—we had established permanent stations. For the third station, Chieng Rāi seemed to present the strongest claim. Politically it was not so important as Nān. But Nān, while very cordial to foreigners personally, was very jealous about admitting foreign influence of any kind. And the absolute control of the people by the princes of Nān would be an obstacle in the way of the acceptance of Christianity there until the princes themselves embraced it. In Chieng Rāi province the governor was known to be favourable to the Jesus-religion. Its broad plains and fertile soil were sure to attract a large immigration from the south, where population is dense and land very dear. The city is about equidistant from the five cities of Wieng Pā Pāo on the south, Mûang Fāng on the west, Chieng Sên on the north, Chieng Kawng on the northeast, and Chieng Kam on the east. In our reports to the mission and to the Board, these facts were urged as arguments for the establishment of a station there. The mission gave its cordial sanction to a temporary occupancy. A longer tour was authorized for the next season; but the heavy debt of the Board forbade the expenditure of more than two hundred and fifty rupees for a temporary house in order to secure the land which had been given us. Our long delay sorely shook the good governor's faith that we would ever come.

The arrival of young missionaries on the field rendered some kind of physical and social recreation necessary. Croquet had formerly been tried, but it gave very little exercise, and had been supplanted by the better game of lawn tennis. In the fall of 1890, Mrs. McGilvary prepared a court in our front lot, and invited the missionaries and the small European community to an "At Home" on Tuesdays at 4:30 P.M. The game furnished the very exercise needed after a day's confinement in school or study. It proved so beneficial to health and to efficiency in work, that the "At Home" was continued, with occasional interruptions from weather or other causes, for thirteen or fourteen years. This was Mrs. McGilvary's little contribution to the health and the social recreation of the community in which we lived; and it was highly appreciated.

In August I had occasion to visit Wieng Pā Pāo. Before I was out of the Chiengmai plain I had an exciting runaway on my big sadaw elephant. A mother cow was grazing at some little distance from her calf. As the elephant approached the calf, the mother became alarmed for its safety, and rushed frantically towards it, bellowing to the utmost capacity of her lungs. This was quite too much for my big timid beast. He started off at a fearful pace, which the driver in vain endeavoured to control. Fortunately it was on an open plain with no woods or trees. The same elephant on a previous occasion, when Mrs. McGilvary was riding him, on some slight alarm rushed off into a thicket of low trees; and once, with me on his back, went crashing through the standing timber in the forest. In both cases it was nothing but the strength of the three-strand rattan girth that saved either howdah or rider. The elephant's fastest run is not a "lope," but a kind of long swing from side to side. It is an awful sensation. I never was in an earthquake, but I imagine the two experiences must be somewhat similar, with the fear in this case of being at any instant dashed from your lofty perch to the ground.

The special reason for this trip was the fear of some collision or trouble between the government and the Christians with regard to the Sunday question. Besides keeping their own Sabbath, the Christians were forbidden to do any manual work on the Buddhist sacred days as well, making altogether eight days in each month. Had the rule been the outcome of conscientious scruples on the part of a religious people at seeing their sacred day desecrated, we should have respected their scruples. But the day was a mere holiday, and, except by a few of the more religious, it was largely spent in hunting and fishing. I had to remind the governor of his beautiful inconsistency. He would not allow the Christians to use an axe or a plow on sacred days, while the people generally were allowed to kill animals, thus breaking the most stringent of Buddha's laws. He must have felt the force of the argument, for before the very next sacred day an order was issued forbidding hunting and fishing on it.

FIRST CHURCH IN CHIENGMAI

DR. McGILVARY'S HOME IN CHIENGMAI

But till the original order was revoked, strict obedience was enjoined upon the Christians.

The Annual Meeting was held in Lakawn early in December. Just before it convened, Dr. and Mrs. W. A. Briggs and Rev. Robert Irwin arrived, together with Dr. and Mrs. Peoples, returning from furlough. For the present these were stationed at Lakawn. At the same time Rev. and Mrs. Stanley K. Phraner were nearing Chiengmai on the Mê Ping fork. But our song of joy over their arrival was destined soon again to have a sad refrain. The two young brides had scarcely reached their husbands' field of labour—which they thought was to be theirs also—when they were both called to a higher sphere.

XXIX

LENGTHENING THE CORDS AND STRENGTHENING THE STAKES

WHILE in the United States, Dr. Peoples had succeeded in procuring a font of Lão type, with the necessary equipment for printing. For twenty-three years we had used only the Siamese Scriptures and literature. With many present disadvantages, it had some compensations. Those who could read Siamese had access to the whole of the Old and New Testaments. The press was set up in Chiengmai, and Rev. D. G. Collins was made manager. The first printing done was Mrs. McGilvary's translation of the Gospel of Matthew.

My daughter had been sent down to aid the Phraners on their river trip. Word was sent ahead that Mrs. Phraner was not well. As they drew nearer, her condition became so critical that Dr. McKean hastened with all speed to meet them. When she reached Chiengmai, her condition, while still critical, was more hopeful. I was ready to start on my tour as soon as the party arrived. When I left home, we were still hopeful that rest, kind nursing, and medical treatment would set her right again.

During my absence this year I was fortunate enough to receive a regular weekly mail from Chiengmai. A staff of engineers were surveying a railroad route for the Siamese government, and had a weekly mail sent to their stations along the line. They were very kind to include my letters also, which was particularly fortunate in that thus I could have news of the invalid left behind.

I have learned to start on my tours with very flexible plans, leaving much to the guidance of providential openings on the way. On this trip, at the village of Pāng Krai—which, because it was a mile or two away from the road, I had not visited in seventeen years—I was delayed three days by a reception so cordial that I could not pass on. On my previous trip a man from the village, Noi Tĕchō by name, came with his little girl across to our camp and begged us to visit it. This I could not then do; but he remained with us till late at night, and seemed to be a believer. I now found that in the interval the man had kept the Sabbath, and had given such other evidence of his sincerity, that we could not refuse his reception to the communion and fellowship of the church. On the last night of our stay we had a baptismal and communion service that was memorable. The man made a good confession before many witnesses, and his little daughter was baptized as a non-communing member.

As in many other cases, this family had been driven by trouble to our religion. Originally he was the slave of a prince in Lakawn. The accusation of witchcraft then settled on the family; but before they were driven off the Prince compelled them to borrow money in order to redeem themselves from him—to do which the man had to give two of his children as security. After a move or two, he was driven by famine from Lakawn, and came to this village.

One morning at Wieng Pā Pāo I was summoned in great haste to attend one of the engineers who was thought to have been nearly killed by a fall from a runaway horse. I found that he had broken a collar-bone, but was otherwise uninjured. I applied all of my amateur surgical skill, and set the bone. But my patient, naturally enough, could not feel quite sure; and thought it safer to go down to our hospital and get Dr. McKean's judgment on the case. He found the bone set all right.

Late one Saturday evening I reached Bān Pā Hōng in Chieng Rāi province, and stopped with the first Christian family. Next day I learned that in the next section of the village there was a Christian girl very low with consumption. Early on Monday morning I moved on, but was only in time to see a lovely form and face apparently in the most natural sleep; but the living soul had departed. I had baptized her two years before, when she was fourteen years of age. She had been sick for seven months, and had spent most of the time in prayer. It made me inexpressibly sad when I learned that her strongest desire was to see her own "Paw Krū" before she departed. On the previous evening, when she heard that we had reached the village near by, she said, "And the Paw Krū is at Noi Lin's, and I cannot see him!" I preached her funeral sermon, and saw her decently buried.

The next Sunday morning, while sitting in the Mê Kawn chapel and preparing for service, I looked up and saw standing on the ground before the door some people in a strange costume evidently not Lāo, looking in as if in doubt whether to enter or not. I immediately recognized them as belonging to the Mūsô tribe, quite numerous in the mountains near by. Their ready acceptance of my invitation to come in showed that they were waiting to be asked, and feared only lest they might be intruders. As the Mūsŏs will be prominent in our narrative of this and the two following years, a word of introduction may be desirable.

They are one of a numerous group of hill tribes which have gradually followed the mountain ridges down from the interior of the continent. They live under a patriarchal government, if it may be rightly called a government at all; and they enjoy great personal freedom, though the authority of the clan approaches very near to absolute despotism. They are worshippers of spirits, which are held to preside over the universe and the destinies of men generally; while as a tribe they are under the guardianship of their own "spirits." They have a twelfth-day sabbath or sacred day, not very definitely marked. They make a great deal of their "kin waw" or New Year feast, when all communication with other villages even of their own tribe is cut off during the five or seven days of their feasting. The religious head of the village is called Pū Chān, and the head Pū Chān of a province holds in his hands the conscience of all his flock.

Their manner of life is as follows: They select a locality, the higher up the better, near the source of a mountain brook. They fell the trees and undergrowth at the close of the rainy season, let them dry during the hot season, and just before the next rainy season set fire to the clearing on a windy day. All that is readily combustible is consumed, leaving the logs on the ground. With a small hoe or a narrow spade they make shallow openings in the earth some ten inches apart, all over the field, and deposit in each a dozen rice grains, more or less. The rains do the rest till the harvest. The second year's crop is the best, but it is seldom that they can compete with the scrub-growth for a third crop. A temporary shack is easily erected, if possible, contiguous to three clearings. When these are abandoned, they move on and repeat the operation elsewhere. By this means all the higher mountains are being steadily denuded of their forests.

Being bound by no system of hoary age and venerable associations, like Buddhism or Brahmanism, most of the hill tribes are very receptive of the Gospel. Their clannishness, however, is such that if they become Christians at all, they come in a body. But it is very difficult for individuals or families to break away from the clan. At the same time their migratory and unsettled habits are by no means favourable to their education and civilization. To any other power than that of the Gospel that would seem to be a hopeless task.

But to return to our visitors at the chapel. There were seven men and boys in the party. The spokesman, Cha Pū Kaw, was tall and well proportioned, with the bearing of one who might be a leader of some position. He understood Lāo better than most of his tribe, and through him it was by no means difficult to draw the others into conversation. They were from three families that had been driven down nearer the plain by accusation of witchcraft. They had learned from our elder that Christians were not afraid of witchcraft, nor of expulsion from the country. They had also talked over with him the plan of salvation for sinful men provided in the Gospel, and had asked to be informed whenever we should come again. They readily consented to remain through the morning service, which was modified to suit the needs of the new audience. It was the first Christian worship they had ever attended, and they were evidently pleased. The Christians invited them to share their dinner, and the most of the afternoon was given up to their instruction. The boys were put to reading the catechism and learning to sing the Lāo version of "There is a Happy Land." They remained with us till there was only light enough left to enable them to find their way home.

Early next morning we crossed the plain to the foot of the mountain, where we struck the little brook along which and in which lay our pathway. The climb was a stiff one, but with noble outlooks over the plain below. In their little hamlet there were three families, or, rather, three divisions of one family, numbering twenty-six souls. By their intercourse with the Christians at the chapel the soil had been prepared for the seed. So from nine o'clock till noon we addressed ourselves to teaching the elders, while the children were becoming more and more interested in the catechism, and especially in the "Happy Land."

While the men and boys were thus engaged, the grandmother and her daughters were busy preparing dinner. When all was ready, the steaming white rice was emptied on a board like that on which our housewives knead their bread. With it was a vegetable curry, sweet potatoes steamed over the rice, bananas, and other fruits, with native sugar in cakes for dessert. The board piled with food was set before me, and I was invited to partake. They were delighted that I could eat and enjoy it.

After all had finished their meal, the exercises of the morning were resumed, with the women now disengaged and free to listen. Long before night Cha Pū Kaw and his brother-in-law, Cha Waw, of about the same age, expressed their firm belief in the truth of our religion, and their acceptance of the Gospel offer as far as they understood it. The women said they would follow their husbands. The sun was already getting low when we had worship together before leaving. When we came to bid our hosts good-bye, we found that we were to be escorted down by the two elder men and the boys, lest a tiger might meet us on the way. It was almost dark when we reached the chapel.—A day never to be forgotten!

At the chapel I found letters from Chiengmai bringing the news that Mrs. Phraner's long and painful sufferings were ended. She died on February 13th. All that three able physicians could do was done; but in vain. Her mother and her family were never willing that she should become a missionary, being sure that she could not endure the strain of a missionary's life. That fact filled the husband's cup of sorrow to overflowing. My letter stated that he was beside himself with grief; that the physicians, and, in fact, the whole mission, strongly advised him to join me on my tour; and that he would reach me not long after the letter.

On the following Friday, while getting the new chapel ready, I heard the shout, "There comes the new teacher!" He was worn and haggard, and visibly older than when I left him; but making a brave effort to be cheerful. He said very little of his great loss.

On Sunday the whole Müsô village was on hand long before the hour for worship. The women came with their babes tied with a scarf to the mother's back, according to their custom. The news that they were become Christians had spread, and drew a larger number than usual of our non-Christian neighbours to the services. The Christians, too, were greatly encour-

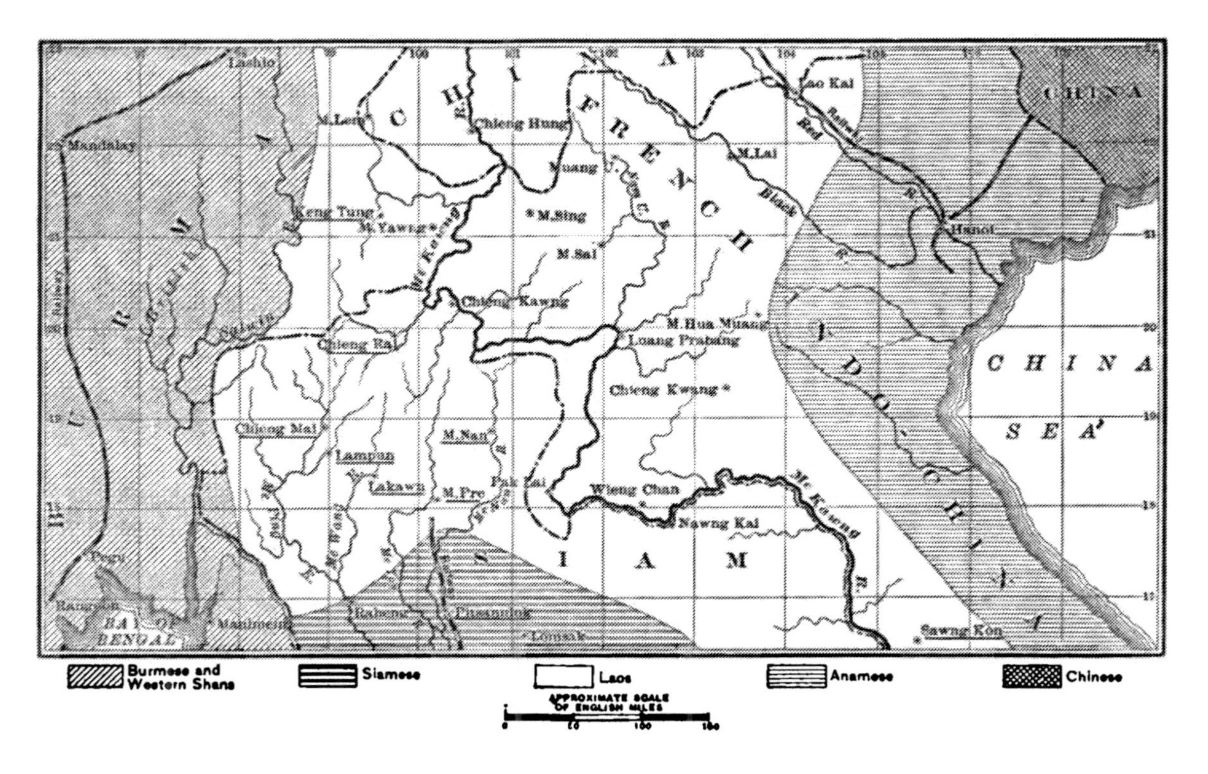

MAP OF NORTHERN SIAM, SHOWING MISSION STATIONS, UNDERLINED.

aged thereby. In the afternoon a few of the tribe from another village were present, and listened with surprise to Cha Pū Kaw's first sermon. He had evidently entered upon his new faith in earnest, and was not ashamed to bear his testimony.

On Monday we moved on to Chieng Răi, where I was to direct the removal of a house to the lot which the Governor had offered us. But Mr. Phraner's condition demanded movement and change of scene. Arrangements were, therefore, made to have the house moved by others, while we went on at once to Chieng Sên. There we found the Chao Uparăt just returned from a trip via Mûang Len to Mûang Sing, some hundred miles or so to the northeast on the other side of the Mê Kōng River. He was profuse in his praise both of Mûang Sing and of the journey thither; and suggested that it would be a fine opening for a mission, and a most interesting tour. The suggestion seemed attractive to us both. So, after a week of work in the church and in the city of Chieng Sên, we started for Mûang Len and Mûang Sing.

Mûang Len is the common market centre of a large number of hill tribes that inhabit the mountain ridges in all directions round about. All the cities and towns north of Chieng Sên hold a fifth-day fair or market. We were fortunate in striking market-day on the Saturday of our arrival. Early in the morning people began to pour into the place from all directions. The mountain tribes came out, their beaux and belles all in gala dress, some to buy and sell, and others because it was their weekly holiday.

From Chieng Sên I had brought along Năn Suwan, the Lû elder, who had come into closer contact with these mountain tribes than had our elders from the south. He could make the men, and especially the head men, understand fairly well. To all who understood the Lāo I could, of course, speak directly. We took our stand at the end of the market, and the crowd gathered about us. None of them had ever seen a missionary. None, save some few of the Lāo men, had ever read a book, or knew even a letter of any written language. They were children of nature, artless and unsophisticated. We pressed home the thought, new to them, that there must be a maker of the world and of all creatures in it. We told them the old, old story of the infinite love of God, our Father, and of Christ, His Son, who suffered and died to save us, and of pardon freely promised to all who believe in Him. This is the final argument that wins these people.

After the merely curious among the crowd had withdrawn, this doctrine of salvation from sin held the more thoughtful, and brought them to our tent in the afternoon, and even far on into the night. The head men especially, who were more free to come to me, expressed a deep personal interest in the new doctrine. The most interested and interesting man was Sên Ratana, the governor of the Kôn quarter of the city. We met him on Sunday. On Monday we called on him and spent most of the morning at his house, explaining to him the plan of salvation and dictating to him portions of Scripture for him to copy; for by this time the Lāo manuscript copies which we brought with us were exhausted. He copied, also, the first few questions and answers of the Shorter Catechism, hoping that with these as a key, he could learn to read the Siamese Gospel and catechism which I gave him.

On our return to our tent on Monday evening we found almost a panic among our people. Some lawless men had lounged about the tent most of the day, asking suspicious questions about how much money we carried, and how many guns, and whither we were going from there, etc., etc. The result was that those who had been most eager for the trip beyond the Mê Kōng to Mûang Sing, began now to beg us to return. Mr. Phraner, moreover, became uneasy about his borrowed elephant, which would be a great prize for robbers. So, after consultation, it was decided to retrace our steps. However disappointing this might be to me, I had at least learned the road to Mûang Sing and Mûang Yawng. The tour to both those places, and to many others, was only deferred to the following year, when we might hope to have at least one printed Gospel in the Lāo language, and a tract or two to distribute. The news of Cha Pũ Kaw's conversion spread far and wide, and was preparing the way for further work among his tribe.

Leaving Mûang Len on Wednesday, we breathed more freely after we had crossed the border into Siam. On reaching Chieng Sên, Mr. Phraner decided to return to Chiengmai. He had reaped all the benefit possible from change of scene. He felt that he ought now to be in his future home, settling down to a systematic study of the language. But I greatly missed his pleasant company.

The object of the missionary's visit to an outlying church like that of Chieng Sên, is to "lengthen the cords and strengthen the stakes"—to awaken the careless, to attract the indifferent, and to deepen impressions already made. Within the range of influence of such a church there are always those who, though taught, indeed, by its native officers, still need further instruction by the missionary—who have objections to be met and doubts to be resolved beyond the power of these officers to cope with. Not infrequently some one who is already a believer has a wife, a husband, or children on whom his own final decision depends. These must be visited in their homes. Their confidence must be won and their friendship gained as a preliminary to awakening their interest in our religion.

For the sake of the Christians personally, as well as for the work in general, it is important to cultivate the friendship of the local rulers. It is to them that the Christians are responsible. And then the Christian families must be visited, their children instructed, their difficulties settled, their sick be treated, and instructed how to treat themselves in our absence; and as much Scriptural teaching is to be given as our time by night and by day will permit. But our most important duty is to instruct the elders themselves, and give them an uplift.

When my work in Chieng Sên was done, I started for Chieng Kawng, taking Nān Suwan along, for he was well known there and in most of the region to be visited as far as Chieng Rāi. The Mê Tam, already referred to as the stream which rises from under the mountain west of the plain, becomes quite a river as it enters the Mê Kōng near Chieng Sên. The bottom land is covered with reedy grass so tall that a large elephant carrying a high howdah can be seen only a short distance away. Here we lost our way completely, and wandered about bewildered for a long time.

When finally we reached the stream, its trough was so deep that we failed in a number of attempts to get down to the water. At last we dug down as best we could the edge of the high sandy bank, and, after much urging, and some protest on his part, my sadaw tremblingly reached forth his front feet, lay down, and slid like an alligator, dragging his hind legs after him, till, with a mighty plunge, we landed in deep water. It was an awful sensation for the rider. The place was in a bayou with "back water" so deep as to be quite over one's head; and, unlike the natives, the rider could not swim! The landing on the further shore was little better. There the elephant struggled up the bank until he got his forefeet on the edge above. Then, with a gigantic effort, he drew himself up so suddenly that the rider had to hold on for dear life to avoid being thrown over his head. It was a feat that only an elephant could perform, and one would much prefer witnessing it from a distance to being on his back during the operation.

At Chieng Kawng I was sorry to find the governor sadly crippled. In descending a flight of steps he had slipped to the ground, dislocating his ankle and bruising the bone. The joint had been barbarously treated, was fearfully swollen, and caries of the bone had evidently set in. I urged him to take an elephant and go to our hospital, as the only possible chance of cure. He was favourably inclined to the idea, and promised to do so after trying somewhat longer the incantations of a noted sorceress, who was believed to have great power over wounds. It almost passes belief that such an intelligent man could have any faith in it. Yet reason and ridicule alike failed to dispel the hope that she might succeed. The result might have been predicted. After giving him great suffering, the treatment cost him his life.

While I was in Chieng Kawng, a Nān prince returning from Mûang Sing brought the news that negotiations then on foot between France and Siam would put a stop to all further settlement of that district; would, in fact, transfer the whole region east of the Mê Kōng to France. The Prince of Nān was greatly disappointed; but little did we think that the transfer would ultimately prove an effectual barrier to our work also. It is surely one of the anomalies and anachronisms of the twentieth century that a Christian nation of Europe should oppose the introduction of Christianity into a region over which it has absolute control!

On the last night before we left, all the princes and officers came to see us, and remained till midnight. They were as loath to have us leave them as we were to go.

The journey from Chieng Kawng was intensely hot; the thermometer standing at 103° in my howdah by day, and on one night in my tent at 96°. On the banks of the Mê Ing I found native white roses in bloom in abundance, and brought home with me a plant which Mrs. McGilvary greatly prized, for this was the only native rose I had found in the Lāo territory.

On the way to Mûang Tông I passed the camp of Chao Wieng Sā, a Nān prince whom I had met in his home on two former visits. He was overseeing the felling and running of teak timber down the Mê Ing and the Mê Kōng to Lūang Prabāng. He had received and read a Siamese New Testament, was quite familiar with the life and teachings of Jesus, and admired His character. A lawsuit afterwards brought him to Chiengmai, where I saw a great deal of him. He was surely a believer at heart. To me he was willing to confess that his only hope was in Jesus Christ, but was not ready to make a public profession of his faith. I love to think of many such whom I have met as like the

MRS. McGILVARY
1893

Gamaliels, the Nicodemuses, and the Josephs of Christ's day.

At Mûang Tông, as soon as I dismounted from my elephant an officer met me to enquire who I was, and to escort me to the public sālā. I soon learned that he was the brother of another officer whom I had found on the road to Chieng Rāi the year before, unable to travel and, apparently, sick unto death with fever. His company could not linger indefinitely in the forest, and so had left him there with two men to watch him, and probably to see him die. A dose of calomel, and the quinine which I left with instructions as to its use, seem to have cured his fever and enabled him to reach his home in safety. He was himself now absent, but his brother's heart had been opened to friendship, and he did all that he could for my comfort. At night he invited his friends to the sālā to meet me, and we had an interesting evening. In all these places Nān Suwan and Noi Siri would often be heard talking to the audience after I had retired, and until sleep closed my eyes.

During our absence from Chieng Rāi a case of oppression, or, at least, of evident injustice, on the part of the Court, had led our friend the governor to take all Christians under his personal protection as his own dependents. The kindness was well meant, and we thanked him for it. But I doubted its wisdom. The only scheme under which Christianity can really establish itself in all lands, is to have Christians stand on precisely the same level before the law as Buddhists or Brahmans or the followers of any other religion.

From Chieng Rāi the elders were sent on to Cha Pū Kaw's village to see how the Mūsôs were getting on. I followed them in a day or two. When I reached the chapel at Mê Kawn, the elders had returned from the Mūsô village with a glowing account of their constancy. This the testimony of Noi Tāliya and of all the Lāo Christians confirmed. They had not missed a single Sunday service; old and young alike came, and mothers, as before, bringing their children tied on their backs. They had shamed the Lāo Christians by their earnestness, getting to the chapel first, studying hard, and returning home late.

On Saturday morning the whole village came down, and we spent the day together. They remained that night as the guests of the Lāo. The next day, Sunday, was largely given up to their instruction. They all had renounced the worship of spirits; they all accepted Jesus as their Saviour; they were all diligently learning to read and to sing. Their conduct was most consistent; they had a good reflex influence upon the church; and their conversion was an astonishment to the non-Christian community.

These Mūsôs had all come, expecting to join the church. They had been taught that public baptism—confessing Christ before men—was the consummating act, the external seal of their initiation into the privileges of the church. Although we impressed upon them that they were not saved by the mere ceremony of baptism, yet somehow they felt that without it they were not quite in the church, and hence probably not quite safe from the spirits. Since it would be nearly a year before they would have another opportunity, it seemed unwise not to receive some of them at this time. The greatest doubt was about Cha Waw. Yet he felt that more than any other he needed whatever protection and assistance the church could afford him. He had begun with his whole strength to break the chains of his opium habit, to seek pardon and be saved. He felt confident that with God's help he would succeed.

The final decision was that, in order to bind them to the service of Christ, they were all to appear before the session and make their profession; but that only the two old men should be received into full communion, and that one grandson from each family be baptized as non-communing members. It was thought best to let the others wait till our next visit; though I have never been satisfied that they should not all have been admitted that day. Three of these Mūsô boys accompanied me to Chiengmai on my return, and entered the Boys' School. It is not at all surprising that, in surroundings so different from those of their mountain homes, they presently grew lonesome and homesick. But they were satisfactory pupils, and remained in school long enough to get a good start in reading and singing.

Cha Waw, after a manful struggle, finally succeeded in breaking away entirely from his opium—by the help of prayer and of quinine, as he always believed and affirmed. When the non-Christian tribesmen with their opium pipes visited his village, he was accustomed to go down to the elders at Mê Kawn, to be away from temptation, and under Christian influence. He lived a number of years after this to attest the reality of his victory—the only case I have ever known where the victory was surely won.

That year there was a famine among all the hill tribes. The upland rice was almost entirely cut off by a plague of rats. I do not believe in "rice Christians"; but when people are famishing with hunger, I believe in feeding them, whether they are Christians or not. These did not ask either for money or for any other aid. But when I left them, I made arrangement with the Lāo elders to furnish them with sixty buckets of rice, for which I paid ten rupees in advance. They were very grateful for the aid.

The days spent among the Mūsôs that week were inspiring. Glowing visions arose before us of a new tribe brought into the Christian church, of which these were the first-fruits. On this whole tour, indeed, only nine adults and seventeen children were baptized. But in addition to the opening of work among the Mūsôs, we had for the first time preached the Gospel beyond the borders of the kingdom of Siam; and our longing eyes were turned toward the Sipsawng Pannā, and beyond the great river. By this time the rains had already begun to fall. A new season was needed to fulfil our desires.

Much as I always enjoy my long tours, when my work is done and my face at last is turned homewards, the gait of my sadaw seems distressingly slow. On reaching Chiengmai I found all in fair health, and all departments of work in full operation. But while I was still on my way, word reached me of the death of Mrs. Briggs in Lakawn, only a month and nine days after that of Mrs. Phraner. So unexpected was it that I was not even aware that she had been ill. In answer to my request for a few particulars from Dr. Briggs, I have received the following, which I know he will excuse me for transferring to these pages:

"Mrs. Alice Hamilton Briggs was from Truro, Nova Scotia. Although within a year of graduation, she gave up her medical course and accompanied her husband to the Lāo mission in answer to the call of the Board. When she bade good-bye to the Secretaries of the Board, Dr. Gillespie said to her, 'It is a pleasure to see you so robust and strong. In this respect you are better off than your husband. There have been so many missionary women who have broken down on the field, that we are glad to see that you have a reserve of health.'

"Before leaving American shores, however, Mrs. Briggs contracted a slight cough which developed in severity during the voyage. On her arrival in Siam it became apparent that the case was one of pulmonary tuberculosis. The disease seemed to respond to treatment, and for months improvement was marked. Up to within twenty-four hours of death Mrs. Briggs was so hopeful of a return to health that she refused to allow her family at home to know of her condition. On Saturday she was cutting out a new dress for herself. On Sunday night she passed away. Dr. Briggs was spending the evening with her, when a call came to attend a child said to be dying just across the road. The doctor said he would be back soon. A few minutes later he was called back too late even to hear a last word of farewell."

The event most interesting to us as a family during the fall of this year, 1891, was the arrival of our son Evander with his young bride, and our daughter Margaret, to carry on the work begun by their parents. Our son had made special preparation for translating the Scriptures into the Lão language, then the most pressing need of the mission.

XXX

AMONG THE MŪSÔ VILLAGES—FAMINE

FOR the tour of 1892 I was to have the company of Dr. McKean as long as he could be spared from Chiengmai, which would greatly enhance the value of the trip. We had also three native evangelist-assistants, and, last, but not least, we were well supplied with Scriptures and tracts in the Lāo dialect. Our start was made on January 5th.

Our first two Sundays and the intervening week we spent in Wieng Pā Pāo, where we established ourselves in the new chapel which the people themselves had built since our last tour. We observed the Week of Prayer with two chapel services daily, and house-to-house and heart-to-heart work in the intervals. The church was formally organized with thirty-six adult members and thirty children, three ruling elders, and two deacons.

From Wieng Pā Pāo we moved on to the village of Mê Kawn, the centre of our very interesting work of the previous year among the Mūsô tribe. The Sunday we spent there was a red-letter day in our missionary life. Of it Dr. McKean writes: "This has been a blessed day. All [of the Mūsôs] desire baptism. Two boys baptized last year were admitted to the communion. Eleven other adults and seven children were baptized, making twenty-two Mūsôs now members of the visible church. One Lāo girl was received on confession, and three Lāo children were baptized. Our Christian Mūsôs were out in full force. A Mūsô officer and others not Christians attended from another village. Before this we had visited these people in their homes. We found that they had built a good chapel for their worship, a better building than either of their own houses. They had been very diligent in observing the Sabbath, in studying the catechism, and in worship."

We could not have been better pleased with our first success. The exclusion of this little group from the large villages made it possible and easy for all of them to become Christians. The whole-hearted zeal with which they entered the church awakened strong hopes for the conversion of their race. Cha Pū Kaw's knowledge of the Lāo tongue was above the average even of their head men. It would be a long time before we could have another such interpreter and assistant. And he was nearly, or quite, seventy years old; so that whatever he was to do in teaching his people must be done soon. It was, therefore, thought best to make a strong effort through him and his family during that season.

At our next stopping-place, Nāng Lé, we came near having a serious casualty. Our boys were out on a deer hunt, and one of them bethought him of a novel expedient for getting the game. He climbed a tree, and had the grass fired on the other side of the open space. The grass was tall and dry, and the wind blew strong towards him. He became so engrossed in looking for the deer that he forgot the fire, till it was too late to flee. He could climb beyond the actual flames; but meanwhile the whole air had become like the breath of a furnace. When, at last, the fire had swept past him, and he was able to descend, he was a mass of blisters. The swiftness of the rush of the fire alone saved his life. Had it been slower, he could not have escaped suffocation.

From Nāng Lê we visited a very large Mūsô village. It was a steep foot-climb of four solid hours, and, to make it longer, our guide missed the way. The first sign of human life we saw was a Mūsô girl alone watching a clearing. She fled for dear life, till, recognizing Cha Pū Kaw's Mūsô speech, she stopped long enough to point the way to the village. Her fleet steps outran ours, and when we reached the village, the people were already assembling to see the unwonted sight of the white foreigners. But the community was greatly disturbed over another matter. One of their leading officers, it seemed, was accused of being the abode of a demon that had caused an epidemic of disease. The authorities were hourly waiting for an order from the court in Chieng Rāi to expel him and his family by force from the province. They had heard of Cha Pū Kaw's conversion, and were anxious to hear from himself his reasons therefor—which he gave and enforced till late in the night. They were expecting, however, on the morrow a regular conflict which might result in bloodshed, and they evidently preferred that we should not be there. The head Pū Chān was several days' journey distant. They would confer together among themselves and with him, would let us know the result, and would invite us up again before we left their neighbourhood.

About midnight a fierce storm of wind and rain broke upon us to our great discomfort. Our thin tent afforded but poor protection. We doubled up our bedding over our clothes, and sat upon the pile under our umbrellas, and laughed at the novelty of our situation and the poor prospect of a night's sleep. But later the storm passed off, and we did get a little sleep. Our visit to that group of Mūsô villages was evidently not well timed. We took the advice of their officers, and returned to Nāng Lê.

Two days later we reached Chieng Sên. Here we received a mail from home, with news that Mrs. McKean was not well, and other members of the station needed the doctor's presence. It was expressed as "the unanimous judgment of the station that he should return immediately." We had planned a regular campaign in the Mūsô districts on both sides of the Mê Kōng—the sort of trip in which the medical missionary finds his best opportunity. But the recall was so imperative that it could not be ignored. So I was left to continue the work alone.

The Mūsô tribe was about equally numerous in the mountain ranges on both sides of the big river. On the east side there were eleven villages. It seemed advisable to take that section first, because they were under Cheng Sên rulers, of whose cordial and sincere interest in our work we were sure. Sên Chai, the head man of the large village nearest to the city, was a friend of Nān Suwan, and was strongly inclined to embrace our religion; but felt the difficulty of breaking the tribal bond. Before this I had made him a visit of two or three days, and saw clearly that our only chance of accomplishing anything was to gain all the head men of the eleven villages. It was actually easier to win over the whole as a unit than to win it piecemeal. This was a formidable task to undertake, but with God's blessing on the labours of Cha Pū Kaw and Nān Suwan, it seemed not impossible.

We set out for the first village one morning shortly aften ten o'clock. It was four o'clock when we stopped for rest at the first cluster of houses on the outskirts of the settlement. The news of our arrival soon reached the main village. When we started again we met Sên Chai with a regular serenade-party of men and boys with native reed instruments, blowing their plaintive dirge-like music, to welcome us and escort us in. Soon the population was all assembled—the maidens in their best sarongs, the mothers and grandmothers each with an urchin strapped to her back by her scarf, the men coming in from their work, and the inevitable crowd of children. Cha Pū Kaw was already answering their questions, with Nān Suwan's sympathetic aid. They were respectfully shy, but there was no cringing. Sên Chai invited the local Pū Chān and all the villagers to assemble after their evening meal to hear the new doctrines. We first had worship with singing, and prayer by Cha Pū Kaw. It was the first time they had heard the Great Spirit addressed in their own Mūsô tongue. There were frequent exclamations of delight that they were able to understand every word.

And then, before that motley crowd, drinking with them their native tea from an earthen teapot, the men seated close around, or reclining as they smoke their pipes, the women and children walking about or sitting on the ground—we tell of God the great Spirit, the Creator, and Father of all—the Bible, His message to men—the incarnation, life, and death of Christ, and redemption through His blood. Before we get through you will hear man after man say, "I believe that. It is true." One man takes up the story from Cha Pū Kaw's mouth and repeats it to another—a story that till now he himself had never heard. Another says, "Nān Suwan has told us this before, but now we hear it from the father-teacher."

Before we retired that night Sên Chai said to us, with the approval of most of his village, "Go on to Sên Bun Yūang and the head men of the other villages. If they agree, we will all accept Christianity. One village cannot accept it alone. If we do not 'kin waw' with them—join in their New Year's feast—we shall be treated as enemies by the whole tribe."

So, next morning, we set out to find the great Pū Chān—the religious head of the province. On our way to his village we fell in with a man to whom Cha Pū Kaw was speaking with great earnestness. I found on approaching him that he was not a Mūsô, but a Kūi—of a tribe which we had planned to visit later. He was the Pū Chān of his village. He had already invited us through Cha Pū Kaw to change our plan, and visit his village first. It was nearer than the village we were intending to visit, and we were already tired enough with our climb to be willing to stop at the nearest place.

The village was a large one, as mountain villages go—of twenty-five or thirty houses, and from two hundred and fifty to three hundred souls—in general not unlike the Mūsô villages we had seen. The Kūi language also, while different from the Mūsô, is cognate with it, so that Cha Pū Kaw could still act fairly well as our interpreter. His talk with the Pū Chān on the way had already laid a good foundation for our work in the evening, when curiosity and interest in our errand brought the whole village together to hear Cha Pū Kaw's new doctrine from his own lips. The news of his conversion had already reached them, and he had made a good impression on the religious head of the village.—And, then, it was something new to see the Mūsô boys able to read and to sing. Nān Suwan and Cha Pū Kaw led in prayer, the one in Lāo and the other in Mūsô. Then our religion was explained in its two leading ideas—rejection of the spirit-cult, and acceptance of Jesus for the pardon of sin and the life eternal. Questions were asked and answered.

At last the Pū Chān suggested that, while we continued our reading and singing with the women and children, he and the men, with Cha Pū Kaw, withdraw to a neighbouring house and talk the matter over. It was evident that they would be more at their ease by themselves, unawed by the presence of the foreign teacher. For some two hours the debate continued. I could hear their earnest voices from the neighbouring house, with only now and then a Lāo word that I could understand. Then they returned to make their report. With oriental politeness, they expressed their gratitude to the "great teacher" who had come so far and at such expense, and had brought with him a fellow-mountaineer of theirs, to teach them, creatures of the jungle, the way to happiness. They had talked these matters over, and understood them somewhat, but not fully. Some were greatly pleased with the teachings, and believed them true. But they could not yet come as an entire village, and they dared not separate. Next morning we parted as friends. They were glad that we had found the way to their village. "Be sure to come again!" That I thought surely I should do; but this proved to be my only visit.

At the Sên Lūang's village, where the great Pū Chān lived, we had the same experience—a good reception, many apparently interested and anxious to escape their own spirit-worship. A number of the head men said, "If such and such a village accepts the Jesus-religion, we will." But no one could be found to face the clan and make a start.

Thinking that our native evangelists might get at the heart of the people all the better if left to do it alone, and being anxious to get my mail from home, I went down on Saturday to Nān Suwan's to spend the Sunday there with the Christians. On Tuesday, to my disappointment, the evangelists returned to me discouraged. They were convinced that in the district east of the Mê Kōng River, no break in the solidarity of the clan could be accomplished that season.

But it was important not to leave these people with the impression that we had abandoned them. I had left Sên Chai's village with the promise to return. So I went up with the Mūsô Christian boys, and spent a last night with them. The village again assembled, and we had an interesting evening. The Sên was greatly disappointed that none of the other villages would join him. But the New Year was at hand, when the clan must be unbroken. They would wait another year, and try to get the other villages to join them. On the whole, I was encouraged. When we left them we were escorted out of the village to the music of their plaintive flutes, more like a victorious than a vanquished army.

After a day or two with the Chieng Sên church, we visited the ridge to the southeast of that city, between it and Chieng Kawng. Our experience there was but a repetition of that from which we were just come—cordial receptions, night audiences, manifest interest, individual believers, anxious consultations, promises for the next year; but the tribal bond was too strong to be broken.

But Cha Pū Kaw was anxious that we should not pass by his own mountain villages on the Mê Kok. So we turned southward again toward Chieng Rāi. This, moreover, was one of those famine years, such as we have already encountered in our story, and shall encounter yet again; many people were on the verge of starvation. In places we could not get food for our own men. And famine was beginning to be followed by disease and death. This was a serious obstacle to our work.

Another serious obstacle was the use of opium, which became more prevalent the further west we went along the Mê Kok range towards Mûang Fāng. We presently reached villages where the poppy was cultivated, until, in the last village, men, women, and boys, and sometimes even girls, were its slaves. Fevers and dysentery prevail during the rainy season. These people have a very scanty pharmacopœia, and no antidotes whatever for these diseases. Opium in some form is probably their surest remedy. Many persons told me that they began by using it in sickness. As sickness recurred the habit grew, until they were fast bound in its chains. These facts largely determined the character of the instruction we gave, and made our tour a kind of anti-opium crusade. Encouraged and disappointed at every village, I was still tempted on by visions of capturing some large village that would prove a more effective entering wedge for the tribe than Cha Pū Kaw's poor little hamlet. The six weeks so spent were at the time the most novel and exciting, as well as most arduous, of all my missionary experiences so far.

We took both the old Mūsô men as assistants, and the younger ones as carriers for our equipment. Our first day's journey was a fair sample of what we had to do continually. In many places it would be a misnomer to speak of the track we travelled as a path. We left the plain in the morning, and it was half-past two in the afternoon when we reached the first summit. It was five o'clock when, desperate with thirst, we came upon a flowing brook. There was, then, still another hard climb before we saw our long looked-for first village ahead. And, in general, because of the habit these people have of planting their villages upon the very highest points where they can get water, the journey from one of these villages to another in plain sight, and, apparently, but a short distance away, would take hours of the hardest travel. Sometimes we would walk weary hours through rain, or through bushes as wet as rain, to visit a village; only to walk back again after sitting three hours in wet clothes trying in vain to awaken some interest in old or young.

One of the most interesting, and, at the same time, one of the saddest, cases we met was that of Mûn Kamprai, the head man of a village which clearly bore the impress of his character in the intelligence and industry of its inhabitants. From opium he had kept entirely aloof until, only a few years before this time, under the stress of a severe illness, he began to take it. The poor man now realized that he was becoming a wreck, but seemed to have no will-power left to make the effort to break away from the habit. He was much interested, however, in his two fellow-tribesmen whom I had brought as my assistants; and Cha Waw's example seemed to afford him a faint gleam of hope. If we would stop a week and teach his people, and would stand by to aid him, he would try. If successful, he would surely become a Christian—and then his village would be the one we had been hoping for to free itself from the tribal bond, and become Christian.

The experiment was, indeed, pathetic. Removing all temptation, he began with a desperate determination to succeed. We encouraged him with human sympathy and the hope of divine aid. We pushed as far as we dared the use of a tonic which Dr. McKean had given me for such cases; and it aided him perceptibly. He held out manfully for several days. But, at last, in an evil hour, he could endure the torture no longer, and before we knew it, he had resumed the use of the drug. For two nights he had not slept. In his own expressive language, it was not his eyes, but his heart that could not sleep. Poor man! his sufferings must have been as near those of the infernal regions as it is possible to experience in the body. And then his absolute wreck of mind, and the contempt he felt for himself when he gave up the struggle as hopeless!

We spared no labour to reach the homes of these people, or their hearts. We tried to become Mūsôs to the Mūsôs that we might win them. Sometimes we had to sleep in their huts—on a floor raised two or three feet from the ground, which the dogs shared with the family, while the pigs and goats were on the ground beneath. In the centre was a raised fireplace on which the native teapot always boiled. Sleeping-mats or thin bedding lay about on the floor, and on this, before bedtime, some of the inmates would lie down and fall asleep even while listening to the conversation.—But everywhere the tribal bond was too strong to be broken.

MŪSÔ PEOPLE AND HUT NEAR CHIENG RAI

By this time the rains had set in. The trails—and the leeches that infested them—were getting worse and worse. Soon the torrent-streams would become impassable. We must return while yet we could. Our six weeks' wanderings we retraced in four days of constant tramping. It had been a hard trip for all of us. I myself had a touch of fever. It seemed good on reaching our camp to have once more the luxury of a chair and a table. And then to be on the sadaw's back travelling homewards, and to meet a good mail on the way! My three-score and fourth birthday was spent in the forest, and I reached home safely on the 18th of May, after an absence of nearly five months.

The peninsula of Farther India is largely exempt from the terrible scourge of famine which has become almost chronic in Hindustan, its greater neighbour on the west. There the population is so numerous that the normal production of food is just sufficient to supply its needs. Even a local or a partial failure of the crops must produce distress. Siam, on the contrary, is happy in that it not only produces an abundant supply for its own people, but is a granary for the surrounding countries. The worst that has ever been experienced in Lower Siam in years of greatest scarcity, has been the necessity of checking the export of rice. The annual floods there cover the whole country, so that a general failure of crops is, humanly speaking, impossible.

In the northern states the land is higher; and considerable portions of it, being above inundation, are directly dependent upon the seasonal and local rains. But with a population by no means dense, this very diversity of the cultivated areas is a source of safety. A season of heavy rainfall which drowns the lowland rice, is apt to prove exceptionally good for the uplands. And, on the other hand, a season of light rainfall, which cuts short the upland crop, is apt to be a good season for the flooded areas. And in considerable sections of the country there is the chance that a second crop in the same season may make good the loss of the first. There is a further security also in the fact that, until communication with the coast becomes such as to make exportation profitable, the excess of fruitful years remains unconsumed in the country, to supply the need of less fruitful ones. It thus comes about that scarcity amounting to a real famine cannot result from the failure of crops in any single year. It requires two consecutive failures to produce extensive suffering among the very poor, and three to result in a real famine.

This last, however, was the case in 1892. In 1890 there was a light crop throughout the land, with less excess than usual to be stored. In 1891 the crop was lighter still. In the eastern provinces, particularly in Lakawn and Prê, there was very little rice to be reaped. Famine conditions began there long before the time for harvest. People were scattering off in squads or by families into Chiengmai and the northern provinces, begging a daily morsel. They were poverty-stricken as well as famishing. The distress led the brethren in Lakawn to make an appeal to friends in the United States for a famine fund. Quite a liberal response, amounting to several thousand dollars, was made to this call, largely by the friends of the Lāo mission. The relief was almost as timely for the missionaries as it was for the famishing people. Otherwise they scarcely could have lived through the long strain on their nerves and sympathies caused by the constant sight of sufferings which they could not even in part relieve.

The province of Chiengmai could have met its own needs until the new crop came in, had it not been for the constant draft upon its reserves to meet the demands of Lakawn and Prê. But, between high prices offered and pity for the less fortunate, those reserves were steadily drained away, until, during the latter months of the year, famine was upon us in Chiengmai, too. Bands of men from destitute villages, maddened by hunger and unable to buy food, began to roam about the country by night, or, sometimes, by day, and seize rice wherever any little remnant of it could be found. The authorities were powerless to restrain them or to keep order. The condition of the more destitute provinces can better be imagined than described.

At last the relief committee in Lakawn were asked if they could not spare us a small portion of their fund, for it seemed that their condition could not be much worse than ours. A letter from Dr. W. A. Briggs brought us three hundred rupees, but with the following *caveat*—the italics are his:

"*Wherever* we can reach the absolutely starving, that is a place to invest. We do not pretend to relieve all the *suffering*. Now, if the need in Chiengmai, or in the district mentioned, is so great that people are actually dying from starvation, and those now living are living on such stuff as the sample enclosed (cocanut-husks, leaves, bark, etc.), *with never a grain of rice*, then I would advise you to form a Famine Committee, and go into the business as we have done. The actual starvation *must* be attended to, *no matter where it is*. But our saddest experience is within Prê. Some one should be sent there at once."

The scenes reported from Prê were harrowing. I will not pain the reader by dwelling upon them. One happy result followed the efforts of the brethren who went to the relief of that district. While administering to bodily wants, they preached the Gospel, making such an impression that there was a strong demand for a permanent station there—which was established the next year, with Dr. and Mrs. Briggs as pioneer missionaries.

It should be stated that, toward the last, the Siamese government sent up supplies of rice; but, because of the distance and the difficulty of transportation, not much reached the suffering people in time to help them; and much was lost in passing through the hands of so many officials.

XXXI

CHIENG RUNG AND THE SIPSAWNG PANNĀ

AT the Annual Meeting of the mission in December, 1892, the broad field of Tai peoples north of the frontier of Siam was discussed, and Rev. Robert Irwin and myself were appointed to make a tour into that region as long and as far as in our judgment might be deemed wise. The tour occupied nearly five months—from January 3d to May 25th, 1893. This time we went fairly well supplied with portions of Scriptures and tracts, and a good outfit of medicine. Of quinine we carried a hundred ounces, and returned with less than twenty-five. We relied on the medicines for the welcome they never yet had failed to win for us. And Mr. Irwin had a cornet which did excellent service throughout the tour. For riding I had my big "sadaw" elephant, and Mr. Irwin had a pony; so we could exchange mounts at our convenience. I pass over the earlier portion of our route, already so often described, and the two weeks spent among the hill-tribes visited on previous trips.

The chief object of our trip was to visit, in their ancient homes, two northern tribes of the Lāo race—the Kôn and the Lû—from which very many of our parishioners in the southern provinces derived their origin. For, under conditions which lasted very nearly down to our own time, there was almost constant predatory warfare going on in this northern country—

stronger states raiding the weaker, and sweeping away the entire population of the districts they overran, to plant them in their own realms. Thus whole villages, and even entire districts, in the Lāo provinces of Siam, are peopled by the descendants of such colonies of captives. We found it unadvisable to attempt both visits in the same season, and the Lû were the more accessible, living on the nearer slopes of the Mê Kông valley. We went up on the west of the river along the edge of the British territory, now known as the South Shan States, and beyond it into Chinese territory, as far as Chieng Rung;[1] then, returning, we made a somewhat wider sweep to the east of the river, through French Indo-China; finally recrossing the river at Chieng Lāp, where we struck once more our outgoing trail.

After leaving Mûang Len, the utmost point of a former trip, we travelled awhile by a fine road along the summit of a ridge so regular as to seem almost like an artificial embankment, and affording noble views over the valley. At Wieng Mai, a recent offshoot of Mûang Yawng, we spent a most interesting Saturday and Sunday. Here the Prince-Governor sent to ask if he should not put up a sālā to shelter us during our stay. In the morning we preached in the market-place, and afterwards I distributed medicine and talked with the people till noon, when I had to flee away to rest under the shade of a big tree by the river. The people seemed hungry for the bread of life. I could not supply all the requests made for copies of the Scriptures.

Mûang Yawng, the older and larger city, we reached

[1]This name appears on some maps as Chieng Hung, initial *r* in the North being generally pronounced as *h*.—Ed.

on Monday forenoon, after a two hours' ride. An officer met us at the gate, and showed us to the sālā. When the Chao Mawm heard of our arrival, he sent for us, meeting us at the door. We had a very interesting interview, but he was not inclined to talk on the subject of religion. He told me that the city and district had been entirely depopulated in 1809 by a force from Chiengmai, when "nothing was left behind but the ground."[1] It had recovered itself, however, and its population was now larger than that of Lampūn. With Nān Su[illegible]an I visited the market and the Court. At the latter place I learned that the British Commissioner would arrive the next day. Knowing that everything would be in confusion, we decided to move on the next morning.

From this point on, our elephant was everywhere an object of great interest. Sometimes the people climbed trees to get a better view of him. A long day's march brought us to Mûang Yū, picturesquely situated on high bluffs, with deep gorges running down to the Mê Lūi. Here we remained only overnight, leaving early the next morning for Mûang Lūi, which we reached about noon. That evening we had a large attendance at worship, the governor and officials remaining till after eleven o'clock. The original population of both these districts, as well as that of Mûang Yawng, are now scattered throughout the provinces of Chiengmai and Lampūn.

[1] This incident is a striking illustration of the methods of warfare in those days. The expedition in question was directed against the Burmese, who had established themselves in Mûang Yāng some sixty miles or more to the north-west. On its way it passed through Mûang Yawng, where it was loyally received. But being defeated at Mûang Yāng, it fell back upon Mûang Yawng, and there gathered up all the inhabitants and swept them off to Chiengmai to prevent their falling into the hands of the enemy!—Ed.

Next morning we crossed the beautiful stream on a raft, while our elephant took the ford. During the forenoon we came upon Captain Davis of the Commissioner's staff, who had been sent to make a detour by Mûang Sing, and was then on his way to join his party. He was resting by the roadside, ill with fever, and was glad to get from me some quinine.

The following day, Saturday, brought us to Mûang Lūang, the largest and most important place in the valley and the southernmost of the old Sipsawng Pannā confederacy. The valley population is wholly Lû. There is scarcely a Ngīu (Western Shan) to be found east of the Keng Tung watershed. Here were the best roads we had seen anywhere in Farther India, with a real arched bridge of stone across the stream at the entrance to the city. Early next morning we were awakened by a noisy crowd about our tent, anxious to see us. It was the great market day, so, instead of attempting a regular service in camp, we chose the market-place. There, whether reading or speaking, we always had some attentive listeners.

On Monday our road lay for many miles along the summit of a low ridge on which at intervals were fifteen large villages, just at the edge of the long fertile plain, where are the rice-fields that feed the country. I never saw in all my touring anything quite to equal that row of villages. It seemed too bad to pass through so many without even stopping.

On the fourth day from Mûang Lūang we reached Chieng Rung, the limit of our northward journey. Its location is strikingly beautiful, on a high steep bluff overlooking the Mê Kōng River, which sweeps in a majestic curve about its base. It is in Chinese territory, and is ruled by a Chao Fā appointed from Yun-

GROUP OF YUNNAN LĀO

nan. An officer from Yunnan was there at the time collecting tribute. The influence of the English was already felt there. Mûang Chê, to the west, had rebelled against the Chao Fā, who thereupon sent out an expedition which captured and brought away some three hundred families of the inhabitants. But England cannot allow border warfare to go on along her frontier. An English officer appeared on the scene, and the thing was stopped.

At Chieng Rung we were still in the midst of an area of Lāo-speaking people—an area which extended far beyond on every side. I gave a portion of Scripture to a Lû whose home was ten days' journey northward; and others to men from as far to the east and to the west.

We had an interview with the Chao Fā by previous appointment. At the door the officer suggested that we pull off our shoes. We replied that it was not our custom, and was unnecessary. He looked very doubtful, but said no more, and we walked in. The Chao Fā received us courteously. We took him to be a man of no great strength of character, about forty years of age, and somewhat weakened by the use of opium. He asked whether we had not some antidote to enable him to stop its use. He listened attentively to our statement of the object of our coming, and said, "You are merit-makers, and that is a good work."

When we called at the court, the presiding officer had a wise suggestion as to how we might further our purpose and establish our religion in the place—a suggestion evidently not originating with himself, but from a higher source. "The favour of the Chao Fā," said he, "will be necessary and all-sufficient. I see you have a fine elephant. Just make a present of him to the Chao Fā. He will be delighted, and your road will be all smooth." I told him that I was an old man, far from home, and dependent on the elephant. So I could not part with him. This same suggestion was pressed upon us several times afterwards, by the highest officials, and quite up to the hour of our departure; though its form was modified from a gift to a sale. I became at last a little anxious about the result, and was somewhat relieved when we actually got away without loss of the elephant.

I may mention at this point an incident of this trip which never came to my knowledge till thirteen years later, showing how we were providentially spared from what would have put a sudden and tragic end to our tour and to our lives. When Dr. S. C. Peoples and Dr. W. C. Dodd were in Keng Tung in March, 1907, the presiding officer of the Court told them that he had met Dr. McGilvary and Mr. Irwin on their way to Chieng Rung; that when the people of Chieng Rung first heard that some foreigners from the south were *en route* to their capital, they planned to kill and plunder them. But when they saw that the foreigners rode elephants and were accompanied by carriers, they decided that this was probably the advance guard of a formidable army, which it might not be well to attack. And then, he said, the kindness of the missionaries so completely won their hearts, that all thought of murder and plunder was given up.

Our return was to be through the region to the east of the Mê Kōng. Its northern cities still belonged to the Sipsawng Pannā. But the rest of it was territory recently ceded by Siam to France. The governing race—the people of the plains—were everywhere Tai, speaking the Lāo language and using the

Lão literature. On its mountain ridges dwelt numerous hill-tribes, especially the Kamu and the Lamĕt.

The route we were to take crosses the river two days' journey south of Chieng Rung; so we had at first to retrace our steps. We left the city on Monday, March 13th, safe from unseen plots, and with our elephant. On the second day, after leaving our upward road to strike across to the river, we entered unexpectedly a large village, where we met with a reception ludicrously hostile. At every door men were standing with guns in their hands. We were surprised; but, supposing that it might be muster-day or something of the sort, we passed innocently along, without challenge, to the monastery, where we dismounted and began to unload. Then guns were laid aside and the head man and villagers came up to see us and to offer assistance. They had heard that foreigners were coming with elephants and men, whether for peace or war no one knew. So they had taken the precaution to be ready. When they found out our peaceful errand, they were ashamed. We had a pleasant visit and worship with them that evening.

The next stage of our road was bad. In some places we had to cut our way through, and there were difficult passages of brook-beds and gorges. We reached the river at Chieng Hā in a pouring rain, and it rained again at night. The next day was the Buddhist sacred day, and we were awakened early by the crowd of merit-makers and worshippers—the women and girls, as usual, in their head-dresses and gay colours, and all anxious to see the elephant and the white faces.

It was 10:30 that morning before we got away. Ourselves, our men, the saddles and luggage, were carried over by the ferry. Nān Suwan alone faced the deep river on the sadaw to guide him through. At the first plunge all of the elephant save his trunk, and half of the rider, went out of sight. Thence on they went, now up and now down, till they struggled out on the further shore. Such an effort is very exhausting to the animal, and he has to have a good rest and breathing-spell after it.

Mūang Ham, on the eastern bank, is larger than its neighbour on the west. Its governor was a Chao Mawm, next in rank to the Chao Fā of Chieng Rung, and his wife was the Chao Fā's sister. I had a long talk on religion with the wife. It was a new thought to her that any one could be greater than the Buddha, though he was neither Creator nor Saviour, but only a man. It is unnecessary continually to state what was everywhere the case throughout this trip; namely, that we had good audiences and interested hearers. We left in every place some books in the hands of those most likely to use them; though we could have used to advantage many more, if we had had them.

From Mūang Ham two days' march brought us on a Saturday to Mūang Nūn, the most important city on our route, and, therefore, a most desirable place to spend Sunday. The city is in the valley of the Nam Bān. It has well paved streets, and a very large monastery on an eminence above, where we camped. The abbot gave us a hearty welcome, and did all he could to make us comfortable. At our night worship the monks and other visitors were very attentive.

On Sunday morning we called on the head officer of the Court, and had a pleasant conversation with him, for he was both intelligent and inquisitive. Just as we were ready for our own morning worship, the Chao

Mawm, a relative of the Chao Fā for Chieng Rung, sent to ask us to call. We sent word in reply that it was our hour for worship, and asked whether he would, perhaps, like to have us worship in his residence. His answer was a cordial invitation to come and do so.

The Prince was young and very pleasant. He had a spacious house, and soon he had it filled with his own family, his officers, and his people. Mr. Irwin, as usual, had his cornet. We find that singing our Gospel hymns, with a short explanation of their central truths, is a better way to hold a mixed crowd where women and children form a goodly proportion, than is a regular service. Nān Suwan's Lû dialect served a very good turn. We had a very interesting morning, and we were cordially invited to hold a similar meeting at night, when many who had been absent in the morning might attend.

At night the house was crowded with a remarkable gathering, for one could hardly call it a congregation. The invitation, the place, the attendant circumstances, were all unique. We sang and prayed and preached with as little restraint as if we had been in our own church in Chiengmai. The part of the service which most impressed them was Nān Suwan's prayer—a direct appeal to a Person unseen, whom he addressed as Father, Redeemer, Saviour, and Friend. Seldom have I felt so strongly for any as for these, that they were as sheep needing a shepherd; hungry souls asking for bread, and getting that which satisfied not. Ethical teaching they had in abundance, but no Divine Voice asking, "Wilt thou be made whole?" or saying, "Thy sins be forgiven thee. Arise and walk!"

Next morning we made our formal call upon the Prince; but he sent to our camp for our books and the cornet, and soon we had another congregation, and were having worship again. In the afternoon the Prince made us a long call. Then there was a continuous stream of visitors, mostly for medicine, and I vaccinated a number of persons. The son of the chief officer of the Court, a fine young man, was almost ready to come with us to Chiengmai to study our religion further. His father, too, was willing that he should come. The young man promised that he surely would do so next year, if we came again. And now, seventeen years after these events, it saddens me to think no missionary has ever been there since. An occupancy, then, of those open Sipsawng Pannā States would have turned the flank of French obstruction, and have ensured an entrance from the north.

Early on Tuesday morning we left Mûang Nūn, after a visit all too short. The Prince, with his officers and a large crowd of people, were on hand to bid us good-bye. That day we found our track very much obstructed by the jungle growth, and had some difficulty in cutting our way through. Another complication presently arose in the illness of my associate, Mr. Irwin. An attack of indigestion developed next day into symptoms of dysentery, which made further travel for the time impossible. So we were laid up until the following Tuesday at Mûang Wên—and anxious nights and days they were. Milder measures failing, we had to resort at last to a most heroic treatment which I had seen used in the hospital, namely, large doses of ipecac. By this means the disease was got under control; and by care and dieting Mr. Irwin was able at length to continue his journey on my elephant, though throughout the rest of our tour he was far from being well.

At Mûang Pōng, one of the three largest cities on the route, we again stopped over from Thursday night till Tuesday. Here I had an ague-chill on the night of our arrival, but, with free use of quinine and a little rest, I escaped further attack. There was a great deal of fever in the place, and I spent much time in ministering to the sick.

On Saturday I called upon the Prince and his chief officer. I was told that the city furnished five hundred men for the Chao Fā's expedition, and had seventy villages within its jurisdiction. In former times it had been raided by an expedition from Nān, and some of the Nān villages to this day are peopled by descendants of those captives.

On Monday the Prince and his chief officer made us long calls. The Prince had never seen a repeating rifle, and seemed incredulous that it could fire twelve shots in unbroken succession, till I fired three by way of demonstration. His look of surprise was ludicrous. He *must* have the gun, he said, to protect his country, and began bidding for it. At last he offered a fine riding pony, which I accepted. He was delighted, saying that we two should always be brothers. If I should never come again myself, he would welcome and aid our assistants. Four years later I did visit the place, but the Prince had been killed.

On Tuesday we reached Mûang Māng, which proved to be one of our most hopeful places. Sitting in front of our tent, with the whole village about us, we talked till midnight. I had a sore throat, but our assistants were inspired with enthusiasm. At last we almost had to drive the crowd away.

Mûang Sing was the objective of this portion of our tour. I first became interested in it when it was about to be occupied as a dependency of the province of Nān. Mr. Phraner and I made an attempt to reach it in 1891, but were turned back. Then, again, it seemed about to fall into British hands, under some old claim by Burma. Even at the time we were there, its status was still uncertain. It gave evidence of having once been a large city, and still had a very large territory under its jurisdiction. Its earlier importance was reflected in the title borne by its ruler, Chao Fā—Lord of the Sky—a title borne by no other Lû ruler south of Chieng Rung. My interest in Mûang Sing had been deepened by acquaintance with a patient in the Chiengmai hospital, of whose case Dr. McKean has kindly furnished the following account:

"This Prayā Singhanāt, a prominent man in the local government, had been for years a great sufferer from vesical calculus and had tried all kinds of remedies without avail. Fearing his disease had been occasioned by offending the spirits in the building of a new house, he tore the house down. This gave him no relief. Although he had spent years in the monastery, and had taken all the degrees of the order, he concluded to re-enter it in the hope of being cured of his malady, spending again six months in the monastery. A travelling merchant who had himself been cured of calculus by an operation in the mission hospital in Chiengmai, advised the Prayā to go there for relief. This he determined to do, not without great opposition from the Prince and from his own family. But he was determined. He sold his possessions, and started with 800 rupees. His journey was long and painful. For weeks or even months at a time he could not travel on account of great pain. Once he was beset by dacoits at night. A part of his money and all his guns were stolen. When he finally reached Chiengmai twelve months after leaving home, he was penniless, and of course still suffering intensely. He was received into the mission hospital and was wholly relieved by an operation. A more grateful patient one rarely sees. He regularly attended service at the hospital and evinced great interest in Christianity."

When we reached Müang Sing, we were disappointed to find that the Prayā was away. But he had loudly sung the praises of the mission hospital, and that was a good introduction for us. The chief officer of the Court was a friend of his, and he proved to be a friend to us, too. Hearing that we were come, the Chao Fā sent for us, and turned out to be a relative of the great Chao Fā of Chieng Rung. Though not of a nature so deeply religious as some, he was interested in religion; and our reply to his first question as to the object of our visit, immediately introduced the subject.

At first he was inclined to cavil, asking such questions as, whether Jesus could rise in the air as Buddha did, and the like. But this was evidently to "save his face" before his officers. For a while he maintained that the universe is self-existent, having come into being by the concurrence of the matter which composes it. But presently he confessed that it is too complicated for that, and plainly shows design—that is, a mind or Mind. At last he asked what argument made us foreigners so certain of our view that we should come to ask them to change their religion for ours. We told him that Jesus Christ Himself was the all-sufficient argument. No matter how the world came into existence, we are here, and we all know that we are sinners. The Buddha confessed himself to be only a man, and himself seeking a refuge like the rest of us. Jesus Christ claimed to have come down from heaven, and to be the Son of God. He challenged the world to convince Him of sin. Those who knew Him intimately saw something in Him not only different and superior, but of a different kind. He showed this not only by His spotless life, but by the miracles that He wrought. He claims to have power to forgive sins. And thousands and millions who have accepted Him believe that He has forgiven them; and show that fact by becoming better men. We talked thus an hour and a half. He evidently felt the force of the arguments.

Sunday was the fifth-day market or fair—the largest and finest we had seen in the north. The hill-tribes, as usual, were out in full force. I was still suffering with sore throat, but Mr. Irwin and the assistants had a fine morning's work, and in the afternoon had a fair attendance at the regular service.

One of the most interesting incidents of our stay was the night service, held in the residence of the Chao Fă at his express request on the evening before our departure. The audience was mainly his own family and dependents, and the Prince was more free than before. During the singing he asked that the cornet be stopped in order that he might hear the words more plainly. When Năn Suwan led in prayer, he wished to know if we always prayed in that way. There was the usual sad refrain—no hope of pardon, bondage to the spirits, the drawing to a better way, but so strong a counter-current! Yet who can tell how many, after all, the truth may have reached?

We left Mûang Sing on Wednesday, April 12th. There is no need to weary the reader with details of the ten days' travel before we reached Chieng Sên, or with the varied incidents of our work.

At Chieng Sên we received letters that were disappointing to my plans. The mission had unanimously decided that, partly for considerations of our health, and partly for reasons of mission policy, Mrs. McGilvary and I should take our furlough at once. We had been ten and a half years on duty in the field. My wife was not really sick, but was not well, and the doctor advised her going. I was very anxious to repeat the same tour the next year, in spite of the few malarial chills I had encountered this time. But arrangements had been completed, and there was no option but to submit.

My companion on this tour was far from well, and it was important that he should hasten home at once. What with daily rains, bad roads, and swollen streams, Mr. Irwin had a hard trip of it alone the rest of the way; and it was some little time before he was well again. For my return there was no such need of haste. The work among the Mūsô had been left, upon the whole, in hopeful condition. The power of the tribal bond, which almost annihilated individual responsibility, had been somewhat weakened. Many head men had promised to enrol themselves as Christians this season. It was certain that no tour among them could be made the coming year. I must visit them now.

The experiences of this visit were entirely like those of the previous ones—everywhere the same warm welcome, interesting night meetings, earnest consultations, and ministering to the sick; days spent in wading brooks, climbing mountain ridges, plunging down ravines, to get from one village to another, where the same round would be repeated. They would all become Christians if only another officer or two would join them. Thus it went on till we had visited nearly all of the eleven villages, and were back at Sên Chai's and Sên Bun Yūang's, where we began. These people were nearer to Nān Suwan's Christian village, had known more of our religion, and, no doubt, were believers in the truth of our teaching. We talked with them till late at night, and our parting with them had a tragic interest. They were apparently on the verge of accepting the Gospel. We used our utmost endeavours to persuade them to join Cha Pū Kaw on the other side of the river, and not wait for the others who might come in afterwards. This was probably my last visit; but if any sufficient number would join the church, the mission would not desert them. If not, in all probability the offer would never be pressed upon them again.

And so it proved to be. About half of the villages were under the governor of Chieng Sên. The inhabitants of these were assured of their safety in taking the decisive step, so far as the rulers were concerned. But some of the larger villages were under the governor of Mûang Len. His opposition was a foregone conclusion, because of his interest in the opium traffic. My failure to gain a large entrance among them was one of the greatest disappointments in my whole work.

That I was not mistaken in the hopefulness of the work among the Mūsôs has since been demonstrated by the many thousand converts won among the same tribe by our Baptist brethren in the Keng Tung region. At the same time they are better prepared for such a work than were we. Their wide experience among the Karens of Burma, and the large number of educated Karens through whom they work, give them advantages in this particular work which our mission does not possess. On the other hand, it is surely to be regretted that our mission should be limited in its access to all branches alike of the Tai population found in the northern states, for which, by identity of race and language and literature, we are far better prepared than our Baptist brethren. For while, to use a legal phrase, the missionary holds a brief for no one particular tribe; while his commission and his duty is to preach the Gospel to all whom he can reach; yet it is a well recognized fact that the Tai family has largely fallen to our mission. And it will be seen from what we have said above, that we returned from this trip with enlarged views and bright prospects of opening up work among our own Tai people in the north. It will take years of hard work and a useless expenditure of time and money for any other missionary organization to reach the point at which we were ready to *begin* work among these people. But this is a complicated question, the tangled web of which it is not possible for any one man to unravel.

XXXII

THIRD FURLOUGH—STATION AT CHIENG RĀI

ON my return to Chiengmai I found preparations well advanced for our departure on furlough. Embarking on June 7th, we reached Bangkok on June 22d, and San Francisco on August 12th, 1893. Of the events of that memorable year, I shall touch upon only two or three.

Dr. J. H. Barrows, the originator and President of the Parliament of Religions, had invited me to attend and participate in its meetings. After, perhaps, a little shock at the boldness of the idea—as if Christianity were to be put on a par with other religions—I sympathized with the object as legitimate and proper. It was merely doing on a large scale what we missionaries are called upon to do on a smaller scale every time that we hold an argument with Buddhists or other non-Christian people. The fairness of the idea, and even its very boldness, might do good; and I believe they did.

On the Sunday before the opening I listened to a really great sermon by Dr. Barrows on "Christ the Light of the World." I attended every session of the Parliament, save at the hour from 11 A.M. to 12, when I usually went over to the Moody meetings to hear John McNeill, as he was familiarly called, preach his trenchant sermons.

If any one went to the Parliament—as possibly some

did—hoping to hear Christianity demolished, he certainly was disappointed. But there was one criticism which occurred to me. Whatever may have been thought of the wisdom of the original conception and inauguration of the Parliament, the Protestant churches might have made a much more imposing front, if the ablest men of the different denominations had not stood aloof, either indifferent or hostile to it. It was surely the opportunity of a lifetime for many, who could not hope otherwise ever to address personally the votaries of non-Christian religions, to bring forward their strong reasons to bear on so many of the most intelligent and presumably the most earnest seekers after the truth.

While attending these meetings in Chicago, I received news that our son, the Rev. Evander B. McGilvary, had felt himself constrained to resign from the Lāo mission. No good can come from now reviewing the issues which led to this step; and it is needless to say how bitter was the disappointment to his parents, who had looked forward to his carrying on their work, and to him, who had specially prepared himself for that work, and for no other. But I must say that bitter as was the disappointment, I sympathized with his position, and respected his motives.

At the meeting of the General Assembly in the following May, to which I was a delegate, the one all-engrossing business was the trial of the Rev. Henry P. Smith, D.D., for heresy on the question of the "Higher Criticism." Viewing the matter from this distance, and entirely apart from the merits of this particular case, I doubt whether critical and scientific questions are proper subjects for trials before such a body. If tried at all, such questions should be tried by a commission of experts. Biblical criticism and science will go on, and the questions involved will be decided according to their own lines of evidence, quite irrespective of the decrees of Popes, Councils, and General Assemblies. I am much mistaken if the good sense and temper of the church would now sanction heresy trials on such questions.

One day some fifteen years earlier than the point we have now reached in our narrative, a letter came to our mission from a Mr. Robert Arthington of Leeds, England. The letter, like all his subsequent ones, was on small sheets of notepaper, written over once, and then written again crosswise, so as to be almost illegible. The writer had somewhere learned of the journey of a French explorer who, from the upper Mê Kōng and the headwaters of the Mê Ū, had crossed to the China Sea through the region now known as Tonking. The traveller had passed through certain tribes possessed of a written language and supposed to be of Aryan stock. By some means Mr. Arthington had heard of our mission, and wrote to enquire whether some of us could not visit those tribes and distribute among them "the Gospels of John and of Luke, and the Acts of the Apostles," particularly "telling them that the Acts followed Luke, *and was by the same author.*"

We had not the slightest idea who the writer was; but the devout spirit of the letter was charming, and such interest in obscure tribes along the northern border of our field was most surprising. His strong desire to send the Gospel message to "the regions beyond" appealed to me. He appeared to be a man of means, for he offered to bear the expense of circulating those three books. At the same time he was evidently somewhat eccentric and impractical in his ideas. He seemed not to have thought that to circulate books among newly discovered tribes would require—since the cessation of the gift of tongues—acquisition of their languages, translation, printing-presses, etc., etc. But the case, at all events, seemed worth following up.

I acknowledged the receipt of his letter, pointing out the obstacles which he seemed to overlook, directing his attention to our own mission as occupying a new and interesting field, with many hill-tribes on our own border which we hoped to reach. I invited his coöperation, stating that as soon as we were properly enforced, we intended to go as far north as we could.

Almost to my surprise, Mr. Arthington replied immediately, expressing his interest in our work, but still reverting to his scheme for evangelizing the "tribes of Aryan stock" found by his French traveller. That was, of course, impossible for us to undertake, though I did propose to Dr. Cushing of the American Baptist Mission in Burma to join me in a tour through that region at Mr. Arthington's expense. This plan had attractions for us both; but Dr. Cushing's college work made it impossible. Still, we might be able to make some compromise with our unknown correspondent. So, for some years, I kept up an occasional correspondence with Mr. Arthington, just sufficient to keep us in touch with each other. He always replied immediately to my letters, breathing the same deep interest in missions, and especially in the tribes hitherto unreached by the Gospel. Touring within my own appointed field engrossed the whole of my available time; but since that field was already in part supplied, it did not specially appeal to him.

After the tour, longer than usual, taken with my

daughter in 1890, I sent him a report of it. In response he sent me thirty pounds, which aided in the work of 1891 among the Mūsô. The tour taken with Mr. Phraner in 1892 was nearer to his idea; and the one taken with Mr. Irwin in 1893 intensely interested him—but chiefly because it seemed to be a stepping stone toward reaching his "Aryan tribes" beyond. He thoroughly approved of that tour; expressed his regret that we could not meet in order to come to a clearer understanding about the geography of the region—since all our maps were defective; and suggested, "I should like your daughter to go with you on your next trip, as I can well conceive the idea that she will be a valuable help." He was, moreover, "particularly interested that the Cambodians also should have the Gospels of Luke and John, and the Acts."

Following up Mr. Arthington's suggestion of an interview, I met him by appointment in Liverpool on my return from the United States. We had only a half hour's interview; but he thought that sufficient to enable us to understand each other's plans. On reaching London I was to make out an order for what sum I needed for my next work. This I did, asking for the modest sum of forty pounds, which I received by return post.

The trans-Mê Kōng tour, however, was inevitably delayed. It was not until the Annual Meeting of the mission in 1896 that Dr. Peoples and I were appointed to make that tour, an account of which will appear later. To complete, however, now the story of my relations with Mr. Arthington, I may say that in advance of the Annual Meeting just referred to, I wrote to him that the projected tour would surely be taken, and suggested that sixty pounds would probably suffice to cover its expense. His reply came the day before our meeting adjourned, with a cheque for seventy pounds. The timely aid seemed to anticipate the divine approval of our attempt. In his letter he suggested, "Perhaps it might be a good precaution for you to let the French know your friendly object, and to get full permission to travel east of the upper waters of the Mê Kōng as far as you deem proper for your purpose. But, dear Brother, seek—and I intend to ask with you—the Lord's counsel and blessed comfort and guidance."

The tour was taken, as I have already intimated, and a full printed report was sent to Mr. Arthington. On the whole, he was pleased; but it is not easy to serve two masters. I had assured him from the beginning that my first duty was to my mission and my own field. Still he was a little disappointed that I had to go so far out of my way to join Dr. Peoples in Nān; and a little more so that we could not get up nearer to Tongking to give his favourite "John, Luke, and the Acts" to the tribes supposed to be of Aryan descent, found by the French traveller. To enable me to do this, he said, "I believe I should have great pleasure in sending you all you will need from me." He even intimated once that he would be willing to provide in his will for the continuance of that work. While not jealous of my connection with the Board, it seemed to him a tantalizing thing that, while I was geographically nearer his goal than any one else, and was, moreover, in sympathy with his devout spirit and evangelistic aspirations to reach the "regions beyond," I was not free to carry out his favourite, though somewhat chimerical, plans.

The last letter I had from him was dated October

22d, 1898. His passion was then as strong as ever to get his three favourite books to "the tribes mentioned by the French traveller, . . . for they are a people for whom I have desired much, since the day I first read of them, that they should have the Gospel." He expressed great sympathy with my disappointment that the French would not permit our labouring in their territory, adding, "Yet the Lord will not be robbed of His own." His death occurred not very long after this. Of the disposition of his large estate I found the following account in the London *Daily Graphic:*

> "The late Robert Arthington of Leeds, left about £750,000 to the London Missionary Society, and the Baptist Missionary Society. The total value of his estate was £1,119,843. It is estimated that the Baptist Missionary Society will receive £415,000 and the London Missionary Society £335,000. The whole of the money must be spent in the next twenty years on new missionary work, and no part of it is to be spent in the United Kingdom."

We reached Bangkok on September 11th, 1894. There we were joined by the Rev. and Mrs. Howard Campbell and Dr. and Mrs. C. H. Denman, who had come *via* the Pacific. Earlier in this same year there had come to the station in Mûang Prê, Dr. and Mrs. Thomas, Mr. and Mrs. Shields, and Miss Hatch; with the Rev. and Mrs. L. W. Curtis and Miss Margaret Wilson for Lakawn.

On our arrival in Chiengmai we found Mr. Phraner very ill with abscess of the liver, and suffering at times intense pain. He had been warned by physicians and friends to desist from his work and take his furlough. But, as chairman of the Evangelistic Committee, he had been pushing the evangelistic work too eagerly to heed these warnings. He refused to leave his post till those who were absent should return. Soon after we arrived he started for the United States, but, alas! it was too late. He died in Singapore on January 15th, 1895, leaving a wife and two little boys to pursue their sad journey alone. Mrs. Phraner—formerly Miss Lizzie Westervelt—had served a useful term in the Girls' School before her marriage. The Phraner Memorial School for small children, erected by the family and friends beside the First Church in Chiengmai, is an appropriate tribute to their labours for the Lāo race, to which they devoted their lives.

The year of our absence had been almost a banner year as regards successful evangelistic work. Mr. Dodd's Training School had furnished a larger number of fairly well prepared evangelists than we ever had before. Between forty and fifty of these had been actually at work in the field for longer or shorter periods during the year, and their work had been very successful. The Annual Meeting convened in Chiengmai soon after our return. In it there was evident, on the part both of missionaries and of native assistants, a degree of enthusiasm and exuberant expectancy which, under the most favourable circumstances, could hardly have escaped the inevitable reaction. Krū Nān Tā, a man of magnetic power among his people, was then in his prime. The great value of his services raised probably to an excessive degree our estimate of the necessity of more *ordained* native labourers. If one had done so much, what might a dozen or a score accomplish? And there were the men, with two, three, or even more years of training in the study of the Bible. Most of them were elders or deacons in the different churches. They had proved faithful in little. Why might they not be trusted with more talents? Nine of these men were presented for examination before the Presbytery.

When we began, it was thought—against the advice of Mr. Dodd, who was on furlough—that one or two might be ordained to meet the immediate needs of the work. Some of them had spent a number of years in the Buddhist priesthood, and had some knowledge of Pali. Others were without such education, but nearly all had learned to read Siamese. In Biblical knowledge they had made fair progress. When the examination was closed, there was a long and anxious deliberation, with special prayer for divine direction. It was quite safe to ordain one or two. But the next candidate was so near the standard of these that it might seem invidious to exclude him—and so with the next, and the next. When the vote was taken, six were chosen for ordination and three for licensure. The millennium seemed drawing near!

With the new title and responsibility, higher wages were naturally to be expected. And it was precisely upon this rock that our hopes and plans suffered shipwreck. The Board, as never before, began to insist on the native churches assuming the support of their own evangelists. The methods of mission work set forth and practised in China by the Rev. Dr. Nevius were urged upon us, and became very popular, especially with the younger members of the mission, though in China they had not passed beyond the stage of experiment. They are best described in Dr. Nevius' own words:

"These two systems may be distinguished in general by the former's depending largely on paid native agency, while the latter deprecates and seeks to minimize such agency.

Perhaps an equally correct and more generally acceptable statement of the difference would be, that, while both alike seek ultimately the establishment of independent, self-reliant, and aggressive native churches, the 'Old System' strives by the use of foreign funds to foster and stimulate the growth of native churches in the first stage of their development, and then gradually to discontinue the use of such funds; while those who adopt the 'New System' think that the desired object can be best obtained by applying principles of independence and self-reliance from the beginning. The difference between these two theories may be more clearly seen in their outward and practical working. The old uses freely, and as far as practicable, the more advanced and intelligent of the native church members, in the capacity of paid Colporteurs, Bible Agents, Evangelists, or Heads of Stations; while the new proceeds on the assumption that the persons employed in these various capacities would be more useful in the end by being left in their original homes and employments."[1]

The result was that the mission took a good thing and ran it into the ground. Economy became almost a craze. The churches were assessed—not heavily, it is true—to support the ministers; and the ministers were exhorted to take whatever stipend was agreed upon, and count any deficiency in it as a voluntary contribution on their part, or as a debt they owed their countrymen for the Gospel's sake. Neither parishioners nor workers understood the scheme. But it was tried for one year; and at the next Annual Meeting (in 1895) the catastrophe came. The churches had been asked to walk before they could stand; and the ministers were to work, as well as walk, by faith and not by sight. As pastors, their expenses were necessarily increased. They had to dress better, and to be an example in clothing, and educating their fam-

[1] *Methods of Mission Work*, p. 4.

ilies, and in hospitality. It seemed to them that they were required to make bricks without straw. A little yielding to demands that were not unreasonable would have satisfied the ministers, and the churches would have been encouraged by the continuance of some support from the Board for evangelistic work, even though the amount was much reduced. The zeal was well meant; but we broke off too suddenly.

For the unfortunate results, the mission, the native ministers, the churches, and, indirectly, the Board should share the responsibility. The advantages gained by our Training School were nullified, and all progress toward a permanent Theological School was at an end. After those two Annual Meetings there was no call for theological training, and no future for a native ministry. So we have to go on appealing to the Board and to the American churches for foreign workers, although the salary of one of these would support half a dozen or more native ministers.

It is easy to say that native ministers and church members should be willing, out of pure gratitude, to labour for the evangelization of their own people, or that such and such other races have done so. As a matter of fact, the Lāo church is largely indebted for its progress to the power exerted by the church itself. And as to the example of other races, we must remember that there are racial differences. Even our nearest Christianized neighbours, the Karens, stand in a class quite by themselves in this respect. We can no more apply one rule to all oriental races than we can enforce western customs in the Orient. But we certainly cannot expect happy results from the application of rules that would have discouraged our own ancestors when the first Christian missionaries found them.

Among the things of more hopeful augury accomplished in the year 1894, two deserve special mention—the establishment of Christian Endeavour Societies in all the Lāo churches, primarily through the efforts of Dr. Denman, and the publication of the Book of Psalms and of a hymnal of over two hundred hymns and tunes. The Psalms were translated by Dr. Wilson, and the hymns were almost wholly from his pen.

At the Annual Meeting, to which reference has already been made, a committee was appointed to consider anew and report on the question whether it was or was not advisable now to occupy the northern portion of the field with a permanent station, and, if it were deemed advisable, to determine the location. I had been anxious to have it occupied two years before this time, but had yielded then to the claims of Prê and of Nān—of Prê because the relief work among the sufferers from famine had furnished a most auspicious opening there; and of Nān because it was a larger city and province than any in the nearer north. Notwithstanding the greater progress of the work in the north, with organized and growing churches in Wieng Pā Pāo, Chieng Rāi, and Chieng Sên, there seemed to be a lingering doubt as to the wisdom of establishing permanent stations in cities so small as these. Most of my colleagues had never visited that northern region. No one save myself had surveyed the whole field. Yet no part of the work of a mission is more important, or requires better judgment, than the location of its permanent stations. Although fully persuaded in my own mind, I did not wish the mission to embark on a new project involving outlay of money and of men, without the mature judgment of the whole mission. Hence it was at my own suggestion that the committee was appointed.

On January 20th, 1896, Dr. Denman and I of this committee started northward. Mr. Dodd joined us later. It is a great thing to have a physician along on such a tour. He relieves a great deal of suffering among a needy people, and so lifts a great load of care from his companion. But beyond this, I myself had quite an attack of fever on this particular trip, and was much indebted to his care for my recovery. Then we had the stereopticon along, and lectured nearly every night to large audiences. The doctor manipulated the lantern, and left the explanation and application to me. Those pictures have made the Gospel story to live in the imaginations of many thousands of people. The occasional introduction of a familiar scene from native life serves to give confidence that the others also are real, while a few comic ones interest the children, old and young. A picture of the King of Siam—their King—with three of his children, one of them with his arms about his father's neck, always attracted great attention, and was often asked for again at the close of the exhibition.

I had some trouble this time with my sadaw elephant. At one stage his back became so sore that I should have left him behind, were it not that he had had a serious encounter with a tusker, and I dared not risk him in that vicinity. He escaped from the encounter with some bruises, and it was fortunate that he inflicted no serious wound on his antagonist. And he was quite well again, before we got home. This was, however, the last tour he made with me. Elephants had become property so unsafe that, before the next season, I disposed of both of mine. In one year, out of three hundred and fifty elephants employed by a timber firm, thirty-two died and twenty-two were stolen. But it was like parting with a friend to see the sadaw go.

The committee visited the three northern churches, and, after full conference both with the local rulers and with the Christians, reached the unanimous decision that there should be a station established in the north, and that it should be at Chieng Rāi. In this we were largely influenced by the central situation of that place with reference to a considerable group of cities and towns within the same watershed, and all, like Chieng Rāi itself, rapidly filling up with an agricultural population crowded out from the dear and densely settled lands further south. And in addition to this was the conviction that the new station would prove a stepping-stone to the large northern section of the Tai race, established in territory which is now English, French, and Chinese. We still think that some amicable arrangement should be made with the American Baptist Missionary Union, by which the Tai race to the north of Siam and east of the Salwin should be left to our mission. The Union has a great work among the hill-tribes—a work for which they are specially adapted and specially well equipped; while we are equally well equipped for work among the Tai.

Dr. Denman viewed the field with special interest, for he had been designated to help in opening the station, and we had the virtual sanction of the Board thereto. It was the prospect of having a physician that specially enlisted the interest of the rulers of Chieng Rāi; though both they and their people were friendly to our work on other grounds. It made us sad to think that our old friend the governor had not lived to see the mission started. But the beautiful lot given by him on the Mê Kok will always be a memorial to him. In due time Rev. and Mrs. Dodd and Dr. and Mrs. Denman moved up and opened the station. The years have abundantly justified the wisdom of this step. In 1910 the accessions to the churches in Chieng Rãi equalled those of the mother church in Chiengmai.

From Chieng Sên we sent out two parties of evangelists, five in each, well loaded with Scriptures and tracts, one northwestward to Keng Tung, and the other across the Mê Kõng to Mûang Sing. This was the very first mission work ever done in the Keng Tung State. These parties carried also a supply of medicines, and were limited in time to two and a half months. They were everywhere well received, and on their return gave interesting reports of their work. Their books were eagerly read, and the supply of them was far too small. There were a number of interesting cases of believers. Some villages were loath to have them leave. The experiment, in fact, was very successful.

As soon as our committee work was done, Mr. Dodd was obliged to return. After visiting the Mũsô villages, Dr. Denman and I moved on to Chieng Kawng. This town is situated on the right bank of the great river within the fifteen-kilometer zone which was reserved as neutral territory upon the cession of the left bank to France. A French military station was on the opposite side of the river, and a small gunboat was lying there—the first that ever came up through the rapids. Among the crew were two or three who could read

PHYA SURA SIH,
SIAMESE HIGH COMMISSIONER FOR THE NORTH

English, and who were very anxious to get English Bibles. This was an unexpected request which we could not then meet. But I applied for some to the American Bible Society, and received them just before I started on my trip of the next year; and, finally, was able to forward them to the men from Lūang Prabāng. The captain of the gunboat was very kind to us while we stayed at Chieng Kawng, and was much interested in having his men get the Bibles.

Letters were presently received by Dr. Denman summoning him back to Chiengmai on account of the illness of his wife. This left me again without an associate, and with the added care of the medical work, which cannot be avoided on such a tour, and which, of course, rests more heavily on a layman than it does on a trained physician. Before returning home I made a call—and I believe it was the last one—at the Mūsô villages beyond the Mê Kōng. Again my hopes were raised of gaining the whole tribe. With such a prospect I would gladly have remained with them several months. But again I had to leave them with only the "next year" promise—which never was fulfilled. I reached home on May 5th, after an absence of three and a half months.

XXXIII

THE REGIONS BEYOND

TWO important tours were undertaken by the Lāo Mission in 1897—one at the opening of the year, eastward and northward beyond the Mê Kōng River into French and Chinese territory; and the other after the close of the rainy season, northward into British territory. The latter tour led to far-reaching results, but it does not come within the scope of this personal narrative. The former was rendered possible by the timely gift of seventy pounds from Mr. Arthington, already mentioned; and represented the nearest approach we could then make toward the fulfilment of his great desire to reach with the Scriptures those "tribes of Aryan origin" in the "regions beyond." Dr. Peoples, then of Nān, was my companion during part of this tour; and we went well supplied with Scriptures and tracts, no less than fourteen carriers being loaded with these alone. I left home on January 12th, going eastward by way of Lakawn and Prê to Nān, where Dr. Peoples was to join me. At each of these stations I spent a busy and a delightful Sunday; and from Lakawn as far as Nān I had the pleasant company of Miss Fleeson and Miss Dr. Bowman, returning to their post from the Annual Meeting.

One night on this portion of the trip we were awakened by the cries of our men and the snorting of the ponies, to find that we had a visit from a night prowler, coming so near that we heard the clatter of the loose stones which he dislodged as he sprang away. The tracks we found in the morning showed him to be a large Bengal tiger. On this same stretch of road, as recently as 1910, the mails for Nān were interrupted by a man-eating tiger, which killed several men and women, till, finally, he was despatched by Dr. Peoples within a few hundred yards of the mission compound.

Ten days were spent in journeying northward through the great province of Nān, stopping night by night in its villages and towns, where we always had good audiences at our evening worship. Sunday we spent at Mûang Ngôn, and then turned eastward, striking the Mê Kōng at Tā Dûa, and making our way up its western bank. At Bān Hūi Kûa we found such interest that we were sorry that we must move on. The Prayā—or Pīa, as the name is called throughout this region—spent an afternoon in transcribing in the Lūang Prabāng character the tract entitled "The Way to Happiness." He had heard something of our religion before this from a former princess-pupil of Miss Cole in the Wang Lang School at Bangkok. As he bade us good-bye he said, pointing upwards, "I hope we shall meet up yonder," and seemed pleased that we had the same anticipation.

The next Sunday we camped in the monastery grounds at Bān Hūa Ling. The people began to assemble before breakfast, and long before it was time for the morning service the grounds were full. The abbot, with his monks and the officers, sat directly before me as I explained the method of salvation through Jesus Christ. The audience listened most attentively. At the close the abbot and the officers remained for further conversation. The abbot expressed surprise at our errand. He had never known of anybody's travelling about simply to teach the people. Some expressed fear of encountering the anger of the spirits if they should no longer worship them. To this the doctor gave the scientific answer that fevers and most other diseases were caused and propagated by specific germs, over which the spirits have no control whatever. This was to them a new idea, but they seemed to comprehend it. Next morning, when we left them, the people followed us with expressions of regret.

When we reached Chieng Mên, a town on the western bank of the river and opposite Lūang Prabāng, we found a European with a group of boys, who turned out to be the French schoolmaster. He invited us to dine with him that evening, and the next day aided us in crossing the river. Our first duty in Lūang Prabāng was to report to the French authorities, M. Vackle, the Commandant Supérieur, and M. Grant, the Commissaire. They had been notified from Bangkok of our coming, and received us with genuine French hospitality. We never met two more perfect gentlemen. They even offered us a house; but, as the abbot of the principal monastery was a personal friend of mine, they yielded to our preference to stop with him, but only on the ground that there would be more comfort and room for our men.

That evening we were invited to dine with M. Vackle. M. Grant and his staff were present; and the dinner was a royal one, to which we were prepared to do full justice. We had the embarrassment of not being able to converse save through a native interpreter not well versed either in French or in English. But our host was most considerate, as were also his French guests. And every evening during our stay we dined with one or another of the officials.

Next day we called on the Lão "King," as he is still euphemistically called, though possessing only such powers as the French give him. When we made our business call on the French officials to ask permission to proceed on our missionary tour through the French territory, they were very obliging. We freely discussed together alternative routes, and they offered us passports for any of them. When at last with some hesitancy, the question of permanent work and a mission station was broached, M. Vackle replied that for that he had no authority. Application would have to be made to the Governor General at Hanoi, and preferably through Washington and Paris. The prospect still seemed hopeful.

On the evening before our departure, M. Vackle invited us to dine informally and spend the evening with him at his beautiful cottage and garden two miles out in the country. On meeting us, our host said, "The other night I was the Commandant Supérieur. To-night I am simply M. Vackle. I want to have a pleasant informal evening with you." And surely we did. We talked of the old friendship between France and the United States, of Washington and La Fayette, the Chicago Exposition, the Parliament of Religions, and of M. Vackle's own work in the new province. He was interested in the Parliament of Religions, and asked if Roman Catholics were equally welcome with Protestants. He had an exaggerated idea of the number of our religious sects. We told him that the great body of Protestants were included in five or six groups somewhat like the orders of the Catholic church, but there were numerous smaller subdivisions. He had heard of one that lived wholly on milk. Of this we had to confess ignorance, unless it were that large group that we call infants.

It was after eleven when we rose to take our leave; and even then he detained us to see by torchlight his beautiful garden, artificially watered, and his bowling alley—insisting that we try a turn on it. This was what I had never done before, but at the first bowl I brought down several pins. This pleased him, and he said that he had never seen a better first play.

On taking our final leave, we spoke a last word for permanent mission work, reminding him that while Catholicism and Protestantism had alike produced great nations, Buddhism never had; and that it was therefore political wisdom to encourage and foster the Christian religion in the provinces. He assented, but said he feared that the "King" might imagine that his subjects would be less loyal if they became Christians. We assured him that the reverse would be true, since it was a fundamental point in our teaching as well as in the Scriptures, that Christians were to be obedient to their rulers.

Among the routes offered we chose the northern one as most nearly meeting Mr. Arthington's desires. Our passport stated that we were Bāt Lūangs, i.e., Catholic priests. We left Lūang Prabāng on Monday, March 8th, crossed the Nam Ū near its mouth, and spent three weeks on our way to Mûang Sai. At one point there was a theft of a considerable amount of our money, which delayed us a day or two, but annoyed us more. The thieves turned out to be some of our own men, who afterwards confessed, and eventually we recovered the money. From Mûang Sai there is a good route to Nān, and as no man had been left in that station along with the ladies, Dr. Peoples felt that he must return to it, while I should go on northward to the Sipsawng Pannā and finally return to Chiengmai along the route which I took with Mr. Irwin in 1893. His departure was a great loss to me personally, and to the effectiveness of the tour. He left us on March 31st.

The next week was one of intense interest to me. One of its days was the thirtieth anniversary of my arrival in Chiengmai, and fraught with memories of the hopes, achievements, and disappointments of all those years. And were we now, perhaps, on the eve of a new opening with wider possibilities than ever? So it seemed. For, one day as I was in the monastery at Mûang Sai, there entered an officer, Sên Suriya by name, who, making the obeisance usually made to priests, explained that, having been absent from home, he had not heard the instruction we had given at our evening worship. His wife, however, had reported that a teacher from a great and distant country was come with Scriptures and an offer of salvation from the great God of all. It was the great desire of his heart to be saved from his sins. His interest was evidently intense, and that roused our interest in him. From three o'clock till nightfall our elders and I explained to him the great truths of revelation, while he listened almost with rapture.

In the midst of this earnest conference the "āchān," or chief officer of the monastery, came in; and Sên Suriya joined us in explaining to this friend the strange news he had heard. The āchān was soon as deeply interested as he. He also desired to know further of this matter. Before we parted that evening,

Sên Suriya had accepted the teaching joyfully; and his friend, with more reservation.

Soon others had joined these two—notably a family of refugees from persecution for witchcraft. They were ready to accept anything which would deliver them from bondage to the spirits. On Sunday at the public service the instruction was directed to the needs of these enquirers, all of whom were present. The cost was to be counted; the cross was to be taken up; but the reward was great. Sên Suriya's wife and family all opposed him. He had spent an anxious night, and was under great strain; but was still firm. He was ready at any cost.

His friend the āchān had received his appointment in the monastery from the Pīa, or head-officer. For honesty's sake he felt he must notify the Pīa and resign his position. It was, therefore, arranged that our elders and I should go with the two friends on that errand that very afternoon. We went, and were kindly received. Sên Suriya, as spokesman, witnessed a good confession. They had been men, he said, who all their lives had sought merit and followed the teachings of the Buddha, but with great anxiety, on account of their failures. Now they had learned of the great refuge of the God who could pardon and save both in this and in the coming world. Their motive was strictly religious. They would be as loyal as ever, and would perform faithfully their government duties. The āchān said that his friend had fully expressed his views, but he wished further to resign his position in the monastery. The Pīa listened with evident interest, but with some surprise. When he spoke, he said: "All that I know of religion I have learned from these two men. They know manifold more than I do. If they see it right, how can I oppose? I will still take them as my religious teachers, and will learn Christianity of them."

I added a word, emphasizing their assurance that being good Christians would only strengthen their loyalty. Thanking the Pïa for his kindness, I retired. How much of his liberality was due to my presence—if it were so due at all—I do not know. But next morning Sên Suriya came to say that he could not withstand the opposition of his wife and family. While his faith was firm as ever, he could do no more this year. By another year he hoped their opposition might be relaxed. Meantime the family of refugees had weakened. I supplied all these with medicine, and urged them to remain steadfast in the faith, reminding them that baptism was not essential to salvation.

I had made further stay in Mûang Sai dependent upon the outcome in the case of these two men. So now it seemed best to continue my journey northward. I went out to a retired wooded hillock, and there spent a quiet season in prayer, commending those in whom I had become so intensely interested to the care of the Divine Teacher, and seeking direction for my further course.

So far we had not met many of the hill-tribes, which had been one of the main objectives of the tour. As I descended from the hill, I found some thirty Kamus just arrived on some government work, and encamped by the road. I turned aside to speak with them, when, to my surprise, one, taller and more intelligent than the rest, answered me in good Lāo. To my greater surprise, when I handed him a tract, he began to read it. It seems that, when a lad, he had been initiated into the monastic order by the Princess of Lūang Prabāng, and was one of the very few of his tribe who was a fairly good Lāo scholar. He was delighted to get the book; but I was like a miner who has found a new gold mine. Had they been ready to return to their homes, I should at once have gone with them. A new vision seemed to open before me of work among that interesting tribe. I had seen the great value of the help afforded by Cha Pū Kaw, the first Mūsô convert, in work among his tribe. But he was not a scholar, and was too old to learn. Here was a Kamu scholar. Might he not have been raised up for this very purpose?

That evening I spent with my elders in their camp. I left with my new friend a number of books, which he promised to read to his people. I took down the names of their villages, and promised if possible to visit them next year—which they all begged me to do. That apparently casual meeting seemed to me a loud call, Come over and help us! And it led to a most interesting work, which was stopped only at the command of the French.

Leaving Mûang Sai, we journeyed northward along the telegraph road, enlivened by noble views of long slopes, deep gorges, and high peaks. We passed some villages of the Yao tribe with whom we could converse only by signs. On the third day out, at Bān Nā Tawng, we left the telegraph road, turning off at right angles to Mûang Lā. At one village the head man assembled his people to meet us, when he learned that here was a man from seven days beyond the great French country! At one place we passed a village of Lentīns, so named from the district in Cochin China from which they came. They showed their Chinese ingenuity by having their rice-pounding done by water-power.

Mûang Āi was the last town in French territory; beyond it one enters the province of Yunnan, China. Here we had scarcely pitched our tent before the governor had read our little tract on "The Way to Happiness," and asked us to stay awhile to teach his people. This we did, remaining from Friday till Tuesday. He invited us to worship in his house, which was filled to overflowing. On Saturday, in company with the governor, I attended a wedding feast. I got along finely with the various dishes until a bowl of blood fresh from a slaughtered hog was passed around, and each guest took a spoonful! My note upon leaving the town was, "It is wonderful how many, especially of the officers and the more thoughtful class, are struck with the self-evidencing truths of the Gospel on its first presentation. And their first thought is the sincere conviction that the Gospel meets their wants. Nor is this testimony invalidated because, when they come to count the cost, they are not willing to pay it."

I was much pleased to hear uniform testimony to the uprightness of French officials. My own respect for French rule had greatly increased since we entered their territory. Is it that the Tai race beyond the Mê Kōng is more religious, or is it on account of the French rule, that people there seem more deeply interested in the Gospel message? But such has been the fact. I have never been cheered by brighter visions of hopeful and speedy results of our labours. It seems almost inconceivable that a European nation should forbid missionary work among its people.

From this point on we were warned not to allow our party to be separated on the march. Shortly before this a merchant travelling with his son had been attacked and killed. I heard of two mountain tribes in this neighbourhood new to me, and of a third further to the northwest, which sacrifices at every rice-harvest a human victim captured from some other tribe. Scarcely any one had ever heard of the name of Jesus.

Not far from the town we passed on a ridge a well-marked boundary stone with the letters R. F. (République Française) on one side, and C. R. (Chieng Rung) on the other, in large Roman capitals. Noticing by the roadside a large stack of bricks, we learned that we were near the salt wells, and that the salt was compressed into bricks for easier transportation on mules. The salt industry makes Bān Baw Rê an important place. No one with white clothes, white hair, or white beard is allowed to enter the enclosure about the salt wells; so I did not see them. I could get no reason for the prohibition, save that the spirits would be displeased.

The time of my visit was unfortunate, being the beginning of their New Year festival, which is always a season of carousal. That night we had a scene that defied description. After supper a man came to tell me to get ready; they were going to "saw" me. I did not know what "saw"-ing might be; but I soon learned, to my disgust. Presently a noisy crowd entered the sālā where I was, with drums, fifes, and other musical instruments, and surrounded me with deafening noise and songs. A great personage had come to their place, and they were come to do him honour. He had great riches, and they expected a treat of fifty rupees. Paying no attention to my attempted disclaimer, they went on: "Give us out your money. Give us fifty rupees! Give us twenty-five!" Pushing my way out of the noisy circle, I was followed with more imperative demands. At last the governor's son came up as a friend and advised me to give them five or six rupees, or they would never depart. Then one of my elders came to me, anxious regarding the outcome, and said that it was only a New Year custom, not a religious one—intimating that I need have no conscientious scruples in the matter. Finally the governor's son said he could get them off with three rupees. I had only one in my pocket, and did not dare open my box before that mob. At last I handed the young man that one, and, with an emphasis which they understood, told him that I would give no more, appealing to his father for protection, and holding him responsible for the consequences. They went off sullenly enough. Having gone so far, I doubt whether they would have desisted without something "to save their face." From me they went to the governor's, and so on, in order, throughout the place, with their hideous noise, which I could hear far on into the night.

At another village further on, the people seemed in doubt how to receive me, till a young man came forward and asked if I were not the man who a few years before travelled through that country with an elephant, and let the Prince of Mûang Pōng have a gun. Then, turning to the head man, he said, "You need not be afraid. He is a teacher of the Jesus-religion." My standing in that village was assured. One of the listeners at our worship in the monastery that night was much impressed, not with the idea of pardon, as is commonly the case, but with that of the Holy Spirit to purify and cleanse. That was what he needed; and he earnestly enquired how to obtain his aid. This led to the subject of prayer to a living, personal God, who has promised this aid. We left him with the hope that his great need would be supplied.

Mûang Lă was the furthest point reached on this

tour. From it we struck westward into our old route of 1893 at Mûang Pōng. The Chao Fā who got my gun had been killed by his people. I was much struck with the judicial aspect of the act as told me. One of the officers said, "He was a bad man, who oppressed the people, fined and executed them unjustly, and, of course, we killed him. That is the way the Lāo do." A nephew and adopted son of the murdered Prince succeeded him, but the authority was largely in the hands of the Prayā Lūang, though the young Prince's mother also had great influence. She invited me to a good dinner, and we had a most interesting conversation. Among other things she asked, "How is it that you say Buddhism cannot save?" and she seemed much impressed with the answer: "Because Gautama Buddha is gone, and it is more than twenty-five hundred years before the next Buddha is expected."

We were now travelling southward, and soon came once more upon the tricolour floating over the French post at Mûang Sing. I felt like saluting it. I was greatly surprised to find an Englishman, Mr. Eva, in charge. He fairly shouted to hear his mother tongue once more. He had scarcely heard a word of it for three years. Seeing that I was spent with my long, hot ride, and that my carriers would not get in till nightfall, he kindly offered to hunt me up some luncheon. This I declined, if only I might have a cup of tea and a piece of dry bread. Holding up both hands, he exclaimed, "You've got me there! I've almost forgotten how wheat bread tastes." He insisted on my taking up my quarters in his bungalow, till I said, "If you were on French business, you would wish to stop where you could best accomplish it, would you not? I am here on missionary work, and my business is with the people. The monastery grounds will suit me better." "Looking at it in that light," said he, "you're right. I'll say no more." I knew that in the home of a French official I should have no visitors at all.

He was the son of an English Wesleyan minister; but, being a wild lad, he had wandered away and drifted into the French army, where he rose to an official position. But the influences of his early days had not been lost. We had many heart-to-heart talks together. He wanted an English Bible. Having only my "Oxford" along, I could not spare him that, but brought him one on my next tour. On Sunday he attended the service led by the elders, pleased at the evidence they gave of the reality of our missionary work. He had six thousand Kamus in his district.

The opium habit is very common. We found but few monasteries in the Sipsawng Pannā whose abbots and monks did not use opium. One man, when asked whether he used it, made a significant answer: "When I have money, I do. When I have none, I don't."

The Chao Fā of Mûang Sing was busy preparing for the marriage of his daughter with a son of the great Chao Fā of Chieng Rung. So I did not see much of him. I had a long talk, however, with the prospective groom. He doubted the possibility of pardon for sin. I had several interviews with Dr. McKean's patient for calculus, before mentioned. He was not so near Christianity as I hoped to find him, but was profuse in praise of the doctor and the hospital. He had two wives before the operation, and now was utilizing his new lease of life by taking another younger one. I saw here some peaches not quite ripe—which was very tantalizing. But I did get some ripe plums.

When I left Mûang Sing on April 28th, Mr. Eva escorted me six miles on my way, and we bade each other good-bye four or five times before we could finally part. At Wieng Pūkā I had another warm welcome from the French Commissaire. I had to decline his invitation, also, to good quarters with him; but dined with him at night, and next morning he sent me a nice shoulder of beef. A large number of Kamus were here engaged on some public works. Unlike most of their tribe, these are Buddhists, and there were a number who could read, and who were delighted to get books. It was remarkable that their women spoke Lāo fairly well. Their chief officer had eighteen hundred men under him. After talking with them till near midnight, I turned them over to the elders, and was soon asleep. Next morning my cook came to my tent to enquire whether I were not ill. It was half-past six, and breakfast was ready!

We passed many Kamu villages in this portion of our route. Most of them would welcome a missionary, and seemed ripe for the Gospel. Formerly, under the government of Nān, they had an easy time, with no taxes and almost voluntary service. Now they naturally complained of the stricter régime of the French. I consoled them with the fact that the world over people have to pay taxes to the government that protects them. For this I did not at all need the warning which Mr. Eva gave me, that the one thing which the French would not tolerate was interference with their government work. At Chieng Kawng I took leave of French territory, with nothing but feelings of gratitude for the uniform personal kindness of their officials, and their apparently kind interest in our work. That work I must now dismiss with the very brief outline I have given. I believe that light was conveyed to many seekers after truth, and seed was sown which will not be lost.

From Chieng Kawng onwards I was on old touring ground, and among friends. I spent a Sunday there, made a short visit to the Müsö hills, and found a warm welcome in Chieng Rāi from the two missionary families who were now established in that station, as well as from my many native friends. Here I received my long-desired mail. Its good cheer was tempered by one sad piece of news—the death of my sister Mary and my brother Evander, the last of my own mother's children. On May 16th I entered upon my own threescore and tenth year. Leaving Chieng Rāi on the 18th, I reached home on the 26th, after an absence of four and a half months.

Meanwhile the work in our own and in all the other stations had been energetically prosecuted by a faithful band of younger workers, better prepared than the old ones to carry it on to completion. And the other long tour to the English territory, planned for the later portion of the year, was successfully carried out by Dr. Briggs, Rev. Mr. Dodd, and Rev. Mr. Irwin.

XXXIV

THE CLOSED DOOR

THE tour of 1898 was undertaken with two special objects in view: (1) to follow up the auspicious beginnings of work among the Kamu and Lamĕt tribes, the largest and most important within the mountain area explored during the previous season, and, apparently, ready as a body to accept the Gospel; and (2) to secure the sanction of the French government for continued work in French territory. I was unable to secure a missionary colleague for the tour, and therefore went accompanied only by native evangelists. I took the most direct route, crossing the Mê Kōng at Pāk Bêng, following the Bêng River to its source, and crossing by the pass at its head to Mûang Sai, the point at which the most promising work of the previous tour was begun. The journey so far occupied nearly a month's time.

The tour was organized on notice too short to permit my passport from the United States Minister in Bangkok to reach me in Chiengmai before I started. It was, therefore, sent on direct to the French authorities at Lūang Prabāng. Meantime M. Vackle, the Commandant Supérieur, who was so kind to us the year before, had been superseded by M. Luce; and him, unfortunately, we just missed at the crossing of the Mê Kōng. He passed up in a steamer the day before we reached the river. By the time we reached Mûang

Sai, M. Luce had returned to Lūang Prabāng, and had wired to the office in Mûang Sai that my passport was come, and that I was expected in Lūang Prabāng. No instructions were given regarding my work, and the authorities were in doubt what to do. Under the circumstances, the only passport they could issue was one to the capital, Lūang Prabāng.

They were not particular, however, as to the route I should take. So I chose a circuit to the northeast, leading through the mountain region to the Ū River, down which I could descend by boat to Lūang Prabāng. This would enable me to find Nān Tit, the Kamu scholar whom I met at Mûang Sai on my previous tour, and to visit with him a few Kamu villages. The extent of the work I hoped to undertake that season would depend upon the opening I found there. A passport was given me by that route, and a soldier was sent along as guide and escort.

Nān Tit, as I hoped, had read the books I gave him, had prepared the way for me by teaching the substance of them to his neighbours, and now would assist me in teaching his tribe. With him as interpreter and assistant we visited a number of contiguous villages, holding night conferences, at which the whole population of the village would be present. Everywhere a wonderfully ready response was given to the Gospel. They, too, were oppressed by the dread of spirits, and welcomed deliverance from their bondage. They would accept the Gospel, but, naturally, referred us on to the Pīa.

To his village at last we went. He was a venerable man near seventy, and though for years hopelessly crippled by paralysis of the lower limbs, his bright mind and business talents had raised him to his present position, and given him a commanding influence. I shall never forget our first interview. He had heard the rumour that our religion could overcome the spirits and save from sin. Crawling painfully on his hands to meet us, he welcomed us to his village and his people. He had heard of the Jesus-religion, and wished to embrace it. Since he was old, he must do it soon. This was on Friday afternoon. By Saturday night every family in the place had made the same decision, and would begin by keeping their first Sabbath next day. Our elders entered with heart and soul into teaching them. The young folks soon learned a verse or two of "The Happy Land," and some a verse or two in the Catechism. Next morning, before I was dressed, old and young of both sexes were gathering to learn how to keep the Sabbath. It was a great day, just the like of which I had never seen. It settled the decision of hundreds, possibly of thousands, of people.

Still, everything depended upon the French authorities. They could forbid our teaching, as, in fact, they afterwards did. But up to this point I could not believe that they would. A prompt and candid interview seemed all that would be necessary to settle that matter, and make the Kamus feel safe. If such an opening were found, I had determined to remain with them throughout the season. But in that case my family and the mission must be informed. More medicine and books and some comforts would be required to carry me through. It was, therefore, decided to move on a day's journey to Mûang Lā, a convenient point, leave there two elders to instruct the people, and send back three carriers to Chiengmai for the needed supplies and another elder; while I went on overland to Mûang Kwā, and there took boat down the Ū River.

The mountain scenery along this river is very beautiful, especially so near its junction with the Mê Kōng. We reached Lūang Prabāng on Monday, May 9th, and called at once on M. Grant, who was so kind to us the year before. He gave me a greeting as warm as ever. The king was having an interview with M. Luce that day, so I could not see him till Tuesday. I dined that night with M. Grant, he himself coming at dusk to walk over with me. We had a delightful evening. There had been a regular exodus of Kamus that year to Chiengmai and other southern provinces. M. Grant asked if I had heard any reason assigned for it. I told him that I had heard of three—the dearness of rice, owing to the failure of the last crop; the exhaustion of the mountain lands, and the lack of remunerative employment by which they could earn the money required to pay their taxes.

On Tuesday afternoon the Commandant Supérieur sent his secretary to invite me to an interview. He, too, gave me a cordial greeting. He had received my passport together with a letter of introduction from the Consul Général in Bangkok. I had also a kind personal letter from our United States Minister, Mr. John Barrett. He had used his personal influence, and assured me that it would all be right. My interview was very pleasant. M. Luce enquired about our mission work, the number of our converts, and other similar matters. He then referred to the large emigration of Kamus; asked if I had heard of any reason for it, and how many of our three thousand converts were Kamus. He was much surprised to learn that the converts were almost entirely Lāo, with not a half dozen Kamus among them. Putting his anxiety about the emigration and our work among these people together, it seemed to me later that he must have thought the movement a religious one.

When, at last, I stated my special errand to the city, namely, that a number of villages in his province were interested in our religion, that I wished to teach them further, and that, since they were French subjects, I thought it proper to inform him and secure his sanction, he thanked me for doing so, but his manner at once changed. He said he should have to consult the king about that; the mountain people were hard to teach; the country was unhealthy; the Catholic missionaries in the south were leaving, or had left; the king would fear that the Kamus would become disloyal to him if they became Christians. To this I replied that the native officials had uniformly granted us permission to teach among their subjects; that they realized that it was a benefit to their country, and even gave us their assistance; and that it was the fixed policy of our mission to teach Christians loyalty to their rulers. M. Luce said he would consult with the king, and would let me know the decision. I expressed my wish to pay my respects to the king, which he said was a very proper thing, and, on my leaving, he gave me a cordial invitation to dine with him that night.

Next day, through M. Grant, I secured a very pleasant interview with the king. My long residence in the country and acquaintance with both Siamese and Lāo officials, gave us much common ground for conversation. He was pleased that I had known their Majesties, the present King of Siam and his father, his former liege-lords. Quite in line with native ideas, he thought I must be a man of great merit to be so old and yet so strong. I explained at his request the teaching of our religion, pointing out some of its distinctive differences from Buddhism, in all of which things he was interested. He said that it was all very good, but he was born and reared in the Buddhist worship, and was too old to change. Gradually introducing my errand, I told him of my interest in the Kamus, and of their desire to become Christians; that I had come down to get permission to work among them. We taught them a better morality, of which loyalty to rulers was a fundamental article, enjoined by Jesus on His disciples. He raised the objection that the Kamus were ignorant, and we would find them harder to teach than the Lão. To this I replied that these villagers had become believers, and I was going to spend several months in teaching them. He asked if I did not think I was running great risk in living so long in the forest, and so far away from home. "Well," said I, "I am used to life in the forest and jungle, and you can see for yourself how I have fared." At which he smiled, and made no further objection. I left with the firm conviction that if M. Luce were not unwilling, there would be no difficulty with him.

While at dinner that night, I informed M. Luce of my pleasant audience with the king; how I told him my plans, and he had virtually given his consent. "Is that so?" said he. "I must see the king myself about that." And as I took my leave, he said again, "I will see the king to-morrow, and will let you know the result."

The next afternoon, Thursday, M. Luce had a long interview at the Prince's residence. On Friday afternoon I called on M. Grant on my way to the Commandant's office. He told me that M. Luce wished to see me, but had instructed him to notify me that the king did not understand that I was to spend several months among the Kamus—though he certainly did, or why should he have raised the question of my health? I reminded M. Grant that my passport was not to the king, but to the French authorities. All the world recognized the country as French territory. It would have been considered a discourtesy to the French if the representative of the United States had sent a letter to the Lāo king as such. He admitted that in a limited sense this was true; but they did not treat the king as a conquered vassal. Cochin China had fought the French, and had been conquered and annexed. But Lūang Prabāng had put itself under their protection without firing a gun. M. Grant delivered his message with as much consideration toward my disappointment as was consistent with loyalty to his superior. But my disappointment I could not conceal.

M. Luce, I was informed, was very busy that day, but would be glad to see me on Saturday afternoon. The decision, however, was irreversible. Further pressure would be useless, and might be unwise. In that case, I said, of course I must submit. I had shown proper respect for the ruling authority, and my own desire to avoid future misunderstanding, by making the long and costly journey to Lūang Prabāng. My errand was now ended. I would take my leave at once, and return next morning.

This being reported to M. Luce, he sent word that he must see me before I left. I might come immediately. Personally, again, he was very kind, but made a studied effort to put the responsibility upon the king, who, as he said, had not understood that I wished to make a long stay among the Kamus, which he thought was unsafe for me. Of course, I had no complaint to make of the king, who had been most gracious. I submitted to their decision, and would return home. But my arrangements required my return to the Kamu villages, where I had left my men and my goods, and would be detained there till my messengers should return from Chiengmai—which, he said, was all right. Since the responsibility had been put on the king, and the adverse decision had been based solely on the danger to my personal health and safety, I thought it unwise to raise the question of native assistants, and so felt free to leave these on the ground to teach the new believers, as, indeed, I felt under obligation to do.

Thanking M. Luce for all his personal kindness, I begged to take my leave of him then, so that I might start on my return the next morning. But he evidently was not satisfied with his own part in the matter, and wished to make some personal amends to soothe my disappointment. He hoped I would not leave in the morning, but would remain till Monday, and give him the pleasure of a dinner with me and M. Grant on Sunday night. I hoped he would still excuse me, since, if I remained, that would be our time for public worship. "Then," said he, "we shall be pleased to have you on Saturday night; and if you are not ready now to give an affirmative reply, I hope you will so arrange it as to notify my secretary in the morning." Notwithstanding his evident disingenuousness in trying to shift the responsibility for his own acts to another, there was no reason for making it a personal matter; and it would be impolitic to leave apparently angry. So I decided to remain till Monday, and accepted the invitation for Saturday night.

I feared there would be great constraint on both

sides at the dinner; but in this I was agreeably disappointed. That very day a long telegram had arrived, reporting the declaration of war with Spain, and the particulars of the great naval victory of Manila Bay. On my arrival at his house, M. Luce handed me a full translation of these into English, which he had had made for me. They were much surprised at the victory, for they thought the Spanish navy much larger and stronger than ours; and they were high in their praise of the victors. We really had a delightful time. After dinner our host and M. Grant both laid themselves out to show me beautiful maps and pictures. M. Luce invited me to call on Monday morning, and he would send a long telegram to my wife without charge. This he did, and we all parted friends. The departure on the 16th, my seventieth birthday, was not as joyful as I had hoped.

On my return to Mûang Sai, I found that my carriers had been delayed by sore feet and sickness. I could not leave till they came, for fear of missing them and causing further complications. So my long trip home was thrown into the middle of a very rainy season. I had to apologize as best I could to the new converts for the change in my plan to remain with them. But they were glad to have our elders stay and teach them. If that shady tree on the little hill at Mûang Sai could speak, it would tell of much anxious prayer on leaving the Christians and starting on the long journey before me. My Ebenezer was left on that tree.

That journey was altogether the worst I ever had. I did not reach home till August 6th, after the longest tour I had ever taken. M. Luce's telegram had prepared my family and friends for my changed plans.

A few lines must close the history of the work among the Kamus. In December the three evangelists returned with a most encouraging report. The converts had remained firm, and others were waiting to join them. The next season a native minister was sent to them. In 1903 the mission ventured to send two of our younger men, Dr. Campell and Mr. Mackay. to Mûang Sai, to visit the Christians, and respond to a pressing call to extend the work. Imagine their surprise on reaching Mûang Sai to find that the local commissioner had received orders to forbid our missionaries to visit the Christian community, or to hold any religious service with them, on penalty of being conducted out of the country, by force if necessary. The command was so imperative that the Commissioner dared not disobey. He begged them for his sake to return peaceably. No effort has been made since to reach the Christians at Mûang Sai, or to extend the work.

It will be remembered that a few members of the Chieng Sên church—never more than half a dozen families—lived on the east bank of the Mê Kōng, in French territory. So objectionable was the very presence of a missionary making a few days' visit among his flock, that it was regarded of sufficient importance to warrant an official protest from the authorities at Lūang Prabāng, sent through the Governor General of Hanoi, and the United States Minister at Bangkok. Complaint was made of a visit made by the Rev. ———, who had exhibited Scripture pictures and distributed books among the people—which was so contrary to their policy that they forbade the Roman Catholic missionaries from working in their territory. They begged that the thing be not repeated! For the credit of the French authorities I should have been glad to suppress the latter part of this story. But, on the other hand, I think it should be known, in order that it may become a burden on the prayers of the Christian world of all denominations, that God's providence may open the whole peninsula of Indo-China to the preaching of the Gospel.

XXXV

CONCLUSION

MY advancing age suggests the wisdom of not attempting to continue this personal narrative beyond the account just given of my last long missionary tour. I may venture to add, however, by way of conclusion, a few suggestions and criticisms concerning the work of our mission as a whole, and briefly notice a few of the more important personalities and events of these later years.

Special prominence has been given throughout to the evangelistic work, as being the foundation of all other missionary work. A Christian Church and a Christian constituency must be the first aim in all missions. In this we have not been unsuccessful. Our ideals, it is true, have not been realized. We have not witnessed among the Siamese or the Lāo any racial movement towards Christianity; nor have there been any great revivals resulting in large accessions to the church. Both of these we hope for in the not far distant future. Yet the uniform, healthful growth of the church, as distinguished from spasmodic or sporadic increase, has been most gratifying. Seldom does a week pass without accessions to some of our churches.

An adult membership of four thousand is a good foundation. And it must never be forgotten that the roll of church-membership is a very inadequate index of the real influence and power of a mission. In addition to a much larger constituency of adherents, there is our large roll of non-communing members, the hope of the future church. And signs of most hopeful promise have appeared within the present year. The growth of the Chieng Rāi church during that time has been surpassed only by the results of Dr. Campbell's recent tours, amounting to eighty accessions within a few weeks. The supporters of our missions have every cause for gratitude, and a call for earnest, effectual prayer in their behalf.

A review of our evangelistic work suggests one or two criticisms. On one line at least, with a smaller amount of hard work done by the missionary himself, we might have accomplished more, might now be better prepared for advanced work, and the native church might be better able to stand alone, if we had addressed our efforts more steadily to the development and use of native assistance. While we have not had the material of well educated young men out of which to form a theological seminary and to furnish a fully equipped native ministry, we have not used, to the extent to which we should have used it, the material which was available. For a mission as old as ours, we must confess that in this most important matter we are very backward.

The delay in starting our school for boys was not our fault; it was inevitable. The Lāo rulers of the earlier years were absolutely indifferent to all education, and were positively jealous of any that was given by the mission. But as the church began to increase, we had accessions of men trained in the Buddhist priesthood. Some of these were among the best educated men in the country. They understood—as young men even from mission schools could not be expected to understand—the religion, the modes of thought, the needs of their own people, and how to reach them. Their education, however deficient, brought them many compensations. They form the class from which nearly all of our evangelists have been drawn. When such men have been drilled in the Scriptures, their Buddhistic knowledge makes them the very best men for successful work among their countrymen. They visit and sleep in the homes of their people, and are one with them. The missionary in his work must rely largely on their judgment and advice.

It must not be understood that we have not taught these men or used them. A great deal of labour has been spent in training them; very much in the same way in which in American churches, a generation ago, busy pastors trained up young men to be some of our best ministers. The criticism I make—and in it I believe all my colleagues will concur—is that we have not made as much of them as we should have done. No doubt there have been difficulties in the way. Their families must somehow be provided for during the process. The native churches were not strong enough to undertake their support. We were warned that to aid them with foreign funds would make the churches mercenary. What the missionary himself sometimes did to eke out their subsistence was irregular and difficult, and often unsatisfactory. But the labourer is worthy of his hire. Hungry mouths must be fed. The Board and the churches at home do not begrudge a thousand dollars or more to support a missionary in the field. Should they begrudge the same amount spent upon half a dozen men who will treble or quadruple the missionary's work and his influence? In any business it is poor policy to employ a high-salaried foreman, and then not furnish him cheaper men to do that which unskilled labour can accomplish better than he.

In this matter, as in some others, we might have learned valuable lessons from our nearest missionary neighbours in Burma, even though the conditions of our work have been in many respects very different from theirs. Making all allowance for our conditions, I frankly confess that our greatest mistake has probably been in doing too much of the work ourselves, instead of training others to do it, and working through them. This conviction, however, must not in the least lead us to relax our efforts in the line of general education. For the ultimate establishment of the church, and to meet the demands of the age, we must have workmen thoroughly equipped. Till that time comes, we must, as we should more fully have done hitherto, rely on whatever good working material we find ready to hand.

With regard to plans and methods of work, another thought suggests itself. In a business organized as ours is, where the majority in the Annual Meeting has absolute power, it is difficult to avoid the appearance—and sometimes the reality—of a vacillating policy. New stations are established, and missionaries are located by the ballot of the mission there assembled. From year to year the personnel of the mission is constantly changing by reason of furloughs, breakdown of health, and necessary removals. We make our disposition of forces at one meeting, and at the next an entirely new disposition has become necessary. A family has been left alone without a physician or associate. Missionary enthusiasm, or an earnest minority interested in a particular field or a particular cause, may initiate a policy which a subsequent majority may be unable to sanction, or which it may be found difficult or impossible to carry out.

Again, as between the policy of maintaining one strong central station, and that of maintaining several smaller ones in different parts of the country, it is often difficult to decide. With the aim originally of establishing the Gospel in all the states under Siamese rule, we seem to have been led to adopt the latter policy. Through God's blessing on evangelistic tours, in Lampūn and in the frontier provinces of the north, there grew up churches which called for missionary oversight. The famine in Prê summoned us thither; and to secure the work then done, a missionary in residence was needed. Though no church had been formed in Nān, yet our tours had opened the way to one, and the importance of the province and its distance from our centre demanded a station. In every case these stations were opened with the cordial approval of the mission and of the Board at home. Yet it has been difficult to keep them all manned, as has been specially true in the case of Prê—and there to the great detriment of the work. It is easy to say now that a strong central policy might have been better. And that criticism would probably hit me harder than anyone else, for I have sanctioned the establishment of every one of those stations. It is possible that a more centralized organization might have accomplished more toward the education of native workers—the point last under discussion.

With reference to the establishment of stations in the north beyond the frontier of Siam, there was not until recently absolute unanimity in the mission. But that was not from any diversity of opinion as regards the question in itself, but because a sister denomination had established itself there. There has never been reasonable ground for doubt that the language and race of the ruling class, and of the population of the plains would naturally assign them to the Lāo mission. And no other mission is so well equipped for working that field. A Lāo Inland Mission, somewhat on the plan of the China Inland Mission, would be an ideal scheme for reaching the whole of the Tai-speaking peoples of the north and northeast under English and French and Chinese rule. The obligation to carry the Gospel to those peoples should rest heavily on the conscience of the Christian Church, and on our Church in particular. Who will volunteer to be the leaders?

It has already been noticed that in our educational work the Girls' School had the precedence in time, and possibly in importance. Boys did at least learn to read and write in the monasteries. At the time of our arrival in Chiengmai, only two women in the province could read. The Chiengmai Girls' School has had a wide educational influence throughout the north, and to-day our Girls' Schools have practically no competitors.

The Phraner Memorial School for small children, in connection with the First Church, Chiengmai, under Mrs. Campbell's direction, is preparing material both for High Schools and for the College. We have good schools for girls in Lakawn, Nān, and Chieng Rāi; and parochial mixed schools in most of our country churches and out-stations. The young women who have been engaged in this department, and many self-sacrificing married women, have great reason to rejoice over the work accomplished. No greater work can be done than that of educating the wives and mothers of the church and the land. Educated Christian men are greatly handicapped when consorted with illiterate and superstitious wives. Without a Christian wife and mother there can be no Christian family, the foundation both of the church and of the Christian State.

On a recent visit to Chiengmai, Princess Dārā Ratsami—one of the wives of His late Majesty of Siam, and daughter of Prince Intanon of Chiengmai and his wife, the Princess Tipakēsawn, often mentioned in the preceding narrative—was much interested in the Girls' School, and was pleased to name it the Phra Rajchayar School, after herself—using therefor her title, and not her personal name.

The mission had been founded twenty years before it had, and almost before it could have had, a School for Boys. It is the intention of the mission to make of this school—the Prince Royal College—the future Christian College. Similar schools have been established in the other stations.

Since the Siamese government assumed control in the North, it has manifested a laudable zeal in establishing schools, in which, however, the Siamese language alone is taught. His Majesty is most fortunate in having such an able and progressive representative in the North as the present High Commissioner, Chow Prayā Surasīh Visithasakdi. And the country is no less fortunate in having a ruler whose high personal character and wise administration command the confidence and respect of all classes. He is interested in educating the people, and in everything that advances the interests of the country.

I regard the educational question as the great question now before the mission. The existence of the Siamese schools greatly emphasizes the importance of our own work, and the necessity of maintaining a high standard and a strong teaching force in Siamese, English, mathematics, and the sciences. Their schools then will be tributary to ours.

The ultimate prevalence of the Siamese language in all the provinces under Siamese rule, has been inevitable from the start. All governments realize the importance of a uniform language in unifying a people, and have no interest whatever in perpetuating a provincial dialect. The Siamese, in fact, look down with a kind of disdain upon the Lāo speech, and use it only as a temporary necessity during the period of transition. And the Siamese is really the richer of the two by reason of its large borrowing from the Pali, the better scholarship behind it, and its closer connection with the outside world.

These two forms of the Tai speech—with a common idiom, and with the great body of words in both identical, or differing only in vocal inflection—have been kept apart chiefly by the fact that they have different written characters. All of the Lāo women and children, and two-thirds of the men had to be taught to read, whichever character were adopted; and they could have learned the one form quite as easily as the other. Had the mission adopted the Siamese character from the start, it would now be master of the educational situation, working on a uniform scheme with the Siamese Educational Department. Moreover, the Siamese language in our schools would have been a distinct attraction toward education and toward Christianity. And thus there would have been available for the North the labours of two or more generations of able workers in the southern mission, from which so far the Lão church has been mostly cut off. The whole Bible would have been accessible from the first; whereas now nearly half of it remains still untranslated into the Lão. If the future needs of the Siamese provinces alone were to be considered, it might even be doubted whether it were worth while to complete the translation. When the monks, in their studies and teaching, adopt the Siamese, as it is now the intention of the government to have them do, Lão books will soon be without readers throughout Siam. When for the young a choice is possible in the matter of such a transcendent instrument of thought and culture as language, all surely would wish their training to be in that one which has in it the promise of the future. These words are written in no idle criticism of the past, and in no captious spirit regarding the present; but with full sense of the gravity of the decision which confronts the mission in shaping its educational policy for those who henceforth are to be Siamese.

Meanwhile, Lão type and books in the Lão dialect are needed, not merely for the present generation of older people who cannot or will not learn a new character, but also for the instruction and Christianization of that much larger mass of Lão folk beyond the frontier of Siam as revealed by recent explorations. Removed, as these are, entirely from the political and cultural influence of Siam, and divided up under the jurisdiction of three great nations of diverse and alien speech, it is inconceivable that the Siamese should ever win the ascendency over them. Nor has either of these nations any immediate and pressing incentive toward unifying the speech of its provincials, such as has actuated Siam in this matter. If the field of the Lāo mission is to be extended to include these "regions beyond"—as we all hope that it soon may be—Lāo speech will inevitably be the medium of all its work there. Then all that so far has been accomplished in the way of translation, writing, and printing in the Lāo tongue, will be so much invaluable capital to be turned over to the newer enterprise.

As regards the medical department of the mission, the Lāo field has been an ideal one for its operation and for demonstration of its results. When the field was virtually closed to the simple Gospel, the missionary physician found everywhere an exalted, not to say exaggerated, idea of the efficacy of foreign medicine, and a warm welcome for himself. Dr. Cheek, who virtually founded our regular medical work among the Lāo, had been on the field but a short time when he reported thirteen thousand patients treated in one year. Probably no subsequent physician has had such absolute control of the situation as he had, so long as he gave his time and talents to his calling. But even the layman finds his medical chest an invaluable adjunct to his evangelistic work, as we have had frequent occasion to notice. We are devoutly thankful for—we might almost envy—the influence that our medical missionaries have exerted in the civilization and the Christianization of the Lāo tribes.

Somewhat of the present status and importance of the medical mission may be judged from the following facts: Dr. J. W. McKean's projected Leper Asylum is the largest charitable institution ever planned in the kingdom. The new Overbrook Hospital in Chieng Rāi, the generous gift of the Gest family of Overbrook, Pennsylvania, is the finest building in the mission. The Charles T. Van Santvoord Hospital in Lakawn is another similar gift. Native physicians, trained as far as present opportunities permit in Western surgery and medicine, are now maintained at certain posts by the Siamese government. And especially the work of Dr. Arthur Kerr, the government physician in Chiengmai, and his unremitting kindness to the mission, are deeply appreciated by us all.

I cannot close these remarks without making special reference to the work of my old friend and classmate and early associate in the mission, Dr. Jonathan Wilson. In addition to his other most valuable labours, he spent years of loving and devoted service in the preparation of hymns for Lão worship, which will mould and lead the spiritual life of this people for years to come. The Lão are lovers of music. Many of them have received much of their religious instruction through the use of these hymns. His influence in the Lão church may be compared to that of Watts and Wesley for the English race.

Our long isolation as a mission has enabled us to appreciate the coming to us in late years of a number of distinguished visitors, who have greatly encouraged and strengthened us.

At the Annual Meeting in December, 1900, we were favoured with a visit from our United States Minister, Hon. Hamilton King, and his two daughters. Referring to his visit, the "Lão Quarterly Letter" said: "His addresses to the missionaries and native ministers and elders of the Presbytery were much appreciated, and our large church building was crowded on two successive Sabbaths to hear his eloquent words of encouragement to native Christians, and his warm commendation of Christianity to non-Christians. It has been said that one of the best things which a United States Minister can take to a non-Christian land is a good Christian home. And this is just what Mr. King has brought to Siam."

At the Annual Meeting of the following year, in Lakawn, we received the first official visit we ever had from one of the Secretaries of our Board, in the person of Rev. Arthur J. Brown, D.D., accompanied by his good wife. The importance of these secretarial visits to distant missions can hardly be overestimated. It is impossible to legislate intelligently for a constituency twelve thousand miles away. No amount of writing can give the varied kinds of information necessary for a full understanding of the people, the missionaries, their surroundings, and the needs of the field, which a single visit will convey. Then, too, there are questions of administration and mission polity, requiring settlement in the home Board, which can with difficulty be understood through correspondence. Dr. Brown's official visit was most helpful, as also his words of encouragement, his sermons and addresses. The pleasure derived from the personal visits of Dr. and Mrs. Brown to various members of the Mission will always linger in our memories.

Another notable visit to Chiengmai was that of the Crown Prince of Siam, now His Majesty Mahā Vajiravudh, in the winter of 1905-6. On this visit His Royal Highness very graciously accepted the invitation of the mission to lay the corner stone of the Will-

HIS MAJESTY, MAHĀ VAJIRAVUDH,
KING OF SIAM

iam Allen Butler Hall, the recitation hall of the new Boys' School. On that occasion he delivered an address, of which the following is a translation:

"Ladies and Gentlemen:—I have listened with great pleasure to the complimentary remarks which have just been made. I regard them as indisputable evidence of your friendship for the whole Kingdom of Siam.

"During my visit to the United States, the American people were pleased to give me a most enthusiastic welcome. I may mention particularly the sumptuous banquet with which your Board of Foreign Missions honoured me. I perceived clearly that the American people received me whole-heartedly and not perfunctorily. This also made it evident to me that the American people have a sincere friendship for the Kingdom of Siam. Of this fact I was profoundly convinced, and I certainly shall not soon forget my visit to the United States.

"This being so, I feel compelled to reciprocate this kindness to the full extent of my ability. As my Royal Grandfather and my Royal Father have befriended the missionaries, so I trust that I too shall have opportunity, on proper occasions, to assist them to the limits of my power.

"Your invitation to me to-day to lay the corner stone of your new School Building, is another evidence of your friendship and goodwill toward Siam. I have full confidence that you will make every endeavour to teach the students to use their knowledge for the welfare of their country. Therefore I take great pleasure in complying with your request, and I invoke a rich blessing on this new institution. May it prosper and fulfil the highest expectations of its founders!"

In response to a request from the Principal that he would name the new school, His Royal Highness sent the following reply:

"CHIENGMAI, January 2d, 1906.

"I have great pleasure in naming the new school, the foundation stone of which I have just laid, The Prince Royal's College. May this School which I have so named, be prosperous, and realize all that its well-wishers hope for it. May it long flourish, and remain a worthy monument of the enterprise of the American Presbyterian Church of Chiengmai. This is the wish of their sincere friend,

"VAJIRAVUDH."

Little did we then think that His Royal Highness would so soon be called to fill the high office left vacant by the lamented death of his distinguished father, King Chulalangkorn, which occurred October 22d, 1910.

In December, 1908, Mrs. McGilvary's brother, Professor Cornelius B. Bradley of the University of California, while on a visit to the land of his birth and of his father's labours, paid us a visit in the North. He was present at our Annual Meeting in Lakawn, and on Sunday preached the Communion sermon, and again in Chiengmai. It was to the astonishment of all who heard him, both natives and foreigners, that he could converse fluently and flawlessly, and could so preach, after an absence of thirty-six years. It was upon this visit to Siam that he made a special study and translation of the Sukhōthai Stone—the earliest known monument of the Siamese language.

In company with Professor Bradley came Mr. William McClusky, a business man, on a visit to his daughter, Mrs. M. B. Palmer. The significance of this visit lies in the fact that Mr. McClusky has remained among us, and has identified himself with the work of the mission, endearing himself to all.

In 1905 Mrs. McGilvary returned to the United States for a much-needed change. I remained on the field until 1906, when I was cabled for on account of the very serious state of her health. I found her very low, and my visit was devoted to the restoration of her health. In the autumn she was sufficiently recovered to make our return possible, and the voyage was undertaken in compliance with her own ardent wish. She was greatly benefited by the sea-voyage, and since her return her health has been fully restored.

On May 16th, 1908, my daughter, Mrs. William Harris, gave a dinner in honour of my eightieth birthday, at which all our missionary and European friends in Chiengmai were guests. Dr. McKean expressed the congratulations of my friends in an address, from which I quote the following: "Eighty years of age, sir, but not eighty years old! We do not associate the term old age with you, for you seem to have drunk of the fount of perpetual youth." But the sentiment to which I most heartily subscribe is the following: "There is a common maxim among men to which we all readily assent; namely, that no man is able to do his best work in the world without having received from God that best of all temporal gifts, a helpmeet for him. We most heartily congratulate you that, early in your life in Siam, Mrs. McGilvary was made a partner in this great life work. And no one knows so well as yourself how large a part she has had in making possible much of the strenuous work that you have done. To her, likewise, we offer on this happy occasion our hearty congratulations and our fervent wishes for an ever-brightening future!"

On December 6th, 1910, Mrs. McGilvary and I celebrated our Golden Wedding. As this occurred during the Annual Meeting of the Mission, most of our missionary friends, as well as our friends of the foreign colony, were present. It was a matter of great regret, however, that Dr. Wilson, who was present at the wedding fifty years before, was too feeble to come to Chiengmai on this occasion. The many beautiful gifts received were another token of the loving regard of our friends and dear ones in this and in the homeland. Among the many letters and telegrams received was a cablegram from our children in America. "It was like a hand-clasp and a whisper of love flashed around the world." Dr. Arthur J. Brown, speaking for himself and the members of the Board of Foreign Missions, wrote: "We greatly rejoice in your long and conspicuously devoted and influential service for the Lāo people. We share the veneration and love with which we know you are regarded by the people among whom your lives have been spent, and by the missionaries with whom you have been so closely associated. It would be a joy if we could join the relatives and friends who will be with you on that happy day in December. We invoke God's richest blessings on you both. Mrs. Brown and all my colleagues in the office unite with the members of the Board in loving congratulations."

One of the most valued of these messages came from H. R. H. Prince Damrong, Minister of the Interior: "I just learn from the local papers of the celebration of your Golden Wedding. I wish you and Mrs. McGilvary to accept my sincere congratulations and best wishes that you both may be spared to continue your great work for many more years. Damrong."

Our good friend, H. E. Prayā Surasīh Visithsakdī, High Commissioner for the Northwestern Provinces, brought his congratulations in person, presenting Mrs. McGilvary with a very rare old Siamese bowl of inlaid work of silver and gold.

From the native church in Chieng Rāi a message in Lāo was received, of which the following is a transla-

DR. AND MRS. McGILVARY
FIFTY YEARS AFTER THEIR MARRIAGE

tion: "The Chieng Rāi Christians invoke Divine blessings on the Father-Teacher and Mother-Teacher McGilvary, who are by us more beloved than gold."

We were deeply touched by a most unexpected demonstration of the Chiengmai Christians, who assembled at our home, and with many expressions of loving esteem and gratitude presented us with a silver tray, designed by themselves, on which were represented in relief the progress of the city in these fifty years: on one end the old bridge, on the other the new bridge just completed; on the two sides, the rest-house we occupied upon our arrival in Chiengmai, and our present home. The inscription, in Lāo, reads: "1867-1910. The Christian people of Chiengmai to Father-Teacher and Mother-Teacher McGilvary, in memory of your having brought the Good News of Christ, forty-three years ago."—It makes one feel very humble to quote such expressions from our colleagues and friends. But it would not be in human nature to fail to appreciate them.

I would not close this life-story without expressing, on behalf of my wife and myself, our heartfelt gratitude to our friends, native and foreign, for the great kindness shown us in our intercourse with them during these long years; and, above all, our devout gratitude to the Giver of all good, for sparing so long our lives, and crowning them with such rich blessings. Of these the greatest has been in permitting us to lay the foundations, and to witness the steady growth of the Church of Christ in Northern Siam.

INDEX

PRINTED IN THE UNITED STATES OF AMERICA

ROBERT E. SPEER, D. D.

The Foreign Doctor: "The Hakim Sahib"

A Biography of Joseph Plumb Cochran, M.D., of Persia. Illustrated, 12mo, cloth, net $1.50.

Dr. Cochran came to a position of power in Western Persia which made his life as interesting as a romance. He was one of the central figures in the Kurdish invasion of Persia, and was the chief means of saving the city of Urumia. In no other biography is there as full an account of the actual medical work done by the medical missionary, and of the problem of the use of the political influence acquired by a man of Dr. Cochran's gifts and opportunities.

HENRY D. PORTER, M. D., D.D.

William Scott Ament *Missionary of the American Board to China.*

Illustrated, 8vo, cloth, net $1.50.

A biography of one of the most honored missionaries of the Congregational Church, whose long and effective service in China has inscribed his name high in the annals of those whose lives have been given to the uplift of their fellowmen.

MARY GRIDLEY ELLINWOOD

Frank Field Ellinwood *Former Secretary Presbyterian F. M. Board*

His Life and Work. Illustrated, cloth, net $1.00.

A charming biography of one of the greatest missionary leaders of the Nineteenth Century.—*Robert E. Speer.*

ANTONIO ANDREA ARRIGHI

The Story of Antonio the Galley Slave

With Portrait, 12mo, cloth, net $1.25.

"Reads like a romance, and the wonderful thing about it is that it is true. A fervid religious experience, a passion for service and good intellectual equipment were his splendid preparation for a great missionary work among his countrymen in America."—*Zion's Herald.*

GEORGE MULLER

George Muller, The Modern Apostle of Faith

By Frederick G. Warne.

New Edition, including the Later Story of the Bristol Orphan Home. Illustrated, cloth, net 75c.

"What deep attractiveness is found in this life of the great and simple-hearted apostle."—*Christian Advocate.*

KINGSTON DE GRUCHE

Dr. Apricot of "Heaven-Below"

Illustrated, 8vo, cloth, net $1.00.

"No one who has read this book will ever afterwards repeat the threadbare objection, "I don't believe in missions."—*Continent*

ROBERT E. SPEER *The Cole Lectures for 1911.*

Some Great Leaders in the World Movement

12mo, cloth, net $1.25.

Mr. Speer in his characteristic inspiring way has presented the key note of the lives of six of the World's greatest missionaries: Raymond Lull, the crusading spirit in missions; William Carey, the problems of the pioneer; Alexander Duff, Missions and Education; George Bowen, the ascetic ideal in missions; John Lawrence, politics and missions; and Charles G. Gordon, modern missionary knight-errancy.

S. M. ZWEMER, F.R.G.S., and Others

Islam and Missions

12mo, cloth, net $1.50.

This volume presents the papers read at the Second Conference on Missions to Moslems, recently held in Lucknow, India. The contributors are all experts of large experience in such mission effort.

VAN SOMMER, ANNIE, and Others

Daylight in the Harem

A New Era for Moslem Women. *In Press.*

Woman's work for Woman is nowhere more needed than on the part of Christian women for their sisters of Islam. It is a most difficult field of service, but this volume by authors long and practically interested in this important Christian ministry, demonstrates how effectually this work has opened and is being carried forward with promising results.

ROBERT A. HUME, D.D.

An Interpretation of India's Religious History

Introduction by President King, LL.D. of Oberlin College

12mo, cloth, net $1.25.

The author of this careful, though popular, study, is eminently qualified to deal with the subject of his thoughtful volume. Equipped for this purpose through long residence in India and intimate study of India's religious history, what he says will be accepted as the estimate and interpretation of an authority.

MARGARET E. BURTON

The Education of Women in China

Illustrated, 12mo, cloth, net $1.25.

The author of this scholarly study of the Chinese woman and education is the daughter of Prof. Ernest E. Burton, of the University of Chicago. ...... The work is probably the most thorough study of an important phase of the economic development of the world's most populous country that has appeared.

Z. S. LOFTIS, M. D.

A Message from Batang

The Diary of Z. S. Loftis, M.D. Illustrated, 12mo, cloth, net 75c.

Dr. Loftis went out to Tibet as a medical missionary of the Disciples Church. His diary contains the events of the outgoing trip together with incidents of the daily life of a missionary in this "closed" land.

HON. WILLIAM JENNINGS BRYAN

The Fruits of the Tree

16mo, boards, net 35c.

This is the address which Mr. Bryan delivered at the World's Missionary Conference at Edinburgh and contains his views on missions—views which are the result of his personal and painstaking investigation on foreign fields.

HELEN S. DYER

Pandita Ramabai

The Story of Her Life. *Second Edition.* Illustrated, 12mo, cloth, $1.25.

"The story of a wonderful life, still in the midcareer of high usefulness. 'Pandita' should be known to all American women."—*The Outlook.*

MINERVA L. GUTHAPFEL

The Happiest Girl in Korea

And Other Sketches from the Land of Morning Calm. Illustrated, 12mo, cloth, net 60c.

These sketch stories of actual life in Korea by a missionary of experience and insight portray conditions of real life; they combine humor, pathos and vivid description.

JOHN JACKSON

Secretary to the Mission to Lepers in India and the East.

Mary Reed, Missionary to the Lepers

New Edition. Illustrated, 12mo, cloth, net 50c.; paper, net 25c.

G. T. B. DAVIS

Korea for Christ

Illustrated, paper, net 25c.

An effective report of the recent revivals in Korea told by an eye witness, who himself participated in the work.

MISSIONARY

JULIUS RICHTER

A History of Protestant Missions in the Near East

8vo, cloth, net $2.50.

A companion volume to "A History of Missions in India," by this great authority. The progress of the gospel is traced in Asia Minor, Persia, Arabia, Syria, and Egypt. Non-sectarian in spirit, thoroughly comprehensive in scope.

JOHN P. JONES, D.D.

The Modern Missionary Challenge

Yale Lectures, 1910. 12mo, cloth, net $1.50.

These lectures, by the author of "India's Problem, Krisha or Christ?" are a re-survey of the demand of missions in the light of progress made, in their relation to human thought. The new difficulties, the new incentives, are considered by one whose experience in the field and as a writer, entitle him to consideration.

ALONZO BUNKER, D.D.

Sketches from the Karen Hills

Illustrated, 12mo, Cloth, net $1.00.

These descriptive chapters from a missionary's life in Burma are of exceptional vividness and rich in an appreciation for color. His pen pictures give not only a splendid insight into native life, missionary work, but have a distinctive literary charm which characterizes his "Soo Thah."

JAMES F. LOVE

The Unique Message and Universal Mission of Christianity

12mo, cloth, net $1.25.

A volume dealing with the philosophy of missions at once penetrating and unusual. It is perhaps one of the most original and valuable contributions to the subject yet made.

WILLIAM EDWARD GARDNER

Winners of the World During Twenty Centuries

Adapted for Boys and Girls.

A Story and a Study of Missionary Effort from the Time of Paul to the Present Day. Cloth, net 60c; paper, net 30c.

Children's Missionary Series

Illustrated in Colors, Cloth, Decorated, each, net 60c.

Children of Africa. James B. Baird.
Children of Arabia. John C. Young.
Children of China. C. Campbell Brown.
Children of India. Janet Harvey Kelman.

The World Missionary Conference

The Report of the Ecumenical Conference held in Edinburgh in 1910. In nine volumes, each, net 75c.; the complete set of nine volumes, net $5.00.

A whole missionary library by experts and wrought up to the day and hour. The Conference has been called a modern council of Nicea and the report the greatest missionary publication ever made.

Vol. 1. Carrying the Gospel.
Vol. 2. The Church in the Mission Field.
Vol. 3. Christian Education.
Vol. 4. The Missionary Message.
Vol. 5. Preparation of Missionaries.
Vol. 6. The Home Base.
Vol. 7. Missions and Governments.
Vol. 8. Co-operation and Unity.
Vol. 9. History, Records and Addresses.

Echoes from Edinburgh, 1910

By W. H. T. GAIRDNER, *author of "D. M. Thornton."*

12mo, cloth, net 50c.

The popular story of the Conference—its preparation—its management—its effect and forecast of its influence on the church at home and the work abroad. An official publication in no way conflicting with the larger work—which it rather supplements.

HENRY H. JESSUP'S AUTOBIOGRAPHY

Fifty-three Years in Syria

Introduction by James S. Dennis. Two volumes, illustrated, 8vo, cloth, boxed, net $5.00.

"A rich mine of information for the historian, the ethnologist and the student of human nature apart from the labors to which the author devoted his life. A thoroughly interesting book that will yield endless pickings."—*N. Y. Sun.*

ROBERT E. SPEER

Christianity and the Nations

The Duff Lectures for 1910.

8vo, cloth, net $2.00.

Among the many notable volumes that have resulted from the well-known Duff foundation Lectureship this new work embodying the series given by Mr. Robert E. Speer in Edinburgh, Glasgow and Aberdeen, will rank among the most important. The general theme, "The Reflex Influence of Missions Upon the Nations," suggests a large, important, and most interesting work.

G. T. B. DAVIS

Korea for Christ

25c net

An effective report of the recent revivals in Korea told by an eye witness, who himself participated in the work.

Printed in the United States
215082BV00004B/44/A

9 781437 455274